OGDEN CODMAN

and the

DECORATION

of

HOUSES

*Codman family house, The
Grange, Lincoln, Massachusetts,
photographed c. 1895*

Ogden Codman
and the Decoration of Houses

EDITED BY PAULINE C. METCALF

THE BOSTON ATHENÆUM

DAVID R. GODINE, PUBLISHER

Edited by Debra Edelstein
Designed by Richard C. Bartlett
This book was set in Galliard
  by Crane Typesetting Service
  and printed and bound by
  Arcata Graphics-Halliday
  Lithograph; color plates printed
  by Mercantile Printing
  Company.
Manufactured in the United States
of America.

Cover illustration:
  Principal elevation, Ogden
  Codman residence, La Leopolda,
  Villefranche-sur-Mer, France.

The publication of this catalogue has been made possible in part by a grant to The Boston Athenæum from the National Endowment for the Arts, a Federal Agency

Library of Congress Cataloging-in-Publication Data
Ogden Codman and the decoration of houses.

  Bibliography: p.
  Includes index.
  1. Codman, Ogden—Criticism and interpretation.
2. Interior architecture—United States.   3. Interior decoration—United States —History—19th century.   4. Interior decoration—United States–History— 20th century.   5. Colonial revival (Architecture)—United States.   I. Metcalf, Pauline C.
NA737.C6034   1988   728.3′7′0924   88-71607
ISBN 0-87923-777-5

Contents

Foreword

Ogden Codman's legacy as an interpreter of the classical style and a major force in the transformation of design known as the colonial revival movement is both significant and neglected. As coauthor with Edith Wharton of *The Decoration of Houses*—the first popular work on that subject, published in 1897—Codman received recognition for his approach to design, with his emphasis on eighteenth-century European country houses and palaces. Nevertheless, his reputation as an antiquarian and architectural historian and Edith Wharton's growing fame as a novelist combined to prevent a fuller appreciation of his exquisite and refined designs. We hope to revive Codman's standing as a designer in this study of the career, influence, and, above all, master works of Ogden Codman.

The Athenæum's connections with the Codman family are almost as old as the library itself. Ogden Codman's paternal grandfather, Charles Russell Codman, became a proprietor in 1820 and donated funds to create a lecture room in 1823. Charles Russell Codman, Jr., also a proprietor, served as a trustee for several years until 1863, the year of his nephew's birth. The Codman family ties are also rooted in The Athenæum in the maternal lineage: Ogden Codman's great-grandfather, Josiah Bradlee, was a proprietor and was a member of the trustees' audit committee during the 1840s. His shares remained within the family until 1922, when privileges and benefits of the library were accorded to Ogden Codman and his younger brothers and sisters through the will of Ogden Codman, Sr. Indeed, many distinguished furniture pieces and decorative objects as well as paintings were given to the library by this branch of the Codman family. Codman's connections to the library included the memberships of his close friends: notable typographer Daniel Berkeley Updike, who bequeathed his personal papers to the library; architect Herbert W. C. Browne; and preservation advocate William Sumner Appleton, founder of the Society for the Preservation of New England Antiquities. This circle further included Codman's Boston patrons: Eben Howard Gay, Nathaniel Thayer, Oliver Ames, and J. Randolph Coolidge.

Although Ogden Codman lived in France for the last third of his life, he left many of his personal papers to The Athenæum. In 1953, two years after Codman's death, our director, Walter Muir Whitehill, arranged to accept shipment of the papers. Mr. Whitehill later wrote:

> *Some months passed. On returning from lunch one day I found the Athenæum vestibule nearly filled with packing cases from Messrs. Pitt and Scott in Paris, and on my desk a bill for ocean freight of close to a thousand dollars.*

The expense was well worth it, as the cases contained several hundred loose-leaf binders compiled by Codman during his lifetime. They included detailed research on the genealogy and local history of New England and of the section of France where Codman grew up, and catalogues of the country houses of England, the châteaux of Codman's adopted country, and the works of his countrymen John Singleton Copley and Gilbert Stuart, along with the genealogies of their sitters.

The collection survives as an outstanding revelation of Ogden Codman's personality. Copies of correspondence sent to his lifelong friends Edith Wharton, Elsie de Wolfe, Fiske Kimball, and Herbert Browne are full of his lively opinions on a wide variety of subjects and people. Ranging from changes in social customs to connoisseurship, Codman's letters attest that his interest in detail was a personal as well as professional characteristic. A typical example of this, and of his somewhat eccentric nature, is his exasperation with his London tailor during an exchange of letters in which Codman was trying to order purple vicuna trousers:

> *I do not like any of the patterns that you sent to me, and I want a violet or purple material. The fawn material is too thick and the other materials are much too sombre. . . . I like purple, it goes well with gray hair and does not look too youthful. Surely it must be possible to find such a colour in a light weight in all London.*

I wish to express my gratitude to the principal individuals whose outstanding efforts have made this exhibition and publication possible. First and foremost, I am especially grateful to Pauline C. Metcalf, curator of *Ogden Codman and the Decoration of Houses*, for initiating this renewed appreciation of Codman's contribution to design. Her generous dedication to this enterprise from its inception in 1984 has been truly a labor of love. Pauline Metcalf, who has used the Ogden Codman collection at The Boston Athenæum to write extensively about him, collaborated from the outset with Donald C. Kelley, Director of the Athenæum Gallery; and to him a special thanks must be offered for giving the project its shape and direction. I extend my thanks to Norman P. Tucker, Research and Programs Officer, who prepared the proposal to the National Endowment for the Arts which led to its early support of this project. His continued guidance throughout has been invaluable. Particular gratitude is due to Helen LaFleur, former Assistant to the Gallery Director, who was pivotal in coordinating several stages of organization. My thanks to Melissa K. Rombout, Assistant Project Coordinator, for her multifaceted abilities during the planning and execution of the production phases. For her valuable suggestions and comments throughout the planning of the exhibition, my gratitude to Ellie Reichlin, Director of Archives at the Society for the Preservation of New England Antiquities. The Athenæum exhibition, traveling to New York and Washington, and this publication reflect the superb efforts of this group.

Rodney Armstrong
Director and Librarian, The Boston Athenæum

Preface

Through his designs and writing, Ogden Codman was a major influence on American interiors and architecture at the turn of the century. With Edith Wharton, he wrote *The Decoration of Houses*, a book that has been, since its publication in 1897, the classic primer for traditional interior decoration. Suitability, simplicity, and proportion—the three piers that support Codman's philosophy of design—are the leitmotifs of *The Decoration of Houses*. The ways in which Codman applied these principles provide a basis for analyzing his work as an architect and decorator.

Apprehending the taste and contribution of an individual designer has always been an elusive task, given the ephemeral nature of interior decoration. In Codman's case, however, remarkably well-documented archives (including watercolor renderings, architectural designs and plans, photographs, and business correspondence) and the survival of several commissions nearly intact allow us to examine his work from several angles. Although a pioneer of the revival of classical taste in the late nineteenth century, Codman was nevertheless among a handful of able interpreters on both sides of the Atlantic who advocated authenticity of ornament and furniture, the uncluttering of spaces, and a simplified, lightened effect—achieved most frequently under the guise of the Georgian/colonial or Louis XV and XVI styles. His work has always been seen in the context of *The Decoration of Houses*; but as an architect and decorator, Codman deserves consideration on his own terms, not merely as an adjunct to Edith Wharton.

Codman maintained a practice in America from 1891 to 1920, and his clients were mainly from established, well-to-do families in Boston, Newport, and New York. Although he did the complete design for twenty-one houses and remodeled a number of others, he is known primarily for his elegant interiors, notable for their understated opulence and moderate scale. His role as a tastemaker, however, has been eclipsed for a number of reasons. Despite his success within his milieu, his name and reputation never spread below the "carriage trade." While his work received some publicity and articles were published on several of his houses, he did not have the flair for self-promotion of someone like Elsie de Wolfe, who actually received many of her ideas on interior decoration from Codman. Throughout his life, Codman never reconciled his desire for recognition with his gentlemanly desire to remain above such concerns. In the aftermath of World War I, he did not want to compete with the talented architects and designers who had come on the scene, so he retired to France. The next generation, however, would inherit the ideas expressed by him and Edith Wharton through the teachings of such men as Frank Alvah Parsons, William Odom, and Fiske Kimball.

Codman left more than an artistic legacy. He was also an antiquarian with a passion for detailed knowledge of both buildings and the people who lived in them. During the last thirty years of his life, he devoted his energies to several considerable collections: one of New England town histories and genealogy; another a unique 36,000-entry compendium of all French châteaux; and the third a vast architectural library containing all the important treatises on Western design and ornament.

A less visible legacy is his correspondence. He was the Samuel Pepys of his circle, and his letters, dating from 1880 to the late 1930s, provide incisive commentary on the life and habits of cultured upper-class American society. While many are full of society gossip and scattered with barbs about most of its members, others reveal his preoccupation with the study of eighteenth- and early-nineteenth-century buildings and his appreciation of America's colonial heritage.

Welles Bosworth, an architect and friend of Codman, aptly summarized his approach to life and work: "The word 'grammatical' suited his character as well as his architecture. . . . His motto was 'Order, for the sake of harmony and in the hope of beauty.' "

Acknowledgments

The fruition of the book and exhibition *Ogden Codman and the Decoration of Houses* has involved the assistance, collaboration, and generosity of many scholars, institutions, and colleagues. The magnitude and scope of the Codman archives and the geographical dispersal of its contents has made the coordination of this project a lengthy and complex undertaking. While each of the major repositories of Codman archives, The Boston Athenæum, the Society for the Preservation of New England Antiquities, the Metropolitan Museum of Art, and the Avery Library of Art and Architecture at Columbia University, were interested in the exposure of their Codman collections, it was not possible until this project was conceived to bring together the different components of Codman's unique bequest as architect, decorator, antiquarian, and bibliophile.

My initial interest in Codman began more than ten years ago, when he was the subject for a master's thesis in the Program of Historic Preservation at Columbia University School of Architecture. Codman's multifaceted legacy was the perfect subject for someone from New England with a background in interior decoration, combined with preservation and nineteenth- and early-twentieth-century architectural history. James Marsden Fitch, Director Emeritus of the Columbia preservation program, and Adolf Placzek, former Librarian of the Avery Architectural and Fine Arts Library, must be given credit for initially guiding me to and encouraging my research on Codman. Aiding my research enormously were two previous studies: one a privately printed book by his cousin, Florence Codman, *The Clever Young Boston Architect* (1970); the other, a comprehensive analysis of Codman's work done for an undergraduate thesis at Harvard University (1973) by

Stuart A. Drake. I am extremely grateful to both these individuals for their groundbreaking research and their generosity in sharing their knowledge and insights with me. Florence Codman's experiences with Odgen Codman and her associations with the Codman family have contributed significantly to my perceptions. The late David McKibbin, former art librarian of The Boston Athenæum, used his incredible knowledge of Boston history and the interconnections of the best "Brahmin" families to identify many names and to provide the locations of many commissions. Without his notations in the "Green Book," a notebook in which he gathered Codman's letters dealing with the most well-known of his friends and clients, much of the wit and gossip recorded in those letters would have gone unappreciated.

A number of individuals have been key to making this book and exhibition a reality. Christopher Monkhouse, Curator of Decorative Arts, Museum of Art, Rhode Island School of Design, and Richard Guy Wilson, Professor of Architectural History, University of Virginia, have been involved with the project since its inception and have guided its implementation. It is due to the unflagging faith and perseverance of Donald C. Kelley, Gallery Director of The Boston Athenæum, that The Athenæum agreed to undertake such an ambitious project with so many divergent aspects. John Dobkin, Director of the National Academy of Design, was an eager supporter of the project from the start, especially because the Academy's two buildings were designed by Codman as town houses for Archer Huntington. Judith Schultz, Curator of Exhibitions at The Octagon Museum of the American Institute of Architects, the third host for the exhibition, expressed enthusiasm for and interest in the project immediately. Nicholas King, whose family were patrons of Codman, and Henry Hope Reed, under whose aegis *Classical America* reprinted *The Decoration of Houses* in 1978, have long been Codman enthusiasts and were eager to see recognition for his work. The National Endowment for the Arts recognized the importance of a project that would explore in depth the role played by this American designer in the transformation of taste at the end of the nineteenth century. Without its support it would not have been possible to organize and produce the exhibition or the accompanying publication.

Given the scope of the enterprise, and the number of organizations involved in its realization, it is not possible to name all the individuals to whom thanks are due. As the originators of the project, the staff of The Boston Athenæum must be given tremendous thanks for meeting the many demands that have been made of them during the long organizing process: Rodney Armstrong, Director and Librarian; Norman P. Tucker, Research and Programs Officer; Helen LaFleur, former Gallery Assistant; Joan Bragen, Director of Development; Thelma Cluett, Development Assistant; Stanley Ellis Cushing and the Conservation Department; Ann Wadsworth, Researcher; Sarah Morgan, Print Department; Alfonso Serantes, Chief Engineer, and his staff; Kevin O. Riley, Mailing Room; and Christopher Steele, Photographer.

The Society for the Preservation of New England Antiquities, whose properties include the Codman family estate, The Grange, as well as the vast collection of Codman family papers, has enthusiastically nurtured this project from the beginning. Nancy Coolidge, Director, and Abbott Lowell Cummings, her predecessor, have long been aware of the importance of this project. Among the staff, I am especially grateful to Ellie Reichlin, Director of Archives, for her understanding, encouragement, and support over the many years that were involved in the preparation of the material. Many thanks as well to Lorna Condon, Associate Archivist, for her tireless assistance in locating photographs and drawings; Richard Nylander, Curator of Collections, for his encompassing knowledge of layers of Codman family history and his sensitive interpretation of objects, textiles, and furniture in the SPNEA collections; J. David Bohl, Photographer, for his excellent photographs and care in developing period images; and Lynne Spencer, Special Projects Manager.

The curators and staff at many other museums, libraries, and historical societies have made their collections accessible, answered inquiries, and offered useful suggestions. The generous cooperation of several departments at the Metropolitan Museum of Art has been essential to this project. In the Department of Prints and Photographs, under the Chairmanship of Colta Ives, I offer special thanks to Suzanne Boorsch, Associate Curator, for her endless patience and assistance in arranging for the photography, conservation and loan of Codman drawings and photographs from the collection; and to David W. Kiehl for his long-term research assistance. In the Slide Library, Deanna Cross was always helpful; and I would like to thank James Parker, Curator of Western Decorative Arts in the Department of European Sculpture and Decorative Arts, for making available books that originally belonged in Ogden Codman's library. At the Avery Library, Columbia University, Janet Parks, Research Librarian, and her assistant, Lisa Rosenthal, have been especially helpful and cooperative in making the Codman collection of architectural drawings available. Members of the staff at Edith Wharton Restoration, Inc., have provided much valuable assistance and information, especially Thomas Hayes, Director, and Scott Marshall, Assistant Director, whose endless research has turned up rare documentation about the life of Edith Wharton. Thanks also to Patricia Willis, Curator of American Literature, Beinecke Rare Book and Manuscript Library, Yale University; Denis Lesieur, Librarian of the Lenox Library; Dianne Harris, Archivist, College of Environmental Design, University of California at Berkeley; Phyllis Stigliano and Janice Parente, Curators at the Nassau County Museum of Fine Art, Roslyn, New York; and Richard Winsche, Librarian for the Nassau County Museum Reference Library. At the Museum of Art, Rhode Island School of Design, Franklin W. Robinson, Director; Thomas Michie, Associate Curator of Decorative Arts; and Elizabeth Leuthner, Research Assistant. At the Preservation Society of Newport County, John Cherol, Director; Roxanne Squibbs, Registrar; and John Carpenter, Curatorial Assistant. Finally, I would like to thank the Woman's City Club of Ormond Beach, Florida.

The following individuals have provided invaluable assistance and expertise in a variety of ways: photographers Richard Cheek, Philip Dickenson, Joseph Farber, and Dwight Primiano; Stanley Barrows, James Burke, Richard Chafee, Tony Duquette, Christopher Gray, Sarah Kearns, Edith MacKennan, Laszlo Meszoly, Richard Nelson, Steve Nichols, Michelle St. Bernard, Thomas Seaver, Katherine Webster, Hutton Wilkinson, and John G. Winslow.

Coordinating the expansion and installation of the exhibition at the National Academy of Design required tremendous time and effort on the part of the staff there. I offer particular thanks to Barbara Krulik, Assistant Director, who has arranged for the loan and transport of objects and drawings from a variety of private and institutional sources; Robert Beard, Special Assistant to the Director, and Steven Cantrell, Publicity Director, who have overseen with endless good will the complicated arrangements involved in the implementation of the exhibition. The extraordinarily generous donations of fabric and trimming from the firm of Fonthill, Ltd., and Brunschwig and Fils have made it possible to create a suitable background for the display of objects and drawings that once belonged in the Codman interiors in the Harold Brown house in Newport, Rhode Island. Richard A. Nelson and the workroom of The Red Unicorn have devoted many hours of labor to the installation of fabric for one room of the exhibition, including the hanging of curtains and recovering chairs. I am most appreciative of the contribution made by the landscape architect Eleanor M. McPeck and interior designer William Hodgson in creating a garden room at the National Academy of Design, installed with the same style and elegance Codman originally conceived.

I am especially grateful to the following individuals for their generous consent to the loan of drawings, paintings, and objects from their collections: Mr. and Mrs. John Auchincloss, Edward Lee Cave, Nicholas King, Mr. and Mrs. Anthony Klomen, Alton Peters, Mr. and Mrs. Edmond J. Safra, Mr. and Mrs. John J. Slocum, Countess Anthony Szapary.

This exhibition and accompanying publication would not have been possible without the magnanimous contributions of the following foundations and corporations: the Beinecke Foundation, the Elsie de Wolfe Foundation, the Felicia Fund, the Vincent Mulford Foundation, the National Endowment for the Arts, the Preservation Society of Newport Rhode Island, the Providence Journal-Bulletin, and the Republic National Bank of New York. It has been extraordinarily gratifying to have received support from the following individuals: April Axton, Edward Lee Cave, Sophie F. Danforth, Esther E. Mauran, Estate of Michael P. Metcalf, Constance Hoguet Neel, Adams H. Nickerson, Mary, Viscomtesse Rothemere, Mr. and Mrs. Edmond J. Safra, J. Peter Spang, and Robert and Gertrude Wilmers.

I am most grateful to David Godine for his decision to collaborate with The Boston Athenæum on the production of this book. The outstanding reputation of Godine books plus the talents of Richard C. Bartlett in graphic design guarantee a book of the highest quality. Essential to the success of this publication has been the extraordinary dedication and sensitivity of the editor, Debra Edelstein. She has brought a discerning eye to this collection of essays, combining them into a whole while treating the individual parts with knowledge and discrimination. Finally, I would like to express my heartfelt gratitude to Melissa K. Rombout, Assistant Project Coordinator, for her tireless effort and dedication, her intelligent enthusiasm, and most of all her willingness to assume responsibility for the endless thankless details that have culminated in the successful realization of this project.

Pauline C. Metcalf
Curator of Exhibition

OGDEN CODMAN

and the

DECORATION

of

HOUSES

*Ogden Codman estate, La
Leopolda, Villefranche-sur-Mer,
France*

From Lincoln to Leopolda

PAULINE C. METCALF

IN THE FABRIC OF OGDEN CODMAN'S LIFE, "NEW ENGLAND WAS THE WARP, AND France was the woof."[1] The ideas of architecture, landscape, and decoration these threads wove are embodied in two houses: The Grange in Lincoln, Massachusetts, and La Leopolda in Villefranche-sur-Mer. The first—the Codman family seat, considered in 1800 to be the "handsomest place in America"[2]— was filled with the bounty of successful merchants, diplomats, and country squires and remained throughout Ogden's life a source of taste, an emblem of his aristocratic sensibilities and of all that was best in the restrained yet refined eighteenth-century Anglo-American tradition. The other—the ideal classic villa built in 1929–31 on the site of the former Domaine of Leopold II of Belgium—was Codman's consummate creation, his individual synthesis of three great neoclassical villas. La Leopolda is also the ultimate expression of the philosophy of design and decoration Codman and Edith Wharton espoused in their timeless manual of style, *The Decoration of Houses*. Between these two houses is the career and work of an architect, decorator, and antiquarian whose dedication to the traditions and forms of the eighteenth century was constant throughout his life.

Ogden Codman, Jr., was born on 19 January 1863 at 34 Beacon Street, Boston, the home of his maternal grandfather, James Bowdoin Bradlee. He was the eldest of five children born to Sarah Fletcher Bradlee and Ogden Codman. As a product of generations of intermarriage among old Boston clans, he was assured of connections to numerous prominent families.[3] Ogden spent much of his early youth at The Grange, and, mindful of the history of the property and its architecture, retained an interest in and devotion to the place all his life.[4] Among the children, Ogden was the only one to establish himself away from the family or to enter a profession. His brothers and sisters[5] remained tied to "Mère Cot" (as Sarah Codman was referred to by her offspring) and to each other throughout their lives. They managed the Codman estate after their mother died in 1922, but always relied on Ogden's advice for the interior decoration of The Grange—from the placement of furniture and objects to the selection of paint colors and materials for curtains and covers.[6] To him, the house and its contents symbolized the values of his distinguished ancestry, and he remained concerned throughout his life about its preservation of the family heritage. When two aunts died, for instance, he urged his siblings to acquire the items that were most important

The Codman family and friends at The Grange, c. 1895. Left to right (front row) Thomas Newbold Codman, Alice Newbold Codman, Violet Grey-Egerton, Ogden Codman, Jr.; (back row) Ogden Codman, Sr., Sarah Bradlee Codman (sitting), Lady Grey-Egerton.

to him. "The main thing," he declared, "is to keep them in the CODMAN family."[7] Over the years Ogden collected eighteenth- and early-nineteenth-century furniture he thought would look good in the rooms at Lincoln. Thus, the appearance of the house today bears a strong mark of Ogden's taste, blended with that of the previous generations.

The progression of Codman family taste can be seen in one corner of the drawing room (plate 1). On the wall is a portrait of Richard Codman (1762–1806), an ancestor of particular interest to Ogden. A younger brother of Ogden's direct forebear, John Codman III, he was in many ways Ogden's mentor. Although officially the representative for the family shipping interests in Paris, Richard spent most of his time there indulging in various extravagances: collecting art, speculating in French stocks, and acquiring several châteaux. Painted by John Singleton Copley in London in 1794, his portrait was among the prized family possessions Ogden took with him when he moved to France in 1920.[8] The smaller painting on the right, depicting Adam and Eve in the garden, was acquired by Charles Russell Codman, grandfather of Ogden Jr., who assembled one of the most important early painting collections in Boston. Next to the Federal mantelpiece is a French bergère and footstool, covered in "Les Roses" chintz,[9] a favorite of Ogden's and used by him in several of his houses; the chair is a late nineteenth-century copy of an eighteenth-century model brought to The Grange in the 1920s. On the right is a small round worktable that was supplied

Paneled room, The Grange, c. 1885–93, before Codman's redecoration

Paneled room, The Grange, after 1897, showing Codman's decoration

Paneled room, The Grange,
c. 1741

by the firm of Leon Marcotte,[10] a part of the Victorian redecoration carried out in the 1860s by Ogden Sr. in conjunction with his brother-in-law, the architect John Hubbard Sturgis.[11] The nineteenth-century Vieux Paris porcelain vases and bronze doré clock, purchased as an ensemble from a relative by Ogden Jr., provide the necessary accents of high-quality "bric-a-brac." The French furniture, paintings, and objects throughout the Codman house reflect the family's strong ties to France over several generations.[12]

Over the years Ogden transformed the interior of The Grange by removing the evidence of what he considered the "hideous" taste of the 1870s and 1880s and creating a synthesis of American and French eighteenth-century decor. In the paneled room, the dark wool rep curtains and solid heavy furniture were replaced with blue and white "toile de jouy" cotton curtains[13] and Louis XV and XVI furniture, which created a lighter, uncluttered effect. He was able to combine the best of Codman family tradition and incorporated the taste for eighteenth-century French furnishings with that of the colonial revival. In its classical design with pilasters and well-defined moldings, the paneled room clearly shows the principles of design that Ogden would adhere to so conscientiously in his own work: proportion, symmetry, and the use of an order in the treatment of the wall (plate 2). The eighteenth-century atmosphere at The Grange, with its backdrop of "old-fashioned" furniture and objects, provided a touchstone of taste for Ogden throughout his life.

The comfortable life enjoyed at the Lincoln estate was dramatically altered in 1872. As a result of the great fire in Boston, the Codmans lost a large part of their fortune, as much of it had been invested in real estate and insurance. The family therefore undertook a self-imposed exile to France until 1884, settling in Dinard on the coast of Brittany in the company of numerous other expatriate Americans. Although this early exposure to France and European culture made a strong impression on Ogden, and eventually led to his settling there, the Boston roots nurtured his artistic perceptions. As he recalled years later:

> *There is an old saying that it is better to be born lucky than rich, and as I look back over the years it would seem to have been true in my case. Environment does a lot too, and the good old Boston of the 60's and 70's made a pleasant environment. I spent a great deal of my time in Beacon Street, opposite the common dominated by his [Charles Bulfinch's] simple but dignified State House, and the equally dignified Park Street Church, both painted brick, both pale grey, both unspoiled by excrescences of their less suitable materials. . . . Alas, in those days Boston had a charm and dignity unequaled it seems to me by any other American town. My father's country house at Lincoln was thoroughly of the eighteenth century. When I left Boston, it made a restrained and simple background, and during the eight years I passed in Europe, when I saw a great many more elaborate and pretentious buildings, I think the aforesaid background prevented me from being carried away by eccentricities that otherwise might have proved too seductive.*[14]

With such impressions of New England firmly fixed in his mind, Ogden rejected the stylistic excesses of modern French architecture, such as Charles Garnier's Paris Opèra.

In 1882 Ogden was apprenticed to a German banking firm in Bonn. His dislike of the work was so intense, however, that he returned to Boston the next year to live with his uncle, John Hubbard Sturgis, a partner in the architectural firm of Sturgis and Brigham. That Sturgis had been anxious to assist his nephew's education and to reestablish his New England ties is evident from a letter to Ogden's father, in which he pleaded, "If he is ever to live in America he ought to go home soon and be educated there or he will be more or less unfitted for his life there. Let me, in Fanny's and my own name, again make the offer that . . . he shall come and live with us and finish his education."[15]

In 1884, under the direction of his uncle, Ogden enrolled as a special student in architecture at the School of Technology, now the Massachusetts Institute of Technology. Evidently the experience of supervised instruction was not an especially pleasant one, as he remained there only a year (and fifty-seven years later requested the school to remove his name from the list of former students). Of more importance to his education was Sturgis's guidance in making measured drawings of old buildings. Sturgis had learned this method of studying historic buildings during his years in England and was an early proponent in America of this approach. It is ironic that Sturgis's

Ogden Codman at nineteen in Dinard, France, 1882

alterations to The Grange, so disliked by Ogden, sparked his curiosity about its earlier appearance and thereby provided him with a firsthand opportunity to study and restore an eighteenth-century building. Recalling the experience sixty years later, Ogden wrote, "I suppose that in 1862 no one thought anything old-fashioned was nice at all. Perhaps if he had left everything as it was, I never would have been inspired with putting things back as they were. But that has been a great pleasure to me."[16] Ogden particularly disliked Sturgis's "up-to-date" treatment of the dining and billiard rooms (decorated in conjunction with Leon Marcotte) as well as the "dreadful mantels he designed for the bedrooms."[17] During the 1890s he restored many of the mantels and doors to their original locations; it was probably at that time that he changed the billiard room into a library, incorporating the heavy bookcases formerly placed in the paneled room. Despite his extensive research, Ogden never discovered the possible association of his favorite Boston architect, Charles Bulfinch, with the 1790s additions to The Grange.

Another uncle who influenced Ogden's career was Richard Codman, who, after the family's losses in 1872, had become a successful interior decorator. He wrote in his *Reminiscences* that "there was a good deal of building going on at that time as the whole Back Bay district was just being developed and I soon found my business rapidly increasing and extending to New York, Newport, Chicago and many other places."[18] He was instrumental in introducing the "aesthetic" taste to Boston society, and he imported the wallpapers and fabrics of Morris and Co., as well as other English wares. Although there is no evidence that Ogden worked directly with his uncle, considering the close ties among members of the Codman family, he probably acted as a mentor to his nephew and helped to guide him to a career in the field of interior decoration.

Ogden's letters to his mother, written during 1883–84, show his growing interest in interiors and his awareness of trends as reflected in the Back Bay. "Taste has advanced in some ways wonderfully in the past ten years," he noted, "perhaps a parlor is finished in white paint in the style of the drawing room at Lincoln . . . now the height of fashion. In all the handsomest new houses the more white paint the better."[19] Pages of his letters to his mother are filled with sketches and descriptions of "old-fashioned" furniture in the Queen Anne and Georgian styles with which he had furnished his recently rented rooms. That he was finding his professional niche comes through in his contented declarations: "My rooms are my great pleasure and a constant occupation for every spare moment," and "Do write a long letter about furniture. There is hardly anything I take so much interest in. Houses and furniture and genealogy are my three hobbies."[20]

The tone of Ogden's letters, despite their enthusiasm, indicates his lingering dilettantish approach to his future profession. His reluctance to continue formal architectural training resulted in two "dreary" years spent in an unidentified architect's office in Lowell, Massachusetts. He also mentions working at A. H. Davenport, the well-known furniture and decorating firm, during this time.[21] His next architectural stint was at the new Boston firm of Andrews and Jacques. That experience ended in September 1889 when he received notice from Robert Andrews, who complained that his performance in the office was marked by an "indifference to succeed."[22] Ogden does not comment on his work there, but the heavy, stone Richardsonian style, typical of their work in the 1880s, was the antithesis of what he would later design. Ogden would not embark on his own business for another two years, but clearly he was not motivated by strictures other than those of his own making.

One positive outcome of the time spent there was the friendship made with a fellow apprentice, Herbert W. C. Browne. Browne and another Boston architect, Arthur Little, became his lifelong friends. In 1890 Little and Browne formed their own successful architectural partnership, while Ogden remained on his own and continued his independent studies. During the late 1880s and early 1890s the trio — which Ogden dubbed the "colonial trinity" because of their shared respect for the past — rediscovered neglected buildings, traced their owners, and explored the many architectural charms of the Boston area. The individual ways in which Codman, Little, and Browne expressed their inspiration from the colonial heritage forms an interesting chapter of New England architectural history. Little used colonial fragments in a "confectionary" manner, while Browne's archaeological approach was more like Ogden's literal translation of eighteenth-century detailing in his designs. The differences led to a professional competitiveness, but they nevertheless remained friends throughout their lives.

Always the indefatigable letter writer, Ogden's letters from abroad show the continuing education of the impressionable young decorator. Especially eager for interior photographs of famous villas and palaces, he collected "between 500 and 1000 of all sorts" during his European trip in 1894.[23] Among his favorites were the palaces of Genoa ("much finer than I expected from the photos"), the Villa Madama, and St. Peter's in Rome. He was also "much gone on Bernini," and concluded that "the sixteenth, seventeenth, and eighteenth [centuries] are still my pets and always will be."[24] His prejudice for the eighteenth century involved more than architecture. While he extolled the pleasures of listening to Mozart and Haydn, he characterized the music of Wagner "as vulgar as the Waldorf-Astoria."[25] This anti-Victorian bias even fell on royalty; when he heard the news about the new king, he wrote, "I am so pleased with King Edward VII. I never expected to outlive Victoria, the inartistic, and was afraid he would be Albert I."[26] While abroad he also cultivated a dandyish self-image, and his pride in his sartorial splendor bursts forth when he writes:

> *You would scarcely recognize me I am so smart. Single eyeglass, bouton-niere, grey or brown linen waistcoat, varnishes, boots, top-hat, a cut-away coat and grey or black very smart gloves. Everything from the swellest London people. I constantly see myself in the glass and wonder who it is. Pink, blue, or mauve shirts, butterflys do make a difference. . . . My mustache is curled, the ends set nearly into my eyes.*"[27]

The first official listing of Ogden Codman as an architect and decorator is in the Boston Directory of 1891. He had borrowed one thousand dollars from one of his aunts to begin his business.[28] Among his first clients were old Boston friends and relations, including Daniel Berkeley Updike, Mrs. Charles Paine, and W. S. Otis. From T. Codman II he received a profit of $11.20 for assistance in selecting wallpapers. Codman usually took his clients shopping for furniture, and when he could not find a genuine antique, would go to a source such as A. H. Davenport, one of the largest furniture companies in New England, which was known for its quality reproductions. He would receive a ten-percent commission on each item his client purchased. At times he commissioned work, such as a favorite ancestral piece, the rare caned settee belonging to John Codman IV, which he had copied in mahogany by the Davenport firm.

Codman began making regular summer visits to Newport, Rhode Island, in 1884. There he was given his first decorating job by a cousin, Mrs. John Doughty Ogden — to set columns between double parlors and install a Georgian mantelpiece. Cavorting with relatives, such as the Wetmore sisters, Edith and Maud, at the fashionable seaside resort brought him in contact with a richer and more flamboyant social circle, which he saw as a potentially lucrative clientele. He did not, however, spend an entire season in Newport until after he had officially opened his office in 1891. For introductions to the "smart" crowd, he relied on a Boston friend, Tom Cushing. "It seems much nicer now I know more people," he reported, "I went to a hop and saw lots of *Town Topic* celebrities." On another occasion, he "went for a drive with Mr. Cushing and left lots of cards." The strategy worked, for by August of that summer he had received a commission for a "jolly new job." He wrote to Arthur Little, "Mrs. Cutting has just told me she wants me to do her house as a result of the Wharton house. It is rather encouraging. . . . I am to decorate it in the French taste. And we are to get the furniture in Paris next spring."[29] Pleased with his growing roster of Social Register clients, he happily reported to his mother the next summer, "Imagine Paines, Cuttings, Coolidges, Millers, Winthrops, Whartons—all owing money!"[30] While eager to have the wealthiest clients to fulfill his professional ambitions and support his expensive tastes, Codman, as a member of the more conservative New England set, was often disdainful of the newer arrivals in the summer community. He condemned their manners and behavior as "common" and "vulgar." The discriminating attitudes of the young tastemaker are evident in his remarks: "I hate shabby dilapidated houses and poor cooks and all that sort of thing and no culture or interest in art. . . . What I want is comfort. . . . I always decide against poverty when I see very good bric-a-brac."[31]

The most notable person among Codman's early Newport clients and the one most responsible for his later success was Edith Wharton. Her friendship and patronage were of invaluable assistance to him in obtaining some of his most important clients. Although Codman does not mention when he first met Mrs. Wharton (as he always addressed her), his reference to work on the Wharton house in 1891 indicates that she was among his earliest clients. Possibly he made suggestions about the decoration at Pencraig Cottage, the Whartons' home in Newport before they purchased Land's End in 1893. It was, as she described in her autobiography, during the process of transforming Land's End—"to give a certain dignity" to "an ugly wooden house with half an acre of rock and illimitable miles of Atlantic Ocean"— that she and "the clever young Boston architect"[32] discovered they both believed that "interior decoration should be simple and architectural" and both shared "a dislike of sumptuary excesses."[33] Not until several years later did they actually embark on their literary venture, *The Decoration of Houses*, which delineated their rebellion against the clutter and heavy-handed excesses displayed in many Victorian houses. Edith's crisp prose gave the book its style, while Ogden contributed both a practical understanding of the principles of interior design and many of the illustrations of splendid rooms in the great palaces and country houses of Europe.

Edith Wharton and Ogden Codman shared other bonds—not the least of which was commiseration with one another on the "dullness" of most Newport society, concern for good cuisine, and an overwhelming love and appreciation for the atmosphere and culture in Europe, primarily France and Italy. Their knowledge of European art and culture certainly contributed to the self-confidence with which they prescribed the formula for suitable and appropriate decoration of houses. Codman, full of enthusiasm for the great palaces and residences of European nobility, felt sufficiently well versed in

Ogden Codman, Mrs. Alice Vanderbilt's bedroom, Cornelius Vanderbilt II house, The Breakers, Newport, Rhode Island, c. 1894–95

J. Allard et Fils, dining room, The Breakers

Gertrude Vanderbilt Whitney's bedroom, The Breakers

Bathroom, The Breakers

their architecture and decoration to adapt them according to the needs and aspirations of well-to-do Americans. Bringing the airs of nobility to Newport was not far from his thoughts when he wrote to his mother, "Mr. Vanderbilt drove me down to my office yesterday. It was much the same as driving with the Prince of Wales or a very good Duke."[34]

In December 1893 Codman received the good news that he had been chosen to decorate the "whole upper floors of Cornelius Vanderbilt's Newport villa" (The Breakers). He instantly penned his excitement to his closest confidants. To Arthur Little he described his plans: "The house is enormous and is to be carried out in the utter-most correctness in the Italian and French eighteenth century." And to his mother he crowed: "Just think what a client! The nicest and richest of them all. . . . I am going to thank Mrs. Wharton who brought this about."[35] The Breakers was the last and the greatest of Richard Morris Hunt's Newport "cottages," and Codman was to share the decorating responsibilities with the firm of J. Allard et Fils, the most highly regarded French firm of the era.

Hunt, who had built a number of houses for branches of the Vanderbilt family and had collaborated with Allard in their interior decoration, had little respect for the inexperienced and relatively untrained young man who wished to impose his ideas on the architect's original scheme. Critical of Codman's inadequate specifications, he admonished him, "If I am to make suggestions, it will be necessary to furnish me with carefully made drawings . . . , not mere outlines showing your intentions."[36] Codman had apparently left out of his plans such basic items as gas outlets and electric bells. The relative simplicity of Codman's rooms (plate 3) was in marked contrast to the overwhelming opulence of Allard's downstairs rooms. Codman did many beautiful color renderings for the rooms, sometimes with an overlay to give a choice of color or curtain design (plate 4). The detailing of moldings and door surrounds were carefully delineated, as were the pattern and design of the fabrics.

Another close friend whose connections and talents were of invaluable assistance to Codman during the early Newport years was Daniel Berkeley Updike. A Rhode Islander by birth and an innovative printer and designer, Updike was responsible for introducing Codman to Harold Brown, a member of one of Rhode Island's oldest and wealthiest families. In 1894 Brown hired Codman to design a series of Empire interiors as appropriate settings for the collection of Napoleonic furniture and objects that he and his bride, Georgette Wetmore Sherman, had acquired during their wedding trip to France in 1892. This was one of Codman's largest early commissions and the only one in which he used the Empire style. Upon the Browns' return to Newport, plans were already underway for a stone house designed by a popular local architect, Dudley Newton, in a style reminiscent of Scottish Baronial and typical of many other houses built in Newport during the 1880s and 1890s. Codman's interiors, in total contrast to the exterior, had Empire decoration in every aspect, from the decorative plasterwork to furniture, upholstery, curtains, and even such items as fire tools. For the detailing,

Codman consulted Charles Percier and Pierre Fontaine's *Recueil de décorations intérieures*, the foremost source for the Empire style (plates 5–10).

Both the Vanderbilt and the Brown commissions are important documents of Codman's early work, especially as they have survived remarkably intact.[37] His style of decoration in the 1890s, while literal in the handling of historical motifs, still retains qualities of pastiche that tie his work to the eclecticism of earlier decades (plate 11). Another surviving Newport example from the early years is at Château-sur-Mer, the George Peabody Wetmore "cottage" begun in the 1850s but with extensive additions made by Richard Morris Hunt in the 1870s. The green salon, redecorated for the coming-out season of the Wetmore sisters in 1897, is one of Codman's most correct handlings of Louis XV detail. Adjoining the ballroom decorated by Leon Marcotte in the 1870s, it shows the difference between Codman's treatment of the French rococo style and that of the preceding generation.

Ogden Codman, design of wall, green salon, George Peabody Wetmore house, Château-sur-Mer, Newport, Rhode Island, 1903

The Thayers of Boston were among Codman's most loyal clients throughout his career. The first commission for Nathaniel Thayer was carried out in Newport in 1896 and provided Codman with the opportunity to remodel extensively an 1860s Stick Style cottage designed by a local architect, George Champlin Mason, and to add a connecting gallery and dining/gala room in the rear. The interiors were completely redecorated in the Georgian style, which was also carried over to the classical addition. Although the latter was done in a different scale from the original structure, it was handled so adeptly that it did not conflict with the character of the earlier house.

Ogden Codman, cross section and plan of Nathaniel Thayer house, Edgemere, Newport, Rhode Island, c. 1896–97

Design of north wall, drawing room, Edgemere

Drawing room, Edgemere

Having completed a job that included some original construction, Codman was hopeful that he could gain membership in the American Institute of Architects. He wrote to Charles McKim on 19 February 1897 and asked him to be his sponsor. Given Codman's minimal formal training and his lack of a completed building, McKim could not endorse his candidacy and wrote him that the "execution of interior decoration work alone would not be considered a sufficient qualification for membership."[38] Although his subsequent work as an architect would certainly have made him a suitable candidate, Codman abandoned his attempt to become a member. He realized that his architectural peers, who had been exposed to the rigorous disciplines of the Ecole des Beaux-Arts or one of the recently formed American architectural schools whose curriculum was based on the French model, would never consider him a bona fide professional architect. In the eyes of Richard Morris Hunt or Charles McKim, the foremost proponent of the classical American Renaissance style, it was important to be inspired by the original source but not copy "too slavishly," as McKim had warned.

In 1897 Codman was given the opportunity to design his first house. Mrs. Charles Coolidge Pomeroy commissioned a seaside villa on a wind-blown site on Ocean Drive in Newport. He referred to it in later years as "my poor little first attempt," although, as it was made of stucco, the local inhabitants soon nicknamed it "the mud palace."[39] It was, in fact, not much more than an interrupted cube with a classical pediment, corbels, and arched windows on the first floor. While it was being built, Codman designed another house nearby for Mr. and Mrs. Alfred Coates of Providence. Derived from late-seventeenth-century English models, this house contained many

Ogden Codman, Ethel Burnet Pomeroy house, Seabeach, Newport, Rhode Island, 1895–96

Dining room, Edgemere

Ogden Codman, Alfred M. Coats house, Landfall, Newport, Rhode Island, c. 1895–96

Ogden Codman, Eben Howard Gay house, 170 Beacon Street, Boston, 1900

elements that would recur in his country houses—a hip roof, dormers, and the massing of a central block with projecting wings.

That same year marked the publication of *The Decoration of Houses*, which was an important watershed in Codman's career. Not only was his reputation considerably enhanced by his association with the book, but his work after 1897 shifted also from the purely decorative approach toward an architectural one. He later wrote that in the process of analyzing the advice that he and Wharton had laid down, he had been able to "inwardly digest"[40] the guidelines and apply them to his own work. Such phrases as "if proportion is the good breeding of architecture, symmetry . . . may be defined as the sanity of decoration" and "structure conditions ornament, not ornament structure" were henceforth consistently adhered to by Codman. As the language and structure of *The Decoration of Houses* were formal, ordered, and symmetrical, so was the design of Codman's houses; both reflected the society in which their creators lived. Codman's style had matured by the turn of the century. There would be no further significant changes in his approach to design, although he gradually rid his decorative schemes of the charming but excessive details so characteristic of the Edwardian era.

The years around the turn of the century were extremely busy ones for Codman's office. In 1900 he designed the Villa Rosa for E. Rollins Morse of Boston. No longer standing, it was one of Codman's most beautiful houses in Newport, and its trellis ballroom was the first room in America to incorporate lattice design as a decorative motif. At this time he also designed a large Georgian house in Roslyn, Long Island, for Lloyd Bryce and another in Providence for Alfred Coats; he also remodeled and refronted a town house on Beacon Street in Boston for Eben Howard Gay. A large estate on the North Shore would soon be on the drawing boards for Oliver Ames of

PLATE I. *Drawing room,*
Codman family house, The
Grange, Lincoln, Massachusetts,
redecorated by Ogden Codman
after 1897

PLATE 2. *Paneled room, The
Grange, redecorated by Codman
after 1897*

Boston. In addition, there were visits to his family in Lincoln to supervise the construction of an Italian garden and the annual trips to Europe for sightseeing and shopping with his clients in Paris and London. Thus, when he was approached by his old friends Edith and Teddy Wharton to design a house in Lenox, Massachusetts, there was truth in his statement, "I told them that I was so busy and my work was so scattered I could not be coming to Lenox once a week and go to Providence, Newport, Boston, and Long Island too."[41] There were, of course, many other reasons for their notorious falling out, but given the strains put on their friendship by the imperious personalities of all the characters, it was almost inevitable that such a break would occur. In October 1902, just after The Mount was completed, Codman wrote his mother about its "forlorn" appearance, caused in part by the Whartons' haste to move in before all the last-minute touches were finished. Although he was satisfied with his work for the interior detailing, he was extremely critical of the flaws in the building's design, which he considered the fault of the "semi-artistic" architect, Francis L. V. Hoppin, who had been hired to replace him. He also expressed a genuine regret that he had not been "kinder" to the Whartons.[42] Implied was a deeper regret—that he had missed the opportunity to work with a rare and special client.

Ogden Codman, Lloyd S. Bryce house, Roslyn, New York, c. 1901

Ogden Codman, ballroom,
E. Rollins Morse house,
Villa Rosa, Newport, Rhode
Island, 1900

Ogden Codman's New York career began in 1893. Pleased with a profit of over a thousand dollars from his first year of business,[43] he opened a branch on Bellevue Avenue in Newport and moved his permanent residence and office to New York. He had not forsaken his New England origins, but he was shrewd enough to realize that New York was a better base from which to pursue a more rewarding clientele. The lure of dinners at Delmonico's and Mrs. Astor's balls were worth the risk of leaving the familial security of Boston.

Codman's letters contain some gossipy portraits of well-known figures in New York at the turn of the century. In his circle were the Hewitt sisters, Sarah and Eleanor, who were beginning to collect decorative arts for their new museum; Elsie de Wolfe and Elizabeth (Bessie) Marbury, perhaps one of the first accepted female couples in New York society; and Anne Morgan, the daughter of J. P. Morgan. None of this group escaped his caustic tongue. In letters to his mother he calls Bessie Marbury "fat and vulgar" and dismisses the Hewitt sisters as "common." On further acquaintance however, he realized the benefits of their friendship, as well as their useful social connections. He comes to consider the Hewitts as "kind and nice," and they are redeemed by their "interesting taste and fondness for pretty things."[44] Ogden enjoyed the "little Sunday gatherings" at Elsie and Bessie's, where old New York mixed with the bohemian theatrical and literary circles. In her autobiography, de Wolfe included Ogden among "the brilliant coterie who gathered at our hearth," along with Henry Adams and Walter Gay.[45] Codman's homosexual proclivities did not prevent his enjoyment of female companionship, nor blind him to the professional advantage of a suitable marriage. Apparently he even considered Anne Morgan a matrimonial prospect, but, he reported, she "seems to think me too frivolous and too fond of smart people."[46] He did manage to arrange a tea party at his office to introduce "Annie" to Elsie and Bessie. In due course Morgan's social position helped launch de Wolfe's decorating career, and her money helped restore the Villa Trianon, the neglected eighteenth-century pavilion in the park of Versailles that was purchased by Elsie and Bessie in the summer of 1906.

Like his Boston work of the 1890s, the New York commissions consisted for the most part in alterations to brownstones, primarily installing decorative plasterwork and paneled moldings in the French style. Codman's confections of swags, garlands, and putti usually found their way into boudoirs before he began decorating the areas shared by the male members of the household. Not everyone approved: Henry James described the Whartons' New York house at 882–884 Park Avenue as a "bonbonniere of the last daintiness naturally."[47] In 1901 Codman was hired by Bessie Marbury and Elsie de Wolfe to make alterations to the drawing room at their Irving Place residence. To help create a "salon" with the "mellowed atmosphere of French society," Codman widened the long wall space by installing panel moldings and painted the walls an ivory color. According to Elsie, the doors were "dressed" in mirrors, and one end of the room was given "a graceful aspect" by a niche in the wall for the placement of a statue. Furnished in a mixture of eighteenth-century English furniture and some pieces of Louis XIV and XV furniture that the women had acquired in their travels to France, and adorned with a portrait by Nattier over the mantel, the room acquired the look that would always be associated with Elsie de Wolfe and Ogden Codman.[48]

Codman also advised on the alterations to and decoration of de Wolfe's other New York houses. In 1910 she bought an "old-fashioned high-stooped brownstone" at 131 East 71st Street and decided to conduct an "experiment" in which she and Codman "waved the divining-rod which brought its latent graces to the surface." They removed the stoop and made "a little court . . . paved with stone flagging, . . . surrounded with a high iron grill and planted [with] a . . . clipped evergreen hedge." The entrance door was brought down to the basement level and lacquered a dark green.[49] Inside the entrance hall, Codman suggested "a black and white marble floor, as I think it would be much more suitable, not to say stylish."[50] An old French porcelain stove was set into a recess, a feature recommended for a hall in *The Decoration of Houses* because it combined an understated elegance and simplicity of design with

function. A spiral staircase was placed in the center of the house to allow the dining and drawing rooms as well as the bedrooms the full eighteen-foot width of the house. Codman also recommended the use of mirrors on the landing and the doors to give a greater sense of illusion to the narrow hall. The result, according to de Wolfe, was a singular success:

> *When it was finished Ogden Codman and I gave a reception to which all of New York flocked, and went away applauding this perfect solution of transmuting an unattractive house into a romantic and unusual dwelling place. Soon the process . . . was copied . . . throughout the country in cities . . . long overburdened with the dull and heavy facades of these mid-Victorian relics.*[51]

Perhaps these alterations were not quite as unique nor influential as de Wolfe claimed, but they were successful, and Codman made similar changes to other town houses in New York and Boston.

Virtually the same alterations were made the following year to the brownstone the women moved into on East 55th Street. The drawing room appeared in a photograph in de Wolfe's *The House in Good Taste*, published in 1913, accompanied by a caption asserting that "the drawing-room should be intimate in spirit." The text of the book, actually ghostwritten by the future decorator Ruby Ross Wood, proclaimed the prerogative of women in the decoration of the home and imparted a decidedly feminist perspective: "We take it for granted that this American home is always the woman's home: a man may build and decorate a beautiful house, but it remains for a woman to make a home of it for him. Men are forever guests in our homes, no matter how much happiness they may find there."[52] The book largely rephrased in chatty language the principles outlined by Codman and Wharton in *The Decoration of Houses*, while adding an air of practicality to the advice. The tone of the book shows the changes that had taken place in the intervening years: the emancipation of women had begun, and de Wolfe wisely directed her advice to "modern women who demand simplified living."[53]

On 8 October 1904, at the age of forty-one, Ogden married Leila Griswold Webb, widow of H. Walter Webb, a vice-president of New York Central and Hudson River Page Railroad. Webb died of consumption in 1900, leaving his wife a sizable inheritance and an estate in Scarboro-on-Hudson, New York. Six years older than Ogden, with two sons, she was the ideal wife for him, both socially and financially; and their marriage was apparently happy. *Town Topics* noted that "friendship had ripened into something deeper when he [Codman] was called upon to draw the plans for Mrs. Webb's new house on Fifty-first street near Fifth Avenue." The announcement continued, "As the walls of the house rose on the foundations, so also rose the hopes of the architect that he might be overseeing the construction of a nest for his fondest aspirations." While another article referred to Mr. Codman as "one of the great Boston swells," a third one said that "it had been supposed that he would die a bachelor."[54] Following the ceremony, which was attended by the John D. Rockefellers, the Vanderbilts, and Berkeley Updike, the couple sailed for Europe on the liner *Cedric*. During the six years of their marriage, Ogden and Leila spent as much as half the year in Europe, and leased a small château, Corbeil-Cerf, in Meru et Oise, from the Marquis de Lubersac. It all ended sadly with Leila's unexpected death from complications after surgery on 10 January 1910.

Drawing room, Elizabeth Marbury and Elsie de Wolfe house, 123 East 55th Street, New York, c. 1910–11

One of the reasons the Codmans spent so much time in France was that most of the furnishings for his clients' houses were supplied by French dealers and he needed to coordinate the myriad details. In his opinion France offered both the best quality and the best price, especially for the exact copies of Louis XV and XVI furniture that were made to order for clients. In addition to the furniture, there were the requisite curtains, trimmings, carpets, hardware, statuary, and bric-a-brac to be selected and made up for the clients. A constant flow of letters, cables, photographs, and drawings of works in progress went back and forth across the Atlantic between Codman and his New York office. When his clients arrived in Europe for their annual shopping expeditions, Codman met them in Paris and took them to the various shops where he had selected items or where samples could be seen. Leila Codman was a tremendous asset; not only did she have a discerning eye and an interest in the artistic nature of decorating, but she was also a charming hostess who created the proper ambience for entertaining the clients at the château. It was important for clients to see a place that was furnished in the manner Codman envisioned for their own houses. The Boston historian Walter Muir Whitehill said of Codman that he often provided his clients with splendid houses that were more tasteful than the clients, unaided, would have necessarily thought of wanting.[55]

One client who became quite impatient with Codman's lengthy sojourns in France, and the length of time it took to produce the items from France, was John D. Rockefeller, Jr. While overseeing the furnishing of his father's house, Kykuit, in Pocantico Hills, he wrote to Codman:

Ogden Codman, bedroom of John D. Rockefeller, Jr. house, Kykuit, Pocantico Hills, New York, 1908

Library, Kykuit

*Father's house is practically finished, insofar as possible, until your re-
turn. . . . Mrs. Rockefeller and I feel your absence most seriously. . . . Mr.
Baumgarten [William Baumgarten's firm executed much of the decora-
tion] is also abroad . . . so we are quite helpless . . . to secure the furnishings and ornaments so necessary to give the house the homelike touch which
you and we are desirous it shall have.*[56]

Rockefeller also resented delays in the production of tapestry curtains caused
by Codman's preference for a French design over one by the firm of Herter
Brothers, and he reminded Codman that he was "entirely satisfied with
designs produced in this country."[57] Codman tried to calm his client by
justifying his decisions:

> *My experience has been that it takes a great deal of time and pains to get
> really good things but that in the end it is well worth while. . . . The plea-
> sure that one obtains from the result is so great that one soon forgets all
> the petty annoyance. . . . I have rarely succeeded in producing the effects I
> was striving for. As a rule my clients have only allowed me to go part way,
> and rarely to carry out a whole scheme. . . . It has taken a long time, but
> I have spared no trouble to get the very best I could find of everything.*[58]

Codman was given a budget of three to four thousand dollars "to pick up
pretty things a bit out of the common run for the house." These included
such items as silverware, framed prints, linens, china, fire tools, and bibelots
of all sorts.[59]

It was during his marriage that Codman began cataloguing French
châteaux. In forming a catalogue raisonné documented with photographs

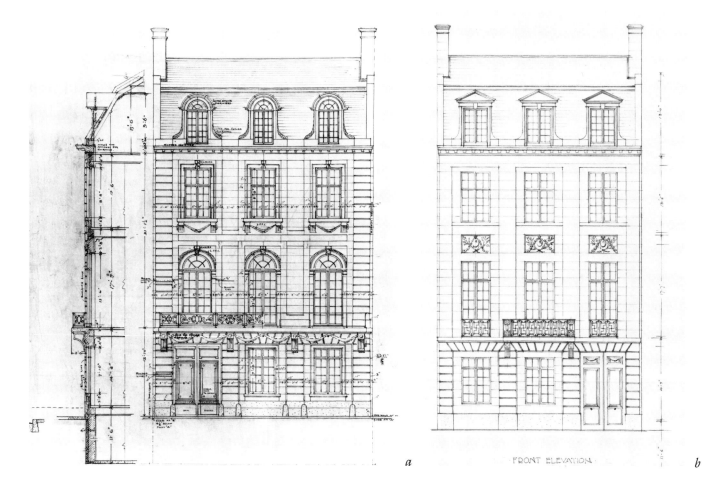

a

FRONT ELEVATION

b

*Ogden Codman, detail of facade
showing porte-cochère entrance,
7 East 96th Street, New York,
1912*

and plans, he transferred his systematic approach to the study of old buildings to the other side of the Atlantic. The couple made trips to the countryside to look at various châteaux, and what he learned through their careful inspection would often appear in later commissions. As he had done with The Grange, Codman absorbed the particulars of his current environment. To a friend and client, Walter Maynard, he described his own château and its grounds:

> *Both are so absolutely simple and logical, and show how much result can be got with a minimum of outlay in money provided the plans are made with a knowledge of good precedent and some taste. It is wonderful how well the formal treatment of the grounds can be carried out on a tiny place and how little labour and expense it involves to keep all in good order. What a pity it is that all this should be so little understood in the U.S.*[60]

Seven years later Codman was able to demonstrate his ideas in a house he would design for Maynard on Long Island.

Leila's death was a tragic loss for Ogden. They had shared similar tastes and ideas, she had encouraged his talents, and together they enjoyed a life

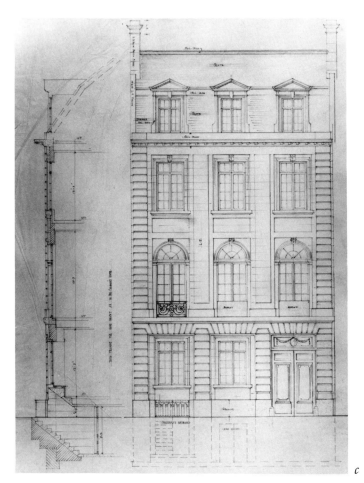

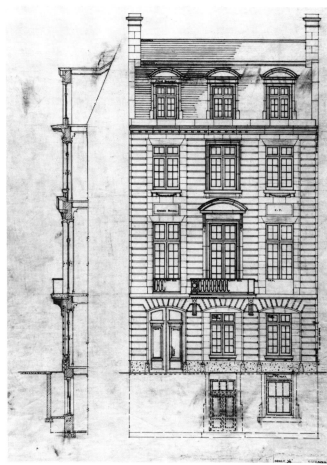

c

d

Ogden Codman, elevations, 7–15 East 96th Street, New York, c. 1912–16
  a. Codman house
  b. Francis de R. Wissman house
  c. Richard Trimble house
  d. Lucy Drexel Dahlgren house

of understated luxury that he had not previously been able to afford. Heart-broken and lonely after her death, he wrote to his brother, "She made all the difference in my being happy, and I could be happy anywhere with her."[61] Among the letters of condolence was one from Whitney Warren, who wrote, "We have . . . in common our ambition to do good work, and you have done such a lot of it and of a quality altogether so extraordinary that consolation must come of your effort."[62]

Codman's efforts did continue, and some of his best houses were built between 1910 and the closing of his office in 1920. There was a house for his cousin, Martha Codman (later Mrs. Maxim Karolik) in Newport, while he completed one for her in Washington, D.C. For the Newport house, he would make good use of his study of eighteenth-century Boston houses, while on the interior he would show his knowledge of English sources. In 1911 he received a commission from the Bayard Thayers for a substantial town house on Beacon Street. He later considered it one of his best works. It was inspired by London town houses, and he and Elsie de Wolfe, with whom he collaborated on the decoration, turned to the English firm of Lenygon & Morant for the interior details.[63]

In 1912 he embarked on an ambitious project for himself at 7 East 96th Street in New York City. Although he had purchased the lot from Andrew

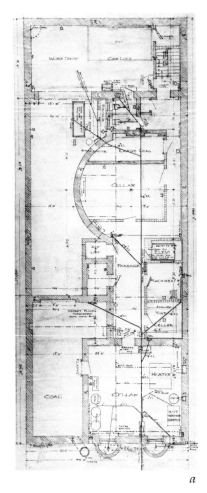

a

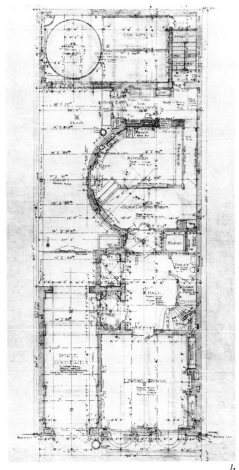

b

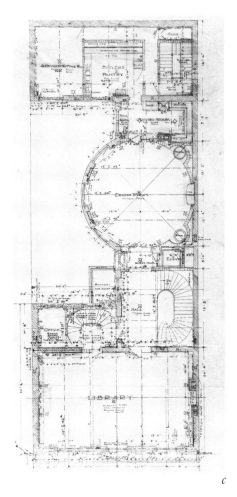

c

Auguste Schoy, facade, maison de porte-cochère, from L'art architectural décoratif et somptuaire de l'époque Louis XVI *(1868)*

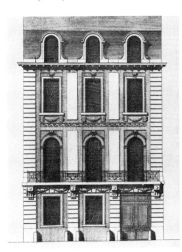

Carnegie in 1908, plans for construction were delayed until after the sale of his 51st Street house.[64] Codman believed the best advertisement of his taste and abilities would be a complete house of his own design, so this move to a relatively undeveloped area of Manhattan (referred to as "the frontier for millionaires' homes" in a 1913 real estate guide), though undoubtedly done in part for land speculation, was made with the hope of attracting other commissions.

As it happened he had a specific source on which to base his conception of a row of elegant town houses. His plan was derived from a series of row houses built in the 1830s, Depau Row, located originally at Bleecker and Thompson Streets in what is now Greenwich Village. Although the houses no longer existed in 1912, Codman had studied them on one of his first visits to New York in 1892 and wrote a description of them to Arthur Little:

> *They say the houses used to open together so when they had balls all the drawing rooms which were on the first floor were ensuite and you could go the entire length of the block, . . . eight or so houses, I wish I had counted. . . . The drawing rooms all have iron balconies . . . like 34 Beacon Street. I had always heard of this place and think it well worth seeing.*[65]

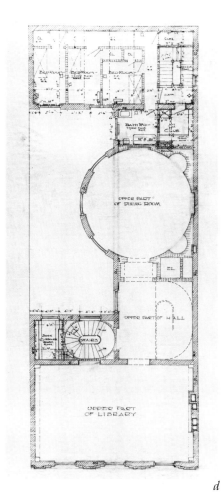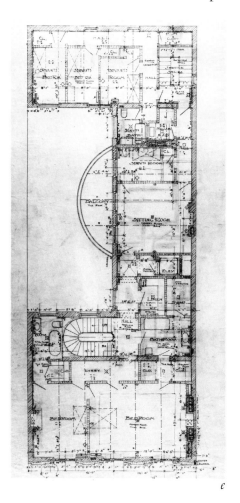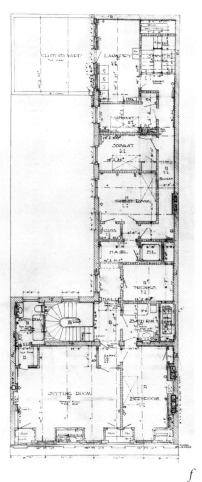

d *e* *f*

Another feature of Depau Row that appealed to him was the French custom of entering the house not from the street, but from a side door beyond the porte-cochère, where a short driveway led to a court and carriage house in the rear. In his house, the porte-cochère entrance led to a garage in the rear, where a turntable enabled the chauffeur to turn the car around with ease.

Codman drew up plans for houses at numbers 9, 11, 13, and 15 East 96th Street; however only number 15 was carried out on the north side and number 12 on the south side of the street. The plans for the others were virtually identical to his own house, and each facade was a limestone variant of an eighteenth-century French *hôtel*. For his own house, Codman used an eighteenth-century French facade based on a plate from Auguste Schoy, *L'Art architectural, décoratif, industriel et somptuaire de l'epoque Louis XVI*. Had all the houses been built, the resulting row would have been Codman's most interesting contribution to the development of the New York town house, as well as an excellent example of the adaptability of an earlier row house design.

Although he received several other important commissions between 1914 and 1917, including two for Archer Huntington at 3 East 89th Street and 1083 Fifth Avenue and a French country house on Long Island for the Walter Maynards, Codman's business was severely diminished because of

Ogden Codman, plans, 7 East 96th Street, New York, 1912
a. Basement
b. First floor
c. Mezzanine
d. Second floor
e. Third floor
f. Fourth floor

World War I. The rattling of the social order had already begun before 1914, but the jolt it received as a result of the war changed the habits of upper-class Americans, and the new generation did not want to return to the old constricted formalities after the war ended. Nearing the age of sixty, Codman felt out of touch with these changes and resented the loss of refinement to life in New York. When his practice ceased to provide him with any personal satisfaction and he felt the competition from the next generation of architects, he closed his office, in the autumn of 1920, and prepared to go to France, the country for which he had always had such an affinity, for at least eighteen months. In fact, he never returned, except for one brief visit in 1928 which he cut short, horrified at the changes that had taken place in the intervening years. He rented his house with its furnishings and loaned a large portion of his architectural library plus his professional drawings, plans, and photographs to the Metropolitan Museum of Art. He did not forget the museum of decorative arts that had been founded by his friends Sarah and Eleanor Hewitt, the Cooper Union, where he sent his eighteenth-century Italian furniture and other objects from his collection.[66] He took two collections with him to France—his genealogies of New England families and his growing catalogue of French châteaux.

During the first years of his retirement Codman lived in several places before he settled on a château to buy. He first had a pied-à-terre in Paris at 60 rue de Varennes (next door to Edith Wharton), then rented a château, Péthagny, in Normandy and another, the Villa Françesca, in Cannes. Several autumns were spent in Venice while he contemplated writing a book on the villas of the Veneto and Brenta. In 1926, restless without a house of his own to decorate, Codman bought a small seventeenth-century château, Grégy-sur-Yerres, situated in a park of fifty acres, eighteen miles southeast of Paris in Brie-Comte-Robert. The restoration of the château and its grounds absorbed his attention for several years. As always, details had to be respected: there must be a small deer park, farm buildings had to be turned into garages and servants' quarters, the kitchen and flower gardens had to be planted. He enlisted the advice of Edith Wharton, who had moved to France in 1912, on what shrubs to plant and where to plant them. After he sold the house on 96th Street in 1927, he brought to France a few of his favorite ancestral pieces to retain a sense of security and remind him of his roots. Others that he thought more suitable for The Grange were sent to his brothers and sisters; always he bore in mind the continuing refinement of the decoration there and its reflection of the Codman heritage.

With the help of a secretary (several came and went over the years), he kept up with his extensive correspondence. One of his most frequent correspondents was Fiske Kimball, with whom he continued to share his love and knowledge of colonial buildings. In the flow of letters (dating from 1917 to 1938) between Kimball and "Horace Walpole" (as Kimball sometimes addressed Codman), one senses the pleasure each derived from the exchange of architectural nuggets about the stylistic development and dating of American buildings. Codman's collection of New England directories of the sev-

enteenth and eighteenth centuries, combined with his extensive knowledge of genealogy, were invaluable in tracing details of ownership and alterations. While the results of Kimball's research arrived on Ogden's desk with high praise for his important contribution, Codman's scholarly efforts were poured into his letters.[67] He made plans for a number of books, but none came to fruition. One was to be about the subjects of portraits by John Singleton Copley, written with Berkeley Updike; another was on London town houses of the eighteenth century; and a third was to be a sequel of sorts to *The Decoration of Houses*, using photographs of houses he had designed and rooms he had decorated as examples of what he called "the eternal verities" prescribed in the book.

Ogden Codman house, Château de Grégy-sur-Yerres, Brie-Comte-Robert, France

Codman preferred the practice of architecture and decoration to writing about it. Although he was not licensed in France or England, he could at least find pleasure as an advisor to expatriot friends on the remodeling or potential purchase of a château, villa, or country house. His most extensive job was at Godmersham Park in England. A much-reworked Georgian house once owned by Jane Austen's brother, it was purchased in the 1930s by Codman's former secretary, Robert Tritton, who had married a rich widow.

Codman enjoyed the challenge of taking the house back to its 1732 form. Among those who also consulted him were a former client, Seton Henry, who owned the villa La Corne d'Or on the Riviera; and a Bostonian, Amos Lawrence, who had purchased the Château De Boussy-Sainte Antoine. Elsie de Wolfe sought his ideas about adapting boiserie for a new room at Villa Trianon, and Linda and Cole Porter consulted him about buying a palazzo in Venice.

Life in France appealed to Americans who sought a gentler pace of life, who preferred to be surrounded by what Edith Wharton described as "the sense of continuity, that 'sense of the past' which enriches the present and binds us up with the world's great stabilizing traditions of art, poetry and knowledge."[68] This group of Francophiles shared the desire to reflect the grace and elegance of eighteenth-century France in their houses. One of its members, the artist Walter Gay, captured the spirit of this world, with all its refinement and charm, in his portraits of their rooms—the nuances of color and subtle balancing of forms played off each other against a well-proportioned backdrop (plate 12). These rooms display, par excellence, the taste espoused by Ogden Codman, Edith Wharton, and Elsie de Wolfe.

Codman's concern with furthering the eighteenth-century revival led him to play a role with the Frank Alvah Parsons School of Design in Paris, known then as The New York School of Fine and Applied Art. His belief that the best training for design students was to study and measure old buildings found an eager supporter in the school's Paris director, William Odom. A longtime friend of Codman's from their New York days, Odom came to Grégy frequently, and even helped with the rearrangement of furniture there. Sharing much the same taste, the two men often went on excursions to the countryside in the never-ending search for antiques to perfect their own collections or to fill a need of a client. Codman was a patron of the Paris school, along with Elsie de Wolfe, Edith Wharton, and Walter Gay. Students were invited to Codman's château to make measured drawings of the rooms. One of these students was the designer William Pahlman, who would carry on many aspects of Codman's taste to the next generation. Pahlman recalled the lasting effect these visits had on the formation of his own taste and style, and he admired Codman's unerring sense of proportion: "He knew what scale to make a moulding." To a young man from Texas in 1929, Grégy was an introduction not only to French country houses, but also to a different concept of their decoration because of the use of chintz for upholstery in the main rooms.[69] This innovative American approach to decor lent a quality of informality and comfort to the profusion of damask that was seen in French salons. The display of chintz in this manner was another Codman motif that was shared with Elsie de Wolfe, and it has been widely used in the decoration of stylish living rooms ever since.

Though Codman enjoyed tinkering with an old house—his own as well as his clients'—it did not produce the same satisfaction as building from scratch. Codman could not resist one last opportunity to design and build his dream house when the perfect site presented itself. In the winter of 1929, while looking for a place to rent on the French Riviera, he saw the Domaine of La Leopolda—a site with a spectacular view overlooking the Mediterranean and a panorama that included Cap-Ferrat, Beaulieu-sur-Mer, and the harbor of Villefranche. Comprised of eighteen small adjoining estates, the Domaine had been created by Leopold II, but his death in 1909 prevented the villa he had planned from being built. When Codman saw it, the land had passed into private ownership and had two remodeled peasants' cottages on it, twelve hundred olive and fruit trees, cypresses, camellias, and Chaliapin roses. Riding the crest of the financial boom of 1927–28, he bought it immediately, realizing this was the perfect spot to create his architectural masterpiece (plates 13, 14).

Codman wanted his villa to be in the style of those that had ornamented the shores of the Mediterranean during the eighteenth century. He selected three examples on which to base his design: the Villa Borelli in Marseilles, designed by Charles Le Brun, the Villa Melzi in Bellagio, and the Villa Belgiojoso in Milan, both designed by Giocondo Albertolli. Although the plan and decorative detailing would be taken from French and Italian eighteenth-century sources, the interior was to incorporate the most modern conveniences of plumbing, heating, and lighting. To perfect the plan, Codman read *The Decoration of Houses* "very carefully"; one result was that he cut out a bedroom and bath on the first floor, "thereby," as he wrote Mrs. Wharton, "giving me the most magnificent room to decorate of my architectural career."[71] This was the Italian salon, or ballroom, a cube of thirty feet on each side, with walls of *bleu-turquin scagliola* and contrasting marble trim. Every detail of the decoration and furnishing throughout La Leopolda was based on a precedent from eighteenth-century palaces and villas of France and Italy.

Codman's joy in his ultimate indulgence was very brief because of the financial debacle of 1929. When Roosevelt took the United States off the

Ogden Codman house, La Leopolda, Villefranche-sur-Mer, France, 1929–31

Scale model, La Leopolda

gold standard, Codman's income was reduced by over forty percent. He alternated between cursing the "Fuhrer Duce Roosevelt," "that socialist in the White House," and himself for having tied up all his assets in property. "Fools build houses for wise men to live in," he commented, "although sometimes the opposite is true."[72] He compared himself to his ancestor, Richard Codman, who had brought ruin to the Codman family by his overindulgence in French real estate. He hoped that Elsie de Wolfe (who had by then become Lady Mendl) and Sybil Colefax, the society "mavens" of the Riviera, would be helpful in finding a buyer or tenant for La Leopolda. When he finally did succeed in renting the villa temporarily, he returned to Grégy, to his genealogies and his gardens.

Codman stayed at Grégy throughout World War II. At the outset he had contemplated making it a refuge for other Americans who wished to remain in France. Instead, after making one futile attempt to leave the country, he resigned himself to making the most of a situation in which he had to share his château with sixty German soldiers. Allowed only one room for himself, his bedroom, he promptly took to his bed, ate chocolates, and read mysteries and eighteenth-century architectural books. After the war, whose end he celebrated by leaving his bed, he gradually succumbed to the infirmities of old age. He died at Grégy on 8 June 1951 in his eighty-ninth year, and was buried in the garden there.[73]

Codman was described by a cousin as being "gifted, intelligent, scholarly, obstinate, ambitious, at once obdurate, caustic, but never boring."[74] Never was he truer to his New England aristocratic sensibilities than in his refusal in 1938 to let La Leopolda to the Duke and Duchess of Windsor. Although they were prepared to pay an adequate sum, they also wanted to change the arrangements and decor — paint the walls and remove most of the furniture, the beautiful carpets, and the statuary — in short, take away "everything that gave the house its artistic character."[75] He drew up a four-page list of conditions and demanded a one thousand pound guarantee against losses and damages. In response, the Windsors, hoping that they could convince Codman to withdraw the stipulation of a deposit, invited him to their Paris hotel to discuss the matter. Codman would not yield to

PLATE 3. *Guest bedroom,*
Cornelius Vanderbilt II house,
The Breakers, Newport, Rhode
Island, 1894–95

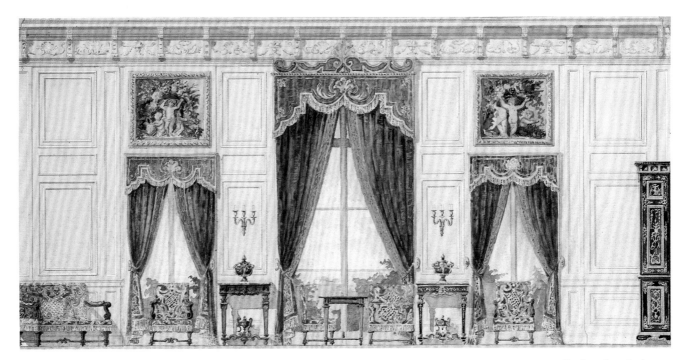

PLATE 4. *Design for window*
wall, bedroom of Cornelius
Vanderbilt, The Breakers

PLATE 5. Design
for stair hall,
Harold Brown house,
Newport, Rhode
Island, 1893

PLATE 6. Design for bay
window in library, Harold
Brown house

PLATE 7. Design for library
bookcase, Harold Brown house

royal prerogative despite the pleas of the duke. As he took his leave, he bowed and said, "Good day, Sir. I regret the House of Codman cannot do business with the House of Windsor."[76] Codman could not compromise on La Leopolda, for it was the ultimate statement of his professional ideals. It remains the finest tribute to his gift for adapting the eighteenth-century tradition, to his unerring taste and his unwavering sense of the meaning of elegance.

NOTES

The following abbreviations are used throughout the notes in this book.
OTNE   Old Time New England, publication of SPNEA
SPNEA   Society for the Preservation of New England Antiquities, Boston
BA   The Boston Athenæum

1. Walter Muir Whitehill, "Introduction," *Index of Obituaries in Boston Newspapers, 1704–1800* (Boston: G. K. Hall & Co., 1968).
2. John Codman to Catherine Amory Codman, 18 July 1800, SPNEA. The Grange was given by the last surviving member of the Ogden Codman family, Mrs. Dorothy Codman, to the SPNEA in 1969, in fulfillment of an agreement between Ogden Codman and William Sumner Appleton in 1920.
3. For further information on the Codman family, see Cora Codman Walcott, *The Codmans of Charleston and Boston, 1637–1929* (Brookline, MA, 1930).
4. Ogden Codman to Charles F. Adams, 7 September 1904, BA. The letter describes Codman's extensive research on the house and family.
5. The brothers and sisters of Ogden Codman are Alice Newbold Codman (1866–1923), Thomas Newbold Codman (1868–1963), Hugh Codman (1875–1946), Dorothy Sarah Frances May Codman (1883–1967).
6. Ogden Codman to Thomas Newbold Codman, 31 May 1923.
7. Ogden Codman to Thomas Newbold Codman, 6 November 1924, SPNEA. For further information see Richard Nylander, "Documenting the Interior of Codman House: The Last Two Generations," *OTNE* 71 (1981).
8. Ogden Codman did extensive research on Richard Codman and his châteaux. Regarding paintings bought by Richard Codman, see Cora Codman Walcott, "A History of the Codman Collection of Pictures," unpublished typescript, 1935, SPNEA. For the life of Richard Codman in France, see Yvon Bizardel, *Deux Yankees et trois demeures parisiennes* (Paris: Librarie Historique Clavreuil, 1980).
9. The original of this fabric was printed in France in the 1850s; it is now reproduced by the firm of Brunschwig & Fils.
10. The New York firm of Leon Marcotte was considered one of the leading decorating firms of the mid-nineteenth century. See *Nineteenth Century America: Furniture and Other Decorative Arts* (New York: Metropolitan Museum of Art, 1970).
11. See Margaret Henderson Floyd, "Redesign of 'The Grange' by John Hubbard Sturgis, 1862–1886," *OTNE* (1981).
12. See Richard Nylander, "Documenting the Interior of Codman House: The Last Two Generations," *OTNE* (1981). Also Lynne M. Spencer, "Codman House," *Antiques* 129:3 (March 1986).
13. "Toile de jouy" refers to a popular French eighteenth-century cotton, similar to the English "copperplate" print, a monochromatic design on an off-white ground; the design was frequently taken from engravings of birds, flowers, and peasant activities. The blue-and-white fabric introduced by Codman was an 1890s reprint of an eighteenth-century design, probably by Francois Boucher, called L'Escarpolette.
14. Ogden Codman to Fiske Kimball, 17 March 1935, BA.
15. John Hubbard Sturgis to Ogden Codman, Sr., 20 November 1880, SPNEA.

16. Ogden Codman to Thomas Newbold Codman, 9 August 1927.

17. Ibid.

18. Richard Codman, *Reminiscences of Richard Codman* (Boston: North Bennet Street Industrial School, 1923), 32.

19. Ogden Codman to Sarah Bradlee Codman, 22 November 1883, SPNEA.

20. Ogden Codman to Sarah Bradlee Codman, 29 January 1884.

21. For information about the firm of A. H. Davenport, see Anne Farnum, "A. H. Davenport," *Antiques* (May 1976).

22. Robert Andrews to Ogden Codman, 16 September 1889, SPNEA.

23. Ogden Codman to Arthur Little, 10 March 1894, SPNEA.

24. Ogden Codman to Arthur Little, 1 February 1889, SPNEA.

25. Ogden Codman to Sarah Bradlee Codman, 26 January 1901, SPNEA.

26. Ogden Codman to Sarah Bradlee Codman, 7 February 1901, SPNEA.

27. Ogden Codman to Arthur Little, 30 March 1894, SPNEA.

28. Francis Bowdoin Bradlee, sister of Sarah Bradlee Codman, loaned Ogden Codman the money. He repaid her on 18 March 1909.

29. Ogden Codman to Arthur Little, 17 August 1891, SPNEA.

30. Ogden Codman to Sarah Bradlee Codman, 13 August 1893, SPNEA.

31. Ogden Codman to Sarah Bradlee Codman, 6 December 1900, SPNEA.

32. Edith Wharton, *A Backward Glance* (New York: Appleton Century, 1934), 106.

33. Ibid., 107.

34. Ogden Codman to Sarah Bradlee Codman, 25 August 1894, SPNEA.

35. Ogden Codman to Arthur Little, 15 December 1893; Ogden Codman to Sarah Bradlee Codman, 13 December 1893, SPNEA.

36. Richard Morris Hunt to Ogden Codman, 13 August 1894, SPNEA.

37. Most of the original furniture remains at the Harold Brown house, now the property of Mr. and Mrs. John J. Slocum. Some of the furnishings for the drawing room and collection of Napoleonic material were given to the Museum of Art, Rhode Island School of Design, by Mrs. Harold Brown in 1937.

38. Charles F. McKim to Ogden Codman, 31 March 1897, Library of Congress.

39. Ogden Codman to Martha Codman, 19 July 1936, BA.

40. Ogden Codman to Edith Wharton, 18 April 1937, BA.

41. Ogden Codman to Sarah Bradlee Codman, 1 March 1901, SPNEA.

42. Ogden Codman to Sarah Bradlee Codman, 8 October 1902, SPNEA.

43. Ibid. Ogden Codman to Arthur Little, 15 January 1892. Codman compares his profit to that of "Uncle Dick" (Richard Codman), who made only three hundred dollars his first year.

44. Ogden Codman to Sarah Bradlee Codman, 13 March 1901, SPNEA.

45. Elsie de Wolfe, *After All* (New York: Harper & Brothers, 1935), 107.

46. Ogden Codman to Sarah Bradlee Codman, 13 March 1901, SPNEA.

47. Leon Edel, *The Life of Henry James, The Master: 1901–1916* (New York: Avon Books), 262.

48. de Wolfe, *After All*, 94.

49. Ibid., 124.

50. Ogden Codman to Elsie de Wolfe, 26 July 1910, SPNEA.

51. de Wolfe, *After All*, 125.

52. de Wolfe, *The House in Good Taste* (New York, 1913), 5.

53. Ibid., 237.

54. These quotes are taken from unidentified newspaper clippings provided by a clipping service, Henry Romeike, Inc., 33 Union Square, New York.

55. In a meeting of the Boston Chapter of the Society of Architectural Historians in April 1978.

56. John D. Rockefeller, Jr., to Ogden Codman, 14 September 1908, Metropolitan Museum of Art.

57. John D. Rockefeller, Jr., to Ogden Codman, 27 April 1909, Metropolitan Museum of Art.

58. Ogden Codman to John D. Rockefeller, Jr., 20 October 1908, Metropolitan Museum of Art.

59. Ogden Codman to John D. Rockefeller, Jr., 12 October 1909, Metropolitan Museum of Art.

60. Ogden Codman to Walter Maynard, 3 September 1909, BA.

61. Ogden Codman to Thomas Newbold Codman, 18 February 1918, SPNEA.

62. This is one of many letters of condolence sent to Ogden Codman, 1910, BA.

63. The Bayard Thayer house at 84 Beacon Street is now The Hampshire House Restaurant.

64. Ogden Codman asked $300,000 for the sale of 15 East 51st Street. The cost to build 7 East 96th Street was $120,000. It sold in 1927 for $250,000.

65. Ogden Codman to Arthur Little, 1 February 1892, SPNEA.

66. Codman's loans did not become actual gifts to the Cooper Union until after his death in 1951. Codman's bequest to the Cooper Union is now part of the Cooper-Hewitt Museum of Design. Some objects were given to the Parson's School of Design at Codman's request in 1948 and were subsequently sold, as were some of the items given to the Cooper-Hewitt Museum.

67. In 1922 Fiske Kimball published *Domestic Architecture of the American Colonies and of the Early Republic*. In the text Kimball thanks Codman for his "constant and disinterested assistance and for the freedom of his unrivalled collection of photographs, measured drawings, and early architectural books."

68. Edith Wharton, *French Ways and Their Meaning* (New York: D. Appleton, 1919), 97.

69. Interview with William Pahlman, November 1981. Stanley Barrows, former member of the faculty at Parsons School of Design and a student at the Paris branch in the last year of its existence in 1939, has recounted many details about the method of study at the school and the influence of Codman and Odom on noted graduates of the program such as Van Day Truex and Eleanor Brown of Macmillan, Inc.

70. To allay the worries of his brother about the potential cost of building and furnishing La Leopolda, Ogden wrote that the increase in the value of his stocks in General Electric and City Bank in 1928 "will more than build and furnish the house, and leave an appreciable margin, and I shall have a place so beautiful that it seems like a fairy tale, and I feel somehow it can not be true." Ogden Codman to Thomas Newbold Codman, 19 January 1929, SPNEA.

71. Ogden Codman to Edith Wharton, 18 April 1937, BA.

72. Ogden Codman to Edith Wharton, 30 September 1931, BA.

73. At the time of his death, Codman left many debts. In addition to his own money, he had spent the inheritance from Leila Codman, which was to have gone to her children, Walter Webb II and John Griswald Webb. There is no accounting for the dispersal of most of the possessions of Grégy, though the Codman family pieces did return to The Grange. Besides two longstanding members of his staff—his secretary, Francis White, and housekeeper, Daisy—he was surrounded by many others who did not serve him well. Shortly after his death, there was a serious robbery at Grégy. The Boston residence of Ogden's brother and sister, 5 Marlborough Street, was sold to raise money to pay the estate debts. Grégy was subsequently acquired by the Catholic church, which stripped the château of all its fixtures. Returned to private ownership, it is now used as a conference center. La Leopolda was sold in 1952 to Giovanni Agnelli; after several other changes of ownership, it remains privately owned. Codman left his Catalogue Raisonné des Châteaux de France, with thirty-six thousand entries, to the French Government, and it is now stored at the Archives Photographiques des Monuments Historiques in Saint-Cyr. His collection of genealogies and New England town histories, Index of Boston Obituaries, and other related materials of New England history were given to The Boston Athenæum.

74. Florence Codman to David McKibbon, 8 April 1968, BA.

75. Ogden Codman to Julian Sampson, 28 April 1930, BA.

76. This story is recounted by Florence Codman, *The Clever Young Boston Architect* (Augusta, ME: Privately printed, 1970), 31.

Clinton and Russell with Ogden Codman, houses of George Gordon King, Edith King McCagg, and Ethel Rhinelander King, 16–20 East 84th Street, New York

Living with Codman

NICHOLAS KING

AT ONE TIME THE NAME OF OGDEN CODMAN SERVED AS A TOUCHSTONE FOR DIS-tinguishing the cognoscenti from the multitude of the be-nighted. Codman and his work, or, as one would have said in those days, his taste, were considered not so much the product of style and education as a guarantee of quality, and therefore a service rendered with full consideration of the proper respect all around.

Today, Codman's reputation has surpassed such narrow boundaries. He has become widely known as an *estampille* traced in pale but authoritative ink on some of the most ambitious plans of American period architecture and design. One says "period" because it is impossible to categorize American building styles in a coherent reference; it is perhaps safest to say that between 1890 and 1930 Codman presented rich and sophisticated Americans with plans and realized architecture in the manner of the high European eighteenth century.

Looking back over the experience of his houses, one's primary reflection is of his consummate authority, authority in a staircase and its railing, a window frame, the paneling of a door, a chimney piece with its glass—in the parts of an ensemble that come to represent the sinews of a house to those who live in it, even if in the case of an engineer or a carpenter or the architect himself the metaphor would evoke something quite different.

There is no question that Codman knew for whom he was designing. His clients were the rich bourgeois of New England and New York, from the Vanderbilts and Rockefellers to the calmer, more solid people who were less well known, but who sometimes possessed almost as much money—although they were considerably more discreet in the displaying of it.

Codman himself came from this sort of background, however colored by Boston eccentricity: he continually made fun, in private if not in public, of the *arriviste* taste of the big-money families. His letter about visiting the newly finished Breakers in Newport with Edith Wharton and their discussion of the vulgarity of the grandiose gold and marble of the ground floor is the essence of the Codman attitude, as is his lofty approval of what took place in "my rooms" on the second floor of the Vanderbilt palace, meaning the bedrooms and boudoirs he had decorated for the family's less-spectacular moments.

He reveled in his contempt for the "common" rich and sneered happily at repeated examples of their lack of education and refinement. But, like all architects in need of customers who can afford their work, Codman had to sing for his early commissions. He went to Newport precisely for that purpose and his malice and satire were clearly his personal compensation for forced affability, even at times servility, toward the powerful and the arrogant — in other words, the classic revenge of the courtier.

However much Codman fumed about Newport (principally in letters to his mother), it was there that he found Mrs. Wharton, an ally of considerable strength and amusement. Together they wrote *The Decoration of Houses*, which proved to be the climax of their association, for in the long years that followed, they were no more than quarrelsome, if tolerant at a distance, friends. Codman in this period helped Mrs. Wharton make her awkward house on the cliffs "possible," but almost nothing remains of his handiwork at the still bleak mass of Land's End. In Newport itself, the majestic white colonial mansion he built for his cousin Martha Codman survives much as it was, its white gates and clapboard walls still sheltering their columned facade on Bellevue Avenue. Codman designed other Newport houses, but they have been so much changed as to have become evocative rather than truly representative of his work.

Other surviving work of a significant nature, apart from the Breakers' rooms, are the Empire salons of the Harold Brown house farther down the avenue. For many years this gabled granite pile was the quiet abode of the widowed Mrs. Brown. In recent times her niece Eileen Slocum has made it sparkle with life and festivity, and the Codman elegance has witnessed the grand style of a later Newport. Across the avenue, the great Wetmore mansion also contains Codman's work, a green Louis XV salon tacked on to a Victorian mass by Miss Edith Wetmore, the sure-footed tastemaker of the "old" Newport who was related by marriage to Harold Brown.

Codman, like other Beaux-Arts architects, for that's what he essentially was, enjoyed being grand and fussy at the same time (though he added a touch of Yankee trader in his accounting to his clients). In this he reflected, as he was bound to, the life that went on around him and for which, inevitably, his houses were built. The assumptions of this life run all through *The Decoration of Houses*, as they run through the novels of his coauthor. Drawing rooms, great halls, monumental staircases, balustrades, and regal terraces were the essential settings for the balls, dinners, receptions, and general mass diversions favored by the entourages of the gregarious rich, and, through them, by the rich themselves.

Money and taste were the two obvious imperatives of the life of Codman's times and consequently of the life of his houses. The third, and most essential of all, was service. It was hardly ever mentioned by his contemporaries (think of the novels of James and Wharton), any more than it is mentioned today. Yet service of that period required immense efforts by immense staffs of people if the meals, the order, and the cleanliness which social activity demanded were to be produced. One has to remember that such houses functioned as closed communities, of necessity self-sufficient to a degree unimaginable today, and above all bound to the repetition of daily and even hourly tasks performed almost entirely by hand with a minimum of mechanical help.

The idea of that life, with its parallel households, one of servants and one of masters, has been conveyed by the television series *Upstairs, Downstairs*, although it tended to gloss over the heavy labor on the part of the servants. For example, in any well-ordered house of Codman's time, by which I mean before the First World War, there was in principle a clean napkin at each meal for each adult member of the family — for those, that is, who ate in the main dining room. Children might be obliged to use napkin rings to make their napkins last a day or two; but napkin rings were taboo otherwise as the despised symbols of the slovenly and parsimonious boarding house. They would not do for a properly served table.

This meant, in a household of let us say two parents, two adolescent or adult offspring, and the resident elderly relation who was then the rule rather than the exception, 15 napkins a day or 105 a week, assuming that meals taken out would be counterbalanced by guests. That means that someone had to wash, dry, and iron over a hundred big linen napkins a week, and this does not include the napkins used by the servants, of whom there were at least four in such a household and more if there were young children.

This, of course, is only napkins; it does not begin to define any of the other voluminous categories of washing — sheets, shirts, lingerie, towels, and so on. And the reader should recall that clothes were far more elaborate then, were changed far more often, and were often more difficult to wash and iron than the equivalents today.

The same kind of catalogue could be drawn up for the work in the kitchen and pantry and in all the public and private rooms of the house. Fresh food was usually delivered at the back door by horse-drawn wagons, as was the all-important ice, which, in huge blocks, had to be manhandled into ice boxes. There were no supermarkets, no convenience stores; almost nothing could be bought ahead of time or otherwise prepared except bread. Meals themselves were far more elaborate and their preparation far more time-consuming, and of course the servants had to eat too.

These were some, but by no means all, of the major tasks in a household of that era. In Newport, as in Lenox or even Long Island, there was not a summer month without a chill evening or two, which meant fires in countless grates. There were the gas mantles and their shades to attend to. There was also the production of hot water by coal furnace or the carrying of it up to bedrooms by hand. There was the maintenance of the gardens and drives, and the endless routines of the grooms and the coachmen, so many of whom were to be painfully (and often dangerously) converted into the chauffeurs of the new motor cars. This was in the country; in New York or Boston daily life was busier and even more elaborate. Architects had to think of all these things and plan carefully for them with clients who often knew little about them.

In a considerably later era, I grew up in a Codman house in New York with cool, almost chaste Louis XVI interiors. (If the interior life of the house was not quite the same as in its early days, the attitudes that governed its life were.) The house, 20 East 84th Street, was built at the beginning of the century, along with numbers 18 and 16, by my great-grandmother Mary Augusta LeRoy King (Mrs. Edward King), for her married children. To give an idea of the rapid growth of New York, nothing had ever stood on that ground between Fifth and Madison avenues.

Built of Flemish brick and limestone, the houses were designed by the architectural firm of Clinton and Russell. Codman was given the commission for the interiors. He had met the King family in Newport and approved of them, according to his letters, as unostentatious people of the contemporary establishment. Furthermore, Mrs. LeRoy King, who was to occupy number 20, was born Ethel Ledyard Rhinelander and was a first cousin of Edith

Entrance, Edith King McCagg and Ethel Rhinelander King houses

*Ogden Codman, salon, Ethel
Rhinelander King house, 1900*

Wharton, a connection that no doubt influenced Codman. And Mrs. Wharton would have been certain to recommend Codman in any matter of arranging a new house.

In accordance with Codman's practice, all the furnishings, tables, chairs, sofas, commodes, mantelpieces, upholstery, screens, and paneling were made to measure in France and shipped over, along with a *contremaître* or foreman who stayed for six weeks at a nearby hotel while the installation was being carried out and everything carefully fitted into its place.

The house had a classic plan. A black and white marble *carrelage* on the ground floor separated the morning room facing the street from the

Ogden Codman, dining room,
George Gordon King house,
1900

dining room in the back. From the center of this hall, which on one side had frosted windows looking out on an areaway, a staircase lined with a bronze and wrought-iron banister rose to the main floor. Here a salon stretched across the entire front and, separated by a hall similar to the one below, a library occupied the rear overlooking the yard. The handsome staircase continued up to the third-floor bedrooms but dwindled to something more modest as it ascended to the bedrooms of the fourth, the children's floor. Like almost every other house of the period, the spacious kitchen was in the basement and the food went up to the serving pantry of the dining room by dumbwaiter.

We never saw the yard because the library's windows were made of an elegant variation of bottle glass, like those of Dutch interiors in the seventeenth century, with a pattern of bright circles that admit the light but blot out any detail of what exists outside. The salon itself ran east and west along 84th Street (plate 15). It was decorated with panels of gray painted wood inset with yellow damask, which was also used for the long curtains and valances. A white marble bust of Marie Antoinette stood on the white Louis XVI mantelpiece in front of a pier mirror which rose to the ceiling.

Just outside the entrance to the salon was a small door cut into the wall; it led to the hall of number 18, so the families could visit one another without going outside. Number 18 was lived in by Edith Edgar (King) McCagg, LeRoy King's sister, and number 16, which also had such a door, was occupied by their brother George Gordon King and his family. The Gordon Kings had asked Codman for decoration in the eighteenth-century English style.

After a formal dinner or some family festival, we would gather in the salon, or drawing room, as it was called. But most of the time we sat in the library, as was usual in old New York houses, and indeed in most houses in America. No doubt it was the "front room" mentality that saw to it that the library was always more cheerful and more cosy, and its chairs more comfortable.

The way of life that Codman created for, and indeed helped create, is gone and cannot return, no matter how much money the rich spend in an attempt to bring it back. Interior decorators can ape the room dressings or spend fortunes on old furniture, but the result is and will be far different.

Just as people search for a Victorian "look" by cluttering tables with knickknacks and family photographs but miss the feelings and beliefs that put the knickknacks there in the first place, so gilded pilasters and Louis XV bergères upholstered in lavish materials cannot recreate the life they stood for if the motives that lay behind a certain kind of civilized life are not there. Codman's great gift was to understand those motives, just as he understood the expression of them. For all those who admire his achievement, this is the point of departure.

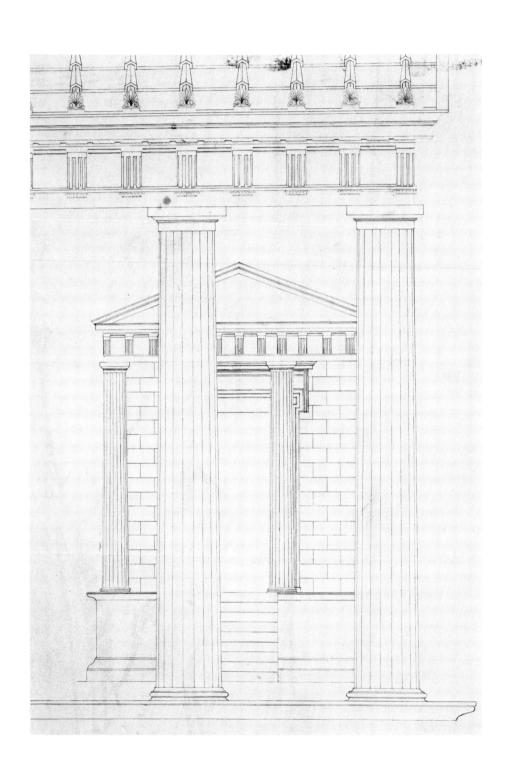

Ogden Codman, Doric temple,
1883

The Making of a Colonial Revival Architect

CHRISTOPHER MONKHOUSE

GDEN CODMAN WAS BORN JUST A STONE'S THROW AWAY FROM THE JOHN HANcock house on the eve of its demolition. Such proximity, both in time and place, to the extinction of one of New England's most historic and architecturally important houses was to contribute significantly to Codman becoming not only an architect, but one deeply committed to the revival of eighteenth-century architecture through close study and the preservation of period examples.[1]

In succumbing to the wrecker's ball, the Hancock house stimulated more interest in colonial architecture than any other building in New England, if not the entire country. Furthermore, as the former home of the first signer of the Declaration of Independence and thus a national shrine, the house was preserved piecemeal through the sale of architectural fragments to those anxious to acquire a relic of a national hero.[2] Although the aesthetic merits of such artifacts were less compelling than their age and association, incorporating them into a new building inevitably placed a seal of approval on the past. It soon became fashionable to be "old fashioned," and the wheel of colonial revivalism was set in fast motion. Within a mere four months of the demolition sale, one of the Hancock house's mantels reemerged in a rural Maine home, where its presence excited notice in the local paper as well as the *Kennebec Journal*:

> The Skowhegan Farmer *states that Mr. S. W. Lawton, who is building a very handsome dwelling on Coburn Avenue, in that town, has placed in his sitting room a relict of "ye olden time," in the shape of a marble mantel and fire piece from the old Hancock House in Boston.*[3]

Unlike the marble mantel, the magnificent front staircase from the Hancock house, with its elaborately turned balusters and newel post, traveled only as far afield as the North Shore, where in 1869 it finally found a permanent home in the new summer residence of Greeley Curtis, then being built from the designs of Ware and Van Brunt at Manchester-by-the-Sea. Curtis acquired the staircase from the Boston architect John Hubbard Sturgis, who had originally purchased it at the 1863 demolition sale. Though Sturgis never got to incorporate the staircase into one of his own projects, he had preserved its original context, if only on paper, by making a set of measured drawings,

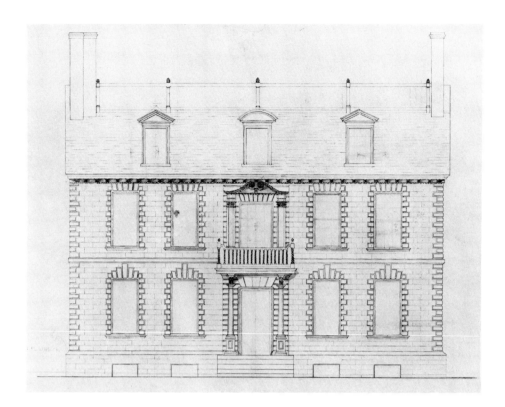

John Hubbard Sturgis, measured drawing of south elevation, Hancock house, Boston, 1863

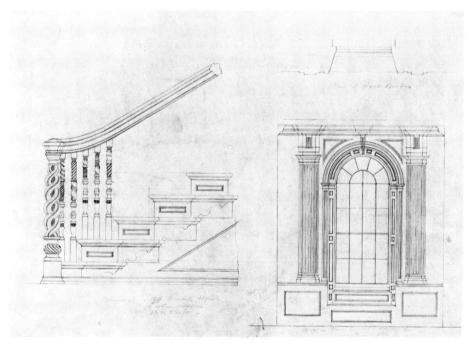

John Hubbard Sturgis, measured drawing of interior details, Hancock house, Boston, 1863

including two floor plans, four elevations, and a sheet of interior details showing the staircase and arched window on the landing. Unlike the staircase, the drawings served Sturgis well: he drew upon them for inspiration in his designs for the Edward W. Hooper house (1872) at 25 Reservoir Street in Cambridge and for the Arthur Astor Carey house (1882), only a block away at 28 Fayerweather Street.[4]

As Sturgis had been partly trained abroad, preparing measured drawings of early buildings was second nature to him. Architectural education was different in this country, and hence his measured drawings have the distinction of being the earliest known American examples. Sturgis also happened to be the uncle of Ogden Codman and served as mentor for him at the outset of his architectural training in Boston. It is therefore not surprising to find that Codman made measured drawings of nearly twenty buildings from the colonial and Federal periods in the 1880s and 1890s.[5]

In 1862, just a year before Codman's birth, his father decided to reestablish the family's colonial roots with the purchase of a large eighteenth-century country house in Lincoln, Massachusetts. Named The Grange by Ogden Codman, Sr., it had been originally built for the Russell family of Charlestown, Massachusetts, shortly before 1741. As the Russells were related to the Codmans by marriage, The Grange eventually came into the possession of John Codman III, who made extensive alterations to it between 1797 and 1799, perhaps with the assistance of Charles Bulfinch.[6] He then bequeathed the house in 1803 to his son Charles Russell Codman, father of Ogden Codman, Sr., who then proceeded to sell it in 1807. After its reacquisition by the Codmans in the middle of the nineteenth century, Ogden Codman, Sr., turned to his brother-in-law, John Hubbard Sturgis, for help with "improvements."

Sturgis proved to be extremely sensitive in dealing with the exterior, and consequently his addition of quoins on the four corners of The Grange has long gone undetected. He also set off the front facade with a balustrade at ground level, added pediments to the windows, and put a porch on the east side, with capitals that echo those on the front portico, carved by John and Simeon Skillin in the late 1790s.

By contrast, Sturgis's work on the interior was more in tune with the 1860s, commencing with the English tile floor in the front hall. Other decorative embellishments characteristic of the era included the strapwork ceiling in the dining room and the dwarf bookcases made by John A. Ellis and Co. of East Cambridge, Massachusetts, in the southeast parlor.[7] While Codman later lamented Sturgis's modern improvements, he also admitted that they gave him the excuse to undertake restoration of several eighteenth-century interior details, such as the fireplace mantels in the bedrooms:

I suppose that in 1862 no one thought anything old fashioned was nice at all. Perhaps if he had left everything as it was, I never would have been inspired with putting things back as they were. But that has been a great pleasure to me.[8]

As a graphic indication of Codman's tendency to view the eighteenth century through the eyes of The Grange, a pencil sketch by him, probably dating from the 1880s, shows the chimney-breast of the southwest bedroom juxtaposed with similar paneling from a house in Salem, Massachusetts.

If his father's reacquisition of The Grange provided Codman with a

Ogden Codman, comparison
of chimney-breast from The
Grange with paneling in a
house in Salem, Massachusetts,
c. 1892

personal training ground for the study of eighteenth-century architecture, the distaff side of his family ensured that it was not seen in isolation. In correspondence with the architectural historian Fiske Kimball, Codman related how Grandmother and Grandfather Bradlee took him regularly on architectural tours of Boston's colonial buildings:

> As a small boy, my grandparents took me with them to King's Chapel very often, and even in those days it seemed to me extraordinarily beautiful. My grandmother desiring to encourage my interest in old buildings and our early architecture, used to take me to other churches for the afternoon service, and in that way I saw the church in Brattle Street, next in beauty to King's Chapel, to the old South where we were much impressed by the chandelier for candles, protected from the draught by tall glasses, like some I may have shown you in my green library at 7 E. 96 st., which came from Joseph Barrell's house in Charlestown, Mass.[9]

Grandmother Bradlee reinforced Codman's attention to interior furnishings by giving his father her May family furniture for use at The Grange. The impact this legacy of colonial furniture had on Codman can be judged in photographs of his Boston and New York bedrooms, where the dominant feature is the May family Chippendale bedstead. And when Codman took up permanent residence in France in the 1920s, he had a May family fireplace mantel shipped over for installation at Grégy. To salve his conscience, he assured his sister Dorothy that the mantelpiece would eventually come back to Lincoln.[10] In a similar vein, he encouraged his clients to incorporate ancestral mantelpieces into new settings, such as the French Empire example

French Empire mantelpiece in
Nathaniel Thayer house,
Edgemere, Newport, Rhode
Island, c. 1896–97

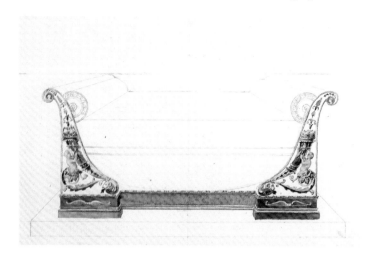

PLATE 8. *Design for sleigh bed, Harold Brown house, copied from Percier and Fontaine, Recueils de décorations intérieures, comprenant tout ce qui a rapport à l'ameublement (1812)*

PLATE 9. *Designs for curtains and chairs, Harold Brown house*

PLATE 10. *Dining room, Harold Brown house*

PLATE 11. *Design for window wall, boiserie, Adele Kneeland house, Fairlawn, Lenox, Massachusetts, c. 1896–1903*

Ogden Codman, bedroom, 100
Chestnut Street, Boston, c. 1890

he used in Nathaniel Thayer's Newport summer house in 1895, which had originally been imported in 1817 by Stephen Van Rensselaer of Albany, New York.[11]

In addition to being surrounded at such an impressionable age by colonial architecture and furniture, Codman, like most of his generation, would have been brought up on the poetry of Henry Wadsworth Longfellow. Perhaps it is not merely a coincidence that the year of his birth also saw the publication of Longfellow's *Tales of the Wayside Inn*, set in a large, gambrel-roofed eighteenth-century tavern on the outskirts of Boston. And shortly after the Codmans moved back to The Grange in the 1860s, a tall case clock appeared on the landing of the double staircase and a flax wheel turned up in the drawing room, bringing to mind Longfellow's celebration of these colonial furnishings in his poems "The Old Clock on the Stairs" (1845) and "The Courtship of Miles Standish" (1858).[12]

With the Boston fire of 1872, which destroyed much of the city's colonial and Federal architecture, Codman's colonial revival childhood came to a close. As his family's wealth largely derived from real estate and insurance, it literally disappeared overnight, thus forcing the Codmans to abandon temporarily their houses, including The Grange, and retreat to France for a self-imposed exile at Dinard, a watering place on the Normandy coast much frequented by foreigners in reduced circumstances. While this quirk of fate allowed Codman to expand greatly his architectural frame of reference, and made him increasingly partial to French decoration, he always insisted that

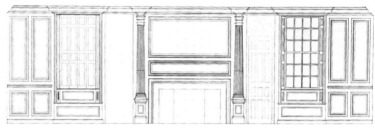

Arthur Little, banquet hall,
Sparhawk House, Kittery,
Maine, from Early New
England Interiors *(1878)*

Ogden Codman, wall design

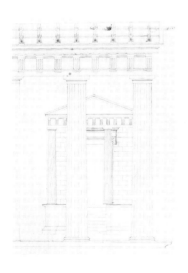

Ogden Codman, Doric temple,
1883

his early appreciation of colonial architecture in Boston prevented him from succumbing to the excesses in design frequently found abroad.

In the aftermath of the Civil War, a nascent interest in our past came into full flower, partly nourished by preparations for the Centennial Exhibition in Philadelphia in 1876. During the 1870s architects who had previously found it worth sketching old buildings only when abroad, now found much of interest in their own backyards. Robert Swain Peabody started off the decade with the publication in 1873 of his *Notebook Sketches* of European buildings drawn while a student at the Ecole des Beaux-Arts[13]; but when two architects who worked in his office published similar volumes, they were exclusively illustrated with sketches of native buildings. William E. Barry's *Pen Sketches of Old Houses* (1874) and Arthur Little's *Early New England Interiors* (1878) contain such a wealth of images of notable colonial and Federal buildings that they helped launch many an architectural sketching tour in quest of the colonial, of which the McKim, Mead, White, and Bigelow tour of 1877 is by far the best known.[14] That their illustrations tended to be more quaintly picturesque than historically accurate suited an age that encouraged architects and designers to take liberties with the past.

Yet at the same time, the increasing use of the camera by the likes of Charles Follen McKim and Stanford White allowed for greater stylistic accuracy, along with speed, and would in due course significantly change both the character of architectural sketching tours and the buildings inspired by them.[15] In a similar vein, the first architecture school established in this country, at MIT in 1865, started in 1874 to require measured drawings of colonial Boston buildings, in keeping with educational practices in England and on the Continent, not to mention the pioneering example set in America by John Hubbard Sturgis.[16] With MIT's curriculum in tune with his own training, it is perfectly understandable that Sturgis should encourage his nephew to study architecture there in 1883.

Although Ogden Codman stayed at MIT for only a year, the measured drawing requirement served him well. From his first feeble attempt at composing Doric temples, he rapidly progressed to making measured drawings of actual colonial buildings. He found this means for studying old buildings

so instructive, in fact, that he continued to execute such drawings into the early 1890s, and, as mentioned earlier, left a legacy of measured drawings for nearly twenty buildings stretching from Maine to Washington, D.C. Many of the buildings he recorded can also be found in the volumes of Barry and Little, and, not surprisingly, a well-thumbed copy of *Early New England Interiors* was in Codman's library. Therefore it is possible to compare Little's chimney-breast at Sparhawk Hall in Kittery, Maine, with the same elevation prepared a decade later by Codman. Here the triumph of accuracy over atmosphere becomes visibly apparent, as it does as well when comparing Barry's elevation of the Morton-Taylor house in Roxbury, Massachusetts, with Codman's. But appearances can be deceptive, and Codman admitted years later to the Boston architect Herbert Browne that he had been too much in a hurry and hence felt his drawings were not always reliable:

> *Alas all my measurements, taken in far too great a hurry, are in the Metropolitan Museum, with my measure books, and the plans I made from them. As I look back on my life I regret I did not devote much more time to taking measurements of old houses and laying out their plans to scale. It was thought a waste of time then, by many people, but it was much more worth while than many things that were thought to lead further.*[17]

Small wonder that in the 1890s Codman gave up his drafting tools and replaced them with a Kodak camera![18]

Among his measured drawings preserved in the library of the Society for the Preservation of New England Antiquities is a sheet labeled "A Really Colonial House." At first glance it might be easily mistaken for an elevation of an existing building, so akin is it to the other drawings. Codman, however, seems to have been in a playful mood, for he manufactured a colonial edifice out of the many structures he had measured. The great gambrel roof might well have been drawn from Sparhawk Hall and the double porches taken from the Shirley-Eustis house in Roxbury. With such visual resources readily at hand, even the most restrained revival architect would find it difficult to

William E. Barry, Morton-Taylor house, from Pen Sketches of Old Houses *(1874)*

Ogden Codman, elevation, Morton-Taylor house, Roxbury, Massachusetts, c. 1889

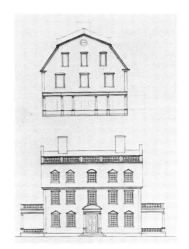

Ogden Codman, "A Really Colonial House"

resist creating colonial conflations, either from scratch or as "improvements" to existing buildings. Therefore, even a building as sacrosanct as The Grange proved vulnerable, and in 1903 Codman produced a pedimented and pilastered scheme for the east elevation. Mercifully, that project remained on paper, unlike a similar one for enhancing the ancestral home of the Nathaniel Thayer family in Lancaster, Massachusetts, in 1902.

Codman found a kindred spirit in Herbert Browne, whom he met during his stint in the office of Andrews and Jacques from 1887 to 1889. Both men had firsthand knowledge of colonial and Federal period buildings acquired through preparation of measured drawings, of which Browne's were particularly proficient and highly detailed. Both recognized the advantage of growing up in houses of architectural significance; for Browne, it was the Crafts house in Roxbury, which Codman may well have recorded by the time they met.[19] Finally, both realized that a thorough knowledge of eighteenth-century architecture depended on the study not only of period buildings, but also of the treatises and pattern books available to the original architects, builders, and their clients.

A similar interest in both old buildings and old books brought the author of *Early New England Interiors* into the fold, and thereafter Codman,

Ogden Codman, Nathaniel Thayer house, The Homestead, Lancaster, Massachusetts

Browne, and Arthur Little referred to themselves as "the colonial trinity."[20] Despite their common interests, they were each cut from a slightly different cloth, as their library interiors readily reveal.

Arthur Little had by far the grandest situation. His library formed an alcove at one end of a two-story ballroom in his Raleigh Street house, which was built to his designs in Boston's Back Bay in 1890.[21] Everything in sight was calculated to impress clients, with ancestral portraits strategically placed to leave no question that his bloodlines were impeccable and stretched well back into the colonial period. As a trophy of the grand tour, the tapestry over the mantel spoke of worldliness, while the books suggested erudition, even though each row was an unbroken horizontal band, never disturbed, it seems, by having a book taken off the shelf.

In marked contrast, the eighteenth-century folios and quartos jammed into the Chippendale bookcases flanking the fireplace in Codman's sitting room at 5 West 16th Street in New York and the Hepplewhite bookcases flanking the fireplace in Browne's Beacon Hill apartment give every impression of having been in constant use. It also appears that the philosophy of simplicity that Codman espoused in public also extended to his private world. In an apparent attempt to reduce his furnishings to a bare minimum, he

W. F. Protz, proposed east facade for The Grange by Ogden Codman, 1903

*Ogden Codman Collection as
installed at The Metropolitan
Museum of Art, New York,
1920*

*Library in alcove, Arthur Little
residence, 2 Raleigh Street,
Boston, 1891*

Sitting room, Ogden Codman residence, 5 West 16th Street, New York, c. 1893

Living room, Herbert W. C. Browne residence, 66 Beacon Street, Boston

Ogden Codman, Hepplewhite
secretary combined with Queen
Anne dressing table

produced a pencil sketch, no doubt partly in jest, in which he combined the top of a Hepplewhite secretary with a Queen Anne dressing table.

Though Browne lived in extremely small quarters, he did not allow them to cramp his style, which like Codman's was classical. But unlike Codman, he subscribed to the "less is a bore" school of interior decoration. His classical souvenirs of countless trips abroad eventually left no surface unadorned.

While Codman and Browne may never have agreed on the number of objects required for furnishing a room tastefully, they were united in believing there could never be too many architecture books at close hand for reference. Codman's opportunity to start building a library of his own came in 1894–95 with his work at Cornelius Vanderbilt's Newport "cottage," The Breakers. Here, Codman recalled, "I did a bit of interior decoration, that brought me in my first big fee, that enabled me to commence my architectural library."[22] As his source for fine and rare architectural folios and quartos, Codman, like other Boston architects, such as J. Pickering Putnam, turned to Batsford's in London.[23] They were indisputably the leading dealers in both new and antiquarian architectural books at the time, a position they enjoyed because they could trace their lineage from such distinguished architectural book publishers as Henry Webley, Isaac and Josiah Taylor, and John Weale.[24]

In order to help both the public and professionals avoid such stylistic aberrations as "so-called 'colonial' houses where stair-rails are used as roof-balustrades and mantel-friezes as exterior entablatures,"[25] Codman opened *The Decoration of Houses* with a list of "Books Consulted."[26] Aware that many of the eighteenth-century titles he cited were virtually unobtainable, even in a city the size of New York, in 1920 Codman loaned, and in 1951 bequeathed, his entire library of architecture books, along with many drawings and photographs, to the Metropolitan Museum of Art. In addition to the books, he "provided bookcases, chairs, tables, a rug, and framed prints, in order that the collection might as nearly as possible be housed as it might have been in an architect's or interior decorator's working library." In this setting Codman intended his library to serve "as a reference collection for mature students and practicing members of the several professions that use this kind of material." He therefore "proposed to let those persons have free access to the shelves, in the hope that thereby they may be enabled with the greatest ease to avail themselves of its sources, and even that some through sheer comfort will be enticed to 'browse.' "[27]

In Boston, Herbert Browne followed Codman's example and left not only his library, but also several pieces of furniture, including his Hepplewhite bookcases, to the SPNEA in 1946. The Browne collection has been augmented by the Codman drawings, sketchbooks, and personal papers that were transferred from The Grange following its bequest to the SPNEA in 1968 by Codman's sister Dorothy. Nearby at The Boston Athenæum, the books and papers kept by Codman at Grégy have come to rest.[28] With so much documentation close at hand, we have a unique opportunity to study the growth of the colonial revival and its contribution in America to the classical language of architecture.

NOTES

1. In addition to being an early member of the Society for the Preservation of New England Antiquities in Boston, Codman served on committees for the preservation of the Royall house in Medford, the Shirley-Eustis house in Roxbury, and Gore Place in Waltham.

2. Margaret Henderson Floyd, "Measured Drawings of the Hancock House by John Hubbard Sturgis: A Legacy to the Colonial Revival," in *Architecture in Colonial Massachusetts*, ed. A. L. Cummings (Boston: Colonial Society of Massachusetts, 1979), 81.

3. *Kennebec Journal*, Augusta, Maine, October 16, 1863. I am grateful to Earle G. Shettleworth, director, Maine Historical Preservation Commission, for bringing this reference to my attention.

4. Floyd, "Measured Drawings," 81–111.

5. For a complete list of Codman's measured drawings, see appendix.

6. R. Curtis Chapin, "The Early History and Federalization of the Codman House," OTNE 61 (1981), 24–46.

7. Margaret Henderson Floyd, "Redesign of 'The Grange' by John Hubbard Sturgis, 1862–1866," OTNE 61 (1981), 47–67.

8. Ogden Codman to Thomas N. Codman, 9 August 1927, SPNEA.

9. Ogden Codman to Fiske Kimball, 5 January 1927, BA.

10. Ogden Codman to Dorothy S. F. M. Codman, 26 January 1926, SPNEA.

11. Originally imported for use in a Philip Hooker designed house in Albany, which was demolished in the 1890s, the mantelpiece came to Newport by way of Stephen Van Rensselaer's descendant, Cornelia Van Rensselaer, who had married into the Thayer family. It is now in the Museum of Art, Rhode Island School of Design, through the generosity of the present owner of the Thayer house, The Viscountess Rothermere. A precedent for Codman's use of ancestral woodwork in a new building can be found in the work of the Boston architectural firm of Cabot and Chandler. Their alterations in

1876 to a country house of 1845 in Beverly Farms for Henry Lee were described as follows: "The interior finish is largely made up of old wainscoting and panels taken from the houses of the ancestors of Mr. and Mrs. Lee, and all new finish is made to correspond" (*American Architect and Building News* 1 [April 1, 1876], 109).

12. For a discussion of "The Old Clock on the Stairs," see Christopher P. Monkhouse, "Cabinetmakers and Collectors: Colonial Furniture and its Revival in Rhode Island," in *American Furniture in Pendleton House* (Providence: Museum of Art, Rhode Island School of Design, 1986), 13. For "The Courtship of Miles Standish," see Christopher P. Monkhouse, "The Spinning Wheel as Artifact, Symbol, and Source of Design," in *Victorian Furniture*, ed. Kenneth L. Ames (Philadelphia: Victorian Society in America, 1982), 154–72.

13. Robert Swain Peabody, *Notebook Sketches* (Boston: James R. Osgood, 1873).

14. For a detailed discussion of the publications of Barry and Little, see Kevin Dean Murphy, " 'A Strol Thro' the Past': Three Architects of the Colonial Revival" (M.A. thesis, Boston University, 1985), 36–44.

15. Walter Knight Sturges, "Arthur Little and the Colonial Revival," *Journal of the Society of Architectural Historians* 32 (May 1973), 148.

16. Bainbridge Bunting, *Houses of Boston's Back Bay* (Cambridge: Harvard University Press, 1967), 353–54.

17. Ogden Codman to Herbert W. C. Browne, 19 May 1936, BA.

18. Thirty-three of Codman's photographs were used by John Mead Howells in his *Lost Examples of Colonial Architecture* (New York: William Helburn, 1931), for which he omitted credit lines on fifteen, much to Codman's consternation; see Florence Codman, *The Clever Young Boston Architect* (Augusta, ME: Privately published, 1970), 30.

19. For an illustration of the Crafts house (also called Elmwood), designed by Peter Banner in 1805, see Fiske Kimball, *Domestic Architecture of the American Colonies and of the Early Republic* (New York: Charles Scribner's Sons, 1922), 198. Codman's measured drawing of the Crafts house, as well as Browne's measured drawings for a number of colonial and Federal buildings, are in SPNEA's library in Boston. One of the latter will be illustrated in James F. O'Gorman, *"On the Boards": An Introduction to Draftsmanship in Nineteenth-Century Boston* (Philadelphia: University of Pennsylvania Press, forthcoming).

20. Ogden Codman to Arthur Little, 17 August 1891, SPNEA.

21. Richard Nylander, curator of collections at SPNEA, kindly brought to my attention the extensive collection of interior photographs of the homes of both Little and Browne.

22. Ogden Codman to Fiske Kimball, 17 March 1935, BA.

23. Ogden Codman to Robert Tritton, 6 June 1936, BA.

24. Hector Bolitho, ed., *A Batsford Century* (London: B. T. Batsford, 1943), 103–8.

25. Edith Wharton and Ogden Codman, Jr., *The Decoration of Houses* (New York: Charles Scribner's Sons, 1897), 12–13.

26. Ibid., xii–xvii. The inspiration for publishing "Books Consulted" might well have come from Codman's cousin, the landscape gardener Henry Sargent Codman, who published a bibliography of "Books on Gardening Art" in the third volume of the periodical *Garden and Forest* in 1890. A shorter version of "Books on Gardening Art" was appended to Mrs. Schuyler Van Rensselaer, *Art Out-of-Doors* (New York: Charles Scribner's Sons, 1893), 387–98.

27. William W. Ivins, Jr., "The Ogden Codman Library," *Bulletin of the Metropolitan Museum of Art* (November 1920), 250–53. Shortly thereafter the collection, as it was bequeathed with its installation, was dispersed. The architectural drawings went to the Avery Architectural and Fine Arts Library, Columbia University.

28. Walter Muir Whitehill, "Introduction," *Index of Obituaries in Boston Newspapers, 1704–1800* (Boston: G. K. Hall & Co., 1968), v–x.

Design and Decoration

PAULINE C. METCALF

OGDEN CODMAN APPROACHED ARCHITECTURE FROM THE INSIDE OUT. FOR HIM the primary purpose of design is to provide the most "suitable accommodation" for "the inmates of the house."[1] As explained in *The Decoration of Houses*, a "definite first conception" is essential not only for determining the spatial flow of rooms, but also for preventing useless rooms and wasted space and achieving a successful harmony between the interior and exterior of the house. "Before beginning to decorate a room it is essential to consider for what purpose the room is to be used"[2]; from there its relative position is established within the hierarchy of other rooms in the house. If, according to Codman and Wharton, "the golden mean lies in trying to arrange our houses with a view to our own comfort and convenience," the consideration of privacy ("one of the first requisites of civilized life"[3]) is of prime importance in the layout of rooms:

> *Each room in a house has its individual uses: some are made to sleep in, others are for dressing, eating, study, or conversation; but whatever the uses of a room, they are seriously interfered with if it be not preserved as a small world by itself. If the drawing-room be a part of the hall and the library a part of the drawing-room, all three will be equally unfitted to serve their special purpose.*[4]

Underlying the reasoning for the taste set forth in *The Decoration of Houses* is a strong belief in the necessity for form and ceremony in the structure of life. These qualities, which permeated the lives of Ogden Codman and Edith Wharton, were essential to Codman's conception of design and decoration.

Codman believed that the architect and decorator should be one, or should act as one, so that the decoration and total ambience of the interior of a house would "harmonize with the structural limitations" of the building and not contribute to a "multiplication of incongruous effects."[5] The introduction to *The Decoration of Houses* states that one of its aims was to correct the unfortunate position of dominance held by the upholsterer, a prime cause of the "deficiency" of house decoration in the nineteenth century. According to Wharton and Codman, the upholsterer had preempted the traditional role of the architect after the first quarter of the century and, because of insufficient training in the ground rules of architecture, was responsible for the sacrifice of "form" to "the piling up of heterogenous ornament."[6] Codman was certainly not alone in advocating the total involvement of the architect in both the exterior and interior of the house, but he was among the minority in the 1890s who operated in such a fashion.[7]

Although Codman was outspoken in his dislike for the architecture produced by contemporary graduates of the Ecole des Beaux-Arts and their American counterparts, his work shows the impact of the Ecole in its planning and use of historical styles.[8] The academic system of the Ecole helped form the aesthetics of the late-nineteenth-century American Renaissance approach to architecture, of which Codman was necessarily a part. The School of Architecture at MIT, where Codman studied in 1883–84, was modeled directly upon the Ecole. His studio instructor was Eugène Letang, a Frenchman who had studied at the Ecole in the 1860s in the atelier of Emile Vaudremer, the favored atelier for many Boston architects.[9] While Codman rejected the external stylistic qualities of design taught by Letang —the heavy massing and blocky forms typical of Second Empire buildings —as well as the use of synthetic eclecticism, he absorbed other important aspects of the Ecole approach. His experience with the firm of Andrews and Jacques undoubtedly reinforced much of this training, as would have most of the prominent Boston architectural firms.

The methodology and teaching of the Ecole system probably affected Codman more than he would have admitted. Even in such fundamental aspects of his practice as the reliance upon source books and the use of measured drawings, he was following time-honored Beaux-Arts practices. For centuries the Ecole had taught the necessity for archaeological research, such as took place at the French Academy in Rome, and all students were taught to do measured drawings. John Hubbard Sturgis, Charles McKim, Arthur Little, and Codman merely extended this practice into their researches of early American architecture.

For Codman the plan was the generator of architectural form. Although the plan might be adjusted to conform with the details of the elevations, the design was still determined by a clear, logical plan. Beaux-Arts planning emphasized symmetrical buildings with a strong processional axis and the particularization of spaces for different room functions. All of Codman's country houses and most of his city houses illustrate these principles. The distribution of the principal rooms of his country houses is based on European seventeenth- and eighteenth-century models, and the plans are usually three or five rooms wide and two or three deep. Many are quite straightforward, with the central axis proceeding directly through the house from the entrance to the garden, as in the Villa Rosa, High Wall, and La Leopolda. A second transverse axis, perpendicular to the first, opens the house from right to left. The lines of visual and directional movement are created by aligning door and window openings, which open the house both internally and to the surrounding landscape. At High Wall there is a slight variant: the entrance axis is split into two parallel axes in the entrance hall, and they lead through double doors on either side of the hall into the drawing room.

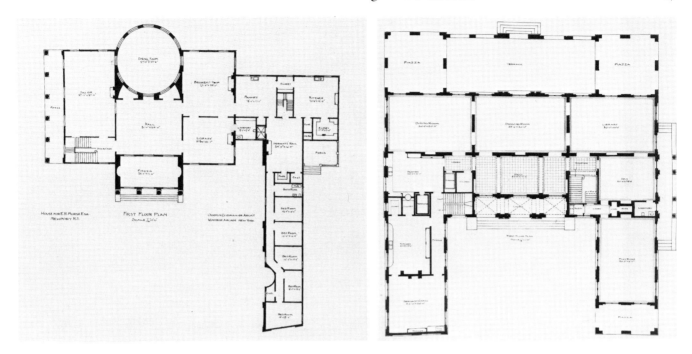

Very different is the plan he partially developed for Edith Wharton's house, The Mount, and used subsequently at Walter Maynard's house, Hautbois. Codman took advantage of the siting of both houses in the side of a hill. The entrance axis on the basement level is immediately deflected toward the staircase on the right, which is contained in the adjoining wing. This placement of a stair hall was customary in eighteenth-century French houses. After entering at the basement level, one proceeded to the main living floor (piano nobile), which opened onto a terrace overlooking the garden. The three principal rooms were arranged across the garden facade in the French manner of an enfilade, a plan that originated with Ange-Jacques Gabriel in the Petit Trianon.

Codman's work is distinguishable from his American contemporaries because he limited his classical and neoclassical sources to those of a specific type and form. He was especially fond of houses designed on a more intimate scale which contained rooms with circular or oval forms, such as those based on the designs of Jacques-François Blondel, the foremost interpreter of French neoclassicism, in the *Maisons de plaisances*. Plans such as those by Blondel had been the inspiration for American models that Codman had measured and drawn, like Woodlands in Philadelphia and the houses of Charles Bulfinch in the Boston area. To Codman, much of the beauty of these houses lay in the adaptability of their spaces; they could provide rooms that were suitable for a variety of functions and levels of entertainment. Much contemporary American architecture, though it alluded to an eighteenth-century source, ignored the scale of the original, thereby distorting the purpose of its reference. He loudly denounced the work of Whitney Warren and Thomas Hastings, which reflected their Ecole training in Paris by accentuating some

Ogden Codman, first floor plan, E. Rollins Morse house, Villa Rosa, Newport, Rhode Island, 1900

Ogden Codman, first floor plan, Oliver Ames house, High Wall, Prides Crossing, Massachusetts, 1904

Ogden Codman, house in Louis XV style

forms and details of classical sources but without necessarily following the original scale. To his friend Fiske Kimball, Codman wrote about this failure as it applied to the Newport "cottages": "I did not think much of the collection of architectural types our multi-millionaires assembled there, utterly neglecting to follow the example set them in colonial times when a number of charming and appropriate houses were built."[10] While Codman's interest in colonial architecture was not unique — Charles McKim and Stanford White, among others, had studied colonial buildings in the 1870s — he had a different aesthetic bias. "Those early houses," he wrote William Sumner Appleton, "were not architectural enough. . . . I want a sort of artistic interest in the design of a house and its plan to give me pleasure. And even then it must be a bit classic."[11]

Codman preached a classicist doctrine of stylistic purity, yet even he at times succumbed to the mixing of architectural metaphors. Early in his career he produced a series of drawings for "model" houses in a range of styles. While most of his designs show his absolute fidelity to an eighteenth-century source — such as the house with a French mansard and projecting center bay, a colonial house (plate 16) clearly based on the Shirley-Eustis house in Roxbury, Massachusetts, and another done in the English Georgian style — Codman also presents a house that is an extraordinary pastiche of styles. The wings are a mixture of English half-timber contrasted with Italian Renaissance, while the main block is composed of English Jacobean and Georgian. In only one instance did he actually compromise his taste to satisfy a client. At Faxon Lodge, built for Frank Sturgis in Newport in 1904, Codman's lack of sympathy for the "Olde English" style his client desired is evident; the resulting Tudor half-timbered exterior hides an interior done in a mixture of Adam and Georgian styles.

In houses of his own design, Codman carried out a well-conceived plan by rigidly following the classical system of symmetry and proportion. Entrance doors were always on axis with a window or panel on the opposite wall, while the fireplace and overmantel formed the focal point for the archi-

Ogden Codman, house in American colonial style

West front of the Shirley-Eustis house, originally built for Governor William Shirley around 1746 by Peter Harrison, Roxbury, Massachusetts, photographed c. 1867

Ogden Codman, house in the Georgian style

tectural decoration of the room. Within a room, a door would face another door or a window, and if such an opening was not possible, a false door had to be created to ensure the balance. Likewise, if a door was required in an asymmetrical position, its outline had to be concealed within the detailing of the wall decoration. The use of a modular system based on proportional ratios aided the planning for such carefully determined rooms. The ratios of one to two and two to three, plus the square, the double cube, and the circle, appear among the seven possibilities recommended by Palladio.[12] *The Decoration of Houses* stressed that the proportion of a room should determine its decoration: "A room with unsuitably proportioned openings, wall-spaces and cornice might receive a surface application of Louis XV or Louis XVI ornament and not represent either of those styles of decoration."[13]

Codman considered work on an existing house more challenging than work on a new one because achieving the desired effects required more ingenuity. Codman frequently "regularized" spaces in town houses built in the 1860s and 1870s, which meant the closing up or moving of asymmetrical openings to symmetrical positions. In some cases the actual floor plan was altered to create a more formal sequence of spaces. Achieving the desired effect in the overall decoration required spaces that had a balance of door and window openings and well-proportioned lines.

His last commission, Godmersham Park, provided Codman with his most serious challenge, for he described it as "the most puzzling house I ever had to think about."[14] An early Georgian house that had become a sprawling mass with two gigantic wings containing servants' offices, kitchens, over fifty bedrooms, and no bathrooms, Codman felt "it must have been planned by a congenital idiot who set out to do it all as wrong as possible." For instance, "to get to the kitchen all the trades people must pass the front door." Codman realized that "it is easy enough to replan it," but he was annoyed that "so much money will go in the tiresome ways that will never show."[15] Codman's advice to his client, Robert Tritton, shows his practical understanding of interior detailing and applies the advice given in *The Decoration of Houses*:

Ogden Codman, house in a pastiche of styles

PLATE 12. *Walter Gay, salon,
Edith Wharton estate, Pavillon
Colombe, Saint Brice-sous-Forêt,
France*

PLATE 13. Grand staircase
leading to Ogden Codman
estate, La Leopolda,
Villefranche-sur-Mer, France,
1929–31

There seem to be radiators in nearly all the places where I should want my best pieces of furniture, and light outlets in all the panels where I should want to hang pictures. . . . A sad example of bad planning is the north side of your library, where a centre doorway occupies the best place for a fine piece of furniture, and two wall radiators take up spaces where you might have placed two smaller pieces. . . . A door at one side as I show . . . in my plan would save both these spaces. . . . If radiators under the South windows are not sufficient to warm the rooms, I should put in the false doors, . . . and put grilles in the door panels, which would let the heat

Robert Tritton estate, Godmersham Park, Kent, England, before Codman alterations

Godmersham Park, after 1936, showing Codman alterations

through without spoiling the design of the decorations, [and] would leave the best places free so you could place furniture and paintings in them.[16]

Codman was extremely critical of the detailing that the office of the English architect Walter Sarel, who was officially in charge of the project, had drawn for the house. He qualified his remarks, however, by telling his client:

As the ordinary architectural draughtsman has no experience in living in a fine house such as Godmersham will be, he should not be blamed for his lack of knowledge even though his client has to spend hundreds of pounds in correcting his mistakes when the work is finished.[17]

Codman, of course, did understand the nuances of upper-class taste and how a large country house should function.

Codman began his career as a decorator, and in later life he recalled the value of this initial experience:

In the old days, when I only did decoration in houses built by other architects, I had to correct so many bad mistakes that it taught me many things that were very valuable when I planned whole houses. . . . American architects only cared for how a house would look from the outside and never gave much thought to the interiors. As I had to begin by only planning decorations, I learned to plan houses with rooms that lent themselves to decoration.[18]

Codman was fortunate that the start of his career coincided with the changing taste among well-to-do families of his social milieu. Fashionable Bostonians and New Yorkers who lived in brownstones built in the 1860s or 1870s were ready for a change of decor and wanted to be *au courant* with upper-class taste of London and Paris. Interior fashions had changed rapidly in the second half of the nineteenth century. After the rather free French Rococo decoration seen in drawing rooms at mid-century, an era of dark heaviness descended and rooms were encased with an "orgy of woodwork" during the 1870s and 1880s. By the late 1880s, however, under the influence of the aesthetic movement, there was a perceptible lightening of form and color. Much of the woodwork was painted white; drawing rooms frequently were furnished in a suitable classical revival style, such as Adam, Federal, or Louis XVI. Along with this came a more authentic approach to the use of historic styles, evidence of which could be seen in the influence of individual collections of antique furniture and the installation of old wood paneling (or boiserie) in drawing rooms. In England, important collections were formed by members of the aristocracy, such as the Marquis of Hertford and Sir Richard Wallace, whose patronage thereby guaranteed the fashion for French eighteenth-century furniture and *objets*. By the 1880s some Americans were also beginning to collect antiques,[19] as the knowledge of ancestral origins and material associations with the Old World became increasingly important marks of social status. Codman, with his cosmopolitan background and knowledge of historical styles, was able to provide his clients with just this sort of atmosphere.

The meticulous watercolor drawings executed by Codman's office in the 1890s provide a rare color documentation of interiors (plates 4, 5, 11, 15, 17–22, 25, 26). Done for presentation to clients, some drawings show several options for the treatment of walls or curtains or give different furniture designs. Although renderings of this sort were customary among European decorating firms, American firms did not produce drawings of this quality, or at least they have not survived. Probably the drawings were done partially for Codman to show his clients that he could carry out interiors with the same finesse as the best French firms. As Codman did not like to draw, it is unlikely that he did any of the drawings himself; he remarked years later that he had employed students from the Ecole des Beaux-Arts to do the drawings for the Cornelius Vanderbilt commission to decorate the second and third floors of The Breakers (plate 4).[20] There is no listing, however, in his account books of payments to individuals for work on the "scrapbooks," as the clients portfolios were called. By 1900 Codman discontinued this practice, an unnecessary expense that was passed on to clients. He evidently heeded Edith Wharton's warning that "it was poor policy to overwhelm your clients by the number of your water-color designs" and listened to her advice that he was "now firmly enough established to be less lavish in this respect."[21]

Codman's method of designing an interior is described by one former draftsman, Emery Roth. A young immigrant from Hungary with some drafting skills, Roth had been assigned by the office of Richard Morris Hunt to prepare architectural data to facilitate Codman's work at The Breakers; he subsequently joined Codman's office after Hunt's death. According to Roth, Codman would choose a room he considered suitable for adaptation from his extensive collection of European design books. Then he would have elements of the room reproduced as faithfully as conditions permitted, down to the minutest details. Most of the designs were drawn from the French tradition, although a few were taken from Italian or English sources.[22] Codman relied on well-known treatises by such noted eighteenth- and nineteenth-century masters as Jacques-François Blondel, C. A. d'Aviler, Daniel Marot, Percier and Fontaine, and Isaac Ware. Most of these titles found their way onto the list of "Books Consulted" in the opening pages of *The Decoration of Houses*.

Codman's rooms, despite his adherence to a specific historical model, in no way resemble genuine period rooms as seen in a museum, nor would one mistake them for the historically inspired rooms done in the 1920s or 1930s, which tend to become rather dry and academic in feeling. In Codman's scientific eclectic approach, parts of the decoration are exactly copied from the source, such as the replication of plasterwork details, but the way in which he combines a number of different details creates a historic scheme that is entirely his own (plates 20, 21). If one compares the drawings of

*Ogden Codman, music room,
Ogden and Leila Codman
house, 15 East 51st Street, New
York, 1904*

*Ogden Codman, designs for
fireplace and curtain, drawing
room, Charles Cooper house, 113
East 21st Street, New York*

*Ogden Codman, design
for table, stool, and lamp,
Harold Brown house, Newport,
Rhode Island, 1893*

*Ogden Codman, designs for
furniture, Harold Brown house*

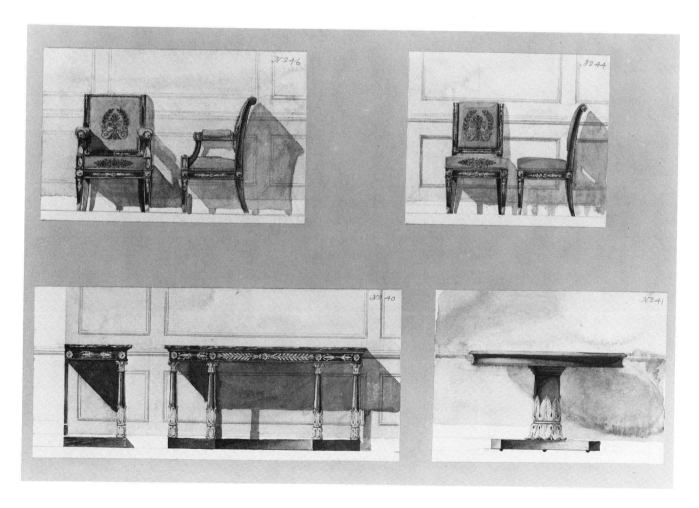

Ogden Codman, design for library showing Napoleonic memorabilia, Harold Brown house

Opposite: Walter Gay, music room designed by Ogden Codman, Eben Howard Gay house, 170 Beacon Street, Boston, Massachusetts, after 1900

Empire furniture done for the Harold Brown house, in which several pieces are labeled "copied from the plates of Percier and Fontaine" (plate 8) with the actual Percier and Fontaine plates showing an entire room, it is evident that Codman copied only certain pieces from the original source, which he then combined with others to create the ambience of an Empire setting (plate 9). Harold Brown had engaged Codman to design a series of Empire interiors as an appropriate setting for his collection of Napoleonic furniture and objects.

Codman also created a backdrop for a particular collection of antique furniture in the Eben Howard Gay house at 170 Beacon Street, Boston, in 1900 (plate 20). Gay wanted his rooms to be decorated in a suitably historical manner that would be appropriate for his collection of Chippendale and other cabinetmaker's pieces. His brother, the painter Walter Gay, recorded a corner of the music room with a Chippendale settee placed against a soft gray wall decorated with plasterwork masks and arabesques and a gilt bracket supporting a Chinese porcelain vase.

Where it is possible to compare a rendering with the actual result, as in the case of the Nathaniel Thayer dining room in Newport, the appearance of the room may not fulfill the level of elegance that the architect had originally conceived (plate 22). The walls did not receive the marbelizing shown in the drawing, nor did the quality of the furnishings give the room the appearance or grandeur Codman would have liked. Like designers of all ages, he had to tolerate the compromises to which his ideas of decoration were subjected by the imposition of the client's taste.

Most of the furniture, fabrics, hardware, and mantelpieces Codman used were imported from France. In order to provide the client with the piece most precisely suited for the room, it was more expedient to copy a model, although there was certainly no difficulty in purchasing antiques at the time. For the bedrooms at The Breakers, for instance, the firm of Pihouée,

Ogden Codman, design for dining room, Nathaniel Thayer house, Edgemere, Newport, Rhode Island, c. 1896–97

Sièges et Meubles d'Art, Paris, supplied photographs and drawings of chairs, chaises, bureaux, beds, tables, and other required items in the various Louis styles. Codman then selected the style, wood, and finish for each piece. The firm of Jansen et Cie was one well-known decorating firm with whom Codman dealt extensively, in particular for curtains and draperies. Codman's bias in using French sources was certainly shared by other decorators, including Elsie de Wolfe, but his reliance on such imports was perhaps more extensive.

Codman used the French firm of F. Audrain to provide the entire contents for the New York drawing room of Ethel Rhinelander King (1900). Codman probably met with his client in Paris to go over the details of the room, and when the house was ready for installation, Audrain shipped the boiseries, cornice moldings, parquet floor, bolts of yellow silk damask to be hung inside the wood panels (plus curtains and lambrequins with their requisite *passementeries*, bergères, fauteuils, various sizes of tables, a chandelier, wall sconces, Savonnerie carpet, and marble chimneypiece). He also sent along a *contremaître* (foreman), who stayed for fifteen days to supervise the installation. Drawings were done by Audrain for all sides of the room, plus one view in perspective, the only drawing among Codman's commissions that shows a room with all of its furnishings (plate 15). Mentioned in the bills are the sources from which the pieces were copied, such as "un

Dining room, Edgemere

guéridon rond bois de rose et marqueterie reproduction d'un modèle du Château de Versailles." Several genuine Louis XVI pieces completed the arrangement. This extensive documentation is a valuable record of how a well-appointed drawing room was assembled at the turn of the century.[23]

It also gives us a glimpse at how Codman's business was run. His practice was exclusively residential, with few exceptions such as a library in Ormond Beach, Florida, and an addition to The Metropolitan Club in New York City. Presumably he hired draftsmen as the need arose, but, besides a secretary, there is in his letters no mention of anyone by name in the office until the arrival of Charles Wulff in 1910. From that date until Codman closed his office, Wulff acted as head draftsman and general office manager.[24] During the months Codman was in France, Wulff entirely ran the office. However, even to the smallest details, final decisions about the choice of materials and designs for both interiors and exteriors were made exclusively by Codman. After 1905, with so much time spent in France, Codman needed an assistant there to attend to the office correspondence, the daily affairs of managing his château, plus the research for his catalogue raisonné of châteaux. The role of secretary was always filled by someone of acceptable social background, and in the later years of his life, he fulfilled the role of companion as well.[25]

The best examples of Codman's work are those in which he acted as both architect and decorator. A comparison of four country houses, plus his own, La Leopolda, demonstrates how successfully he was able to integrate the aspects of plan, design, decoration, and landscaping within a unified conception: Villa Rosa, built for E. Rollins Morse in Newport in 1900; High Wall, built for Oliver Ames in Prides Crossing, Massachusetts, in 1904; Berkeley Villa, built for Martha Codman in Newport in 1910; and Hautbois, built for Walter Maynard in Jericho, Long Island, in 1916. From a variety of eighteenth-century sources, Codman invariably chose as his models houses and villas of a more intimate scale to achieve a combination of elegance and comfort. What had appealed to Bulfinch in the 1780s about French neoclassical architecture appealed to Codman—a plan which incorporated many spatial possibilities and in which privacy and convenience were more important than *parade* and overblown magnificence. Bulfinch had introduced into New England architecture such features as a suite of rooms on the garden side and an oval or circular center room, the subordination of the staircase by moving it to one side, variation in form and height of rooms, and careful planning of service facilities.

Ogden Codman, Oliver Ames house, High Wall, Prides Crossing, Massachusetts, 1904, drawn by Robert Kendrick

Ogden Codman, forecourt with walls, High Wall

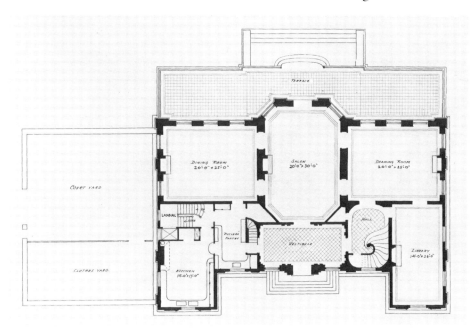

Codman's houses were built during the golden age of country houses in America from 1890 to 1930. American country houses were often distinguished by the relatively small plot of land on which they were built; they were often located in a suburban setting or a summer community where the available land was limited to one or two acres per house. Under such circumstances, creating a sense of place was a greater challenge to the architect than one where natural beauty had determined the choice of site. For instance, two of Codman's Newport houses, Villa Rosa and Berkeley Villa, had addresses on Bellevue Avenue as the prime reason for their site. While High Wall had the advantage of a water view from one side, it was located on a narrow stretch of road between the sea and a public road. Hautbois, situated in a flat, densely wooded area on Long Island, was located there primarily because, according to Codman, the owner "bought a place on Long Island with no view but almost entirely surrounded by Vanderbilts."[26]

For each of these houses, Codman devised adept solutions to the problem of restrictive sites. Once again he showed his indebtedness to the concepts of French planning, the major considerations of which were maintaining a sense of privacy and providing adequate space for a garden in the rear. One flexible solution was to place the house in a forecourt announced by a gateway. His most original variant of that scheme was at High Wall, where he placed the driveway leading to the forecourt at a 45 degree angle, instead of in a direct approach to the house, and included another on the opposite side, also at 45 degrees, leading to the stables. For privacy from the public road, he built a double wall: the outer one, a high, solid wall of concrete with ornamented piers, surrounded the entire property; the inner one enclosed a vast forecourt with gateways providing vistas to the symmetrically planted trees along the drives. Directly opposite the main doorway at the further end of the court was an archway, which lent "a veritable note of triumph"[27] to the composition. Clipped bay trees on either side of the arch and gates gave additional emphasis to the scheme. Taking advantage of the ocean view from the far side of the house, Codman placed the three main rooms — drawing, dining, and library — enfilade and gave them French windows and doors opening onto a terrace and loggias.

An essential aspect of Codman's design for a courtyard was its dimensions in relation to the house. He referred to Edith Wharton's courtyard at The Mount as a "clothesyard" because of its cramped proportions, and he criticized her for not referring to one of the "old books" of architecture which gave instructions for the proper size.[28] In several instances he enabled the courtyard to fulfill both a ceremonial and a functional purpose. At Villa Rosa and Hautbois, Codman made one side of the courtyard wall into a service wing, incorporating the servants' quarters behind the section that extended perpendicular from the house. The arrangement at Villa Rosa was, according to *Town & Country* magazine, "unlike anything of its kind in this country."[29] At both houses, niches filled with statues, trellis panels, and small round windows were among the design elements used to break up the long expanse of wall.

Courtyard facade, Wharton house, The Mount, Lenox, Massachusetts, c. 1904

Ogden Codman, north elevation, Villa Rosa

Statues, stone benches, and consoles — favorite classical devices — were used by Codman to provide decorative relief in formal spaces, such as foyers, terraces, and gardens. Important to the total effect was the design for the base on which a statue or urn rested, which was invariably copied from a classical source. The French sculptor Jules Visseaux made all of Codman's figures and urns, using marble or terra-cotta as the medium. A craftsman whose taste was greatly respected by Codman, he frequently used well-known classical subjects for his models. In one instance Codman had replicated for his cousin, Martha Codman, a statue in the Louvre, *L'Amour et L'Amitié* by Pigalle. It had formerly belonged in the château of Betz, which was owned at one time by their ancestor, Richard Codman.[30]

Treillage (or trelliswork), a popular feature of seventeenth- and eighteenth-century gardens, was included in many Codman houses. Although certainly not unique to him, his extensive use of it for landscaping, roof gardens, and interior spaces helped to popularize its revival in America in the early decades of the twentieth century. This device, which was also much used by and associated with Elsie de Wolfe, who devoted a chapter to it in *The House in Good Taste*, was first used by Codman in the early 1890s for Edith Wharton's garden at Land's End (plate 24). There he designed a trellis screen with panels linked by columns and a trellis niche, derived from a plate in Daniel Marot's *Das Ornamentwerk*,[31] which was a seminal work for many of Codman's ideas on both landscape and decoration. The illustrated volumes of Marot, a French Huguenot whose designs contributed so much to the court of William and Mary, were reprinted and copied extensively throughout the eighteenth and early nineteenth centuries. Marot's designs for outdoor treillage structures — pavilions, screens, and enclosures — placed in formally planted beds were prominent features of seventeenth- and eighteenth-century French and Italian gardens. The great treillage structures in the gardens of Versailles or Chantilly were probably only remnants by the 1880s when Codman and Wharton visited those sites; however, by that date, under the impetus for the revival of eighteenth-century taste, treillage was sometimes used to decorate gala rooms in Paris.[32] Codman's trellis ballroom for Villa Rosa, designed in 1900, is probably the first example of the interior use of treillage in America.

Codman received another opportunity to use trellis in a Newport garden

Ogden Codman, statue in niche, Villa Rosa

*Ogden Codman, vestibule,
7 East 96th Street, New York,
1912*

*Garden, showing niche designed
by Codman and marble statue,
Wharton house, Land's End,
Newport, Rhode Island, 1893*

Copy of Pigalle's L'Amour et
l'Amitié, *entrance hall, Martha
Codman house, 2145 Decatur
Place, Washington, D.C.*

*Ogden Codman and Beatrix
Farrand, garden trellis, J. J.
Van Alen house, Wakehurst,
Newport, Rhode Island,
1896 – 98*

*Ogden Codman, design for
trellis, north side of terrace,
Land's End*

*Daniel Marot, design for a
trellis (detail), from* Das
Ornamentwerk *(1892)*

*Ogden Codman, Italian
garden, Codman family house,
The Grange, Lincoln,
Massachusetts, c. 1900–3*

from a distant relative, James Van Alen, at Wakehurst, a house designed by
Dudley Newton but based very closely on an English Tudor precedent. To
evoke an English medieval garden, Codman designed a lattice fence with a
center pavilion, and Beatrix Jones Farrand, Wharton's niece, designed the
formal geometric layout of beds and paths.

Farrand, one of America's first women landscape gardeners, shared
many of Codman's and Wharton's ideas about landscaping and gardens. She
assisted her aunt with the design of the kitchen garden at The Mount, but
it is still unclear whether she was involved with the gardens at Land's End.[33]
Surprisingly, there is no mention of Farrand in Codman's letters. Undoubtedly they knew one another, as she is known to have visited the Codman
family estate. Possibly Farrand and her aunt assisted with the design for the
Italianate garden at The Grange. Begun in 1899, it captured the spirit of an
Italian Renaissance garden with its reflecting pool, terra-cotta statues, marble
colonnade, and pergola. But with stones from New England walls lining the
pool and terraces, and native plant materials, the garden is also a special
blend of Italy and New England, in much the same spirit described by

PLATE 14. *Principal elevation,
Ogden Codman estate, La
Leopolda, Villefranche-sur-Mer,
France, 1929–31*

PLATE 15. *Design for salon,
Ethel Rhinelander King house,
20 East 84th Street, New York,
1899*

PLATE 16. Garden front,
American colonial style house

PLATE 17. Design for master
bedroom, Frederick W.
Vanderbilt house, Hyde Park,
New York, 1898

Ogden Codman, terrace and garden, Lloyd S. Bryce house, Roslyn, New York, c. 1901

Jacques Gréber, garden, Walter Maynard house, Hautbois, Jericho, New York, photographed 1920

Wharton in her book *Italian Villas and Their Gardens*.[34] Like Wharton and Farrand, Codman extended the principles set forth in *The Decoration of Houses* into the garden—the formal, geometric arrangement of beds defined by gravel paths creates a strong axial configuration and continues the lines of the house into the landscape. Codman's houses often had terraces planted in such a manner, with flower beds and ornamental sculpture, a tradition that had been carried on for centuries in Italy and France.

Among classical revival architects and designers at the turn of the century, there was a great deal of interest in the formal garden, especially in the ways in which the design could be combined with the "naturalistic" flowering one more typical of English and American gardens. On several occasions Codman was assisted in garden design by two noted French landscape architects, Jacques Gréber and Achille Duchêne. Gréber, the great *urbaniste*, had worked on a number of important gardens in America; he collaborated with Horace Trumbauer on several of his grandest commissions, such as Whitemarsh Hall for Edward Stotesbury (1921) and Harbour Hill, the Clarence Mackey estate (1913). Inspired by the totally French atmosphere of Hautbois, designed in the style of a late Louis XV hunting lodge, he reportedly asked the owner, Walter Maynard, if he could do the design for the garden.[35] Its plan balanced perfectly the charm of the house, with its quality of simplified formality. Three series of steps lead down from a terrace to a *tapis vert* bordered by clipped box hedges with flower beds on either side, and terminated with a pool and fountain. Grass parterres with stone

Ogden Codman, Martha Codman house, Berkeley Villa, Newport, Rhode Island, 1910

steps were used at a number of Codman's houses; they are also a feature of the landscaping at The Mount. A traditional landscaping concept that was originally used in Italy, it became popular in England and France during the seventeenth and eighteenth centuries. As part of the landscaping at The Grange, it was therefore a natural component of Codman's taste. Achille Duchêne was originally referred to Codman by Mary Berenson in 1909 for the design of Martha Codman's formal terrace garden at her house in Washington. Considered by Codman to be "the greatest landscape gardener in France," Duchêne was noted for his restoration of historic gardens in France and England, which included Le Nôtre's Vaux-le-Vicomte and the parterres at Blenheim.[36]

A second house for Martha Codman, Berkeley Villa, was built in Newport a year later. One of Codman's most successful country houses, it shows his ability to synthesize American and English eighteenth-century sources and adapt them to the requirements of early twentieth-century life. The exterior of Berkeley Villa was composed of three houses from the Boston area which Codman had measured and drawn years before. Consistent with his prejudice against inappropriately oversized "cottages," he designed a composite "colonial" that was more in keeping with the tradition of Newport architecture. The Shirley-Eustis house in Roxbury, Massachusetts (attributed to Peter Harrison, c. 1746) inspired the story heights, roof line, and dormers; the Eben Crafts House, Elmwood, in Roxbury (Peter Banner, 1805) provided the double columns around the doorway and the projecting vestibule; and the Perez Morton House, also in Roxbury (Charles Bulfinch, 1796), was the source for the octagonal bay with the second-story loggia above. The brick and wood gates with pineapple finials marking the entrance had a Southern colonial antecedent and were copied from the Nathaniel Heyward house in Charleston, South Carolina.

While understatement was appropriate for the exterior, the interior had to provide a suitably elegant ambience for a rich single woman from a distinguished New England family. It was "derived entirely from English

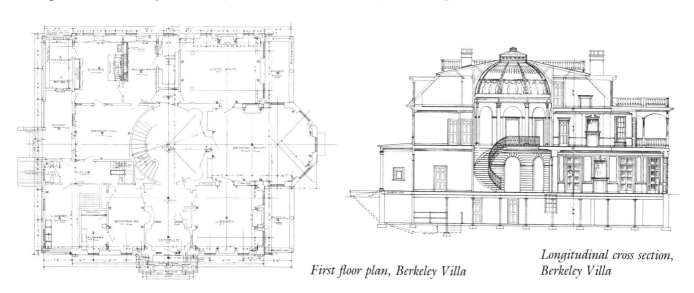

First floor plan, Berkeley Villa

Longitudinal cross section, Berkeley Villa

Staircase, Berkeley Villa

Ogden Codman, garden facade, Walter Maynard house, Hautbois, Jericho, New York, c. 1916–17

sources and is much finer than the exterior, which is very modest, would lead you to expect."[37] A large circular domed hall with a spiral staircase ascending on the left occupied the central space; to the right, the three principal rooms—library, drawing, and dining—were arranged enfilade looking onto the garden. The arrangement and design for the circular stair hall was inspired by several sources. While the one closest in plan appears to be taken from James Paine's Wardour Hall,[38] the detailing of the dome is derived from the stair hall at Home House by Robert Adam; another model Codman mentioned was the circular stair hall of James McComb's New York City Hall. What distinguished Codman's design was his adjustment of these various sources to the proportion of the house. While the space is eminently grand, it is not overpowering. All the details of the decoration are handled in the traditional classical manner.

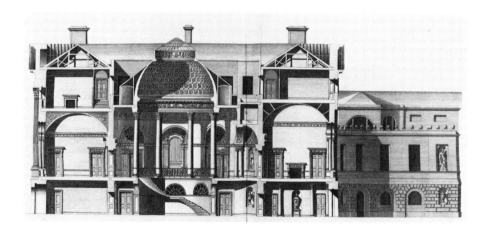

James Paine, longitudinal cross section, Wardour Hall, England, from Plans, Elevations, and Sections of gentlemen's and noblemen's houses *(1767)*

The close relationship between the architect and his client enabled Codman to oversee all aspects of the interior design and decoration. As with the previous house, Codman and his cousin met in London to select the various items, and he reported to his office manager the results of their shopping expedition: "If she does as I believe she now intends to do, and gets everything from Lenygon of 31 Old Burlington Street, she will have as good a house at Newport as she has in Washington, which is saying a lot." Pleased that he had persuaded his wealthy cousin to install the more costly decoration, Codman reported to Wulff, "Miss Codman is thinking of having her rooms panelled in wood, do not discourage her, as it is much nicer and more correct, if somewhat more expensive. I call your attention to it as I attach the greatest possible importance to getting this just as I want it to be."[39] The firm of Lenygon, later known as Lenygon and Morant, provided all the interior fittings for the three principal rooms, including marble mantels, cornice moldings, door trims, and some furniture. The firm was the leading proponent of the neo-Georgian style of decoration in England and America from 1905 to 1940, and Codman relied on them extensively for his interiors in the Georgian style.[40]

Hautbois, the last country house commission by Codman's office, was probably his finest work in the French classic style. Codman and Walter and Eunice Maynard had known each other for many years and shared an appreciation of French art and culture. The architect and client collaborated on this house, and correspondence between Maynard and Codman indicates that Maynard insisted that every aspect and detail of the exterior be stylistically consistent with the overall concept of the house — an early eighteenth-century *manoir* or hunting lodge.[41] To achieve the proper historical reference, Codman relied chiefly on the accuracy of proportions, the design and arrangement of the windows, and the mansard roof line, along with the French tradition of brick trim and quoining contrasted with the white plaster walls. The placement of the principal rooms on the second-story level (piano nobile) was indicated by the increased height of the window frames, and the entrance vestibule on the basement level was treated in the manner of a grotto with the walls left in rough-cast plaster. A similar arrangement had been used by Edith Wharton at The Mount.

The decoration of the drawing room and library at Hautbois exemplify the taste and criteria given in *The Decoration of Houses*. All fixtures, hardware, and mantels were imported from France, while the rooms were furnished entirely with French antiques, the result of many shopping forays by the Maynards and Codman. To give the sense of an architectural order, Codman divided the drawing room walls with paneled moldings and a bracketed cornice. Such a treatment supplanted the decorative plasterwork and fabric-filled rococo panels used by Codman in earlier schemes. With the decoration reduced to the simplest element, a room could accept a variety of stylistic references, though all were compatible with the eighteenth-century mode. The decorative paintings of flowers and urns over the doors were further allusions to late-eighteenth-century French taste and were used in many

Second floor plan, Hautbois

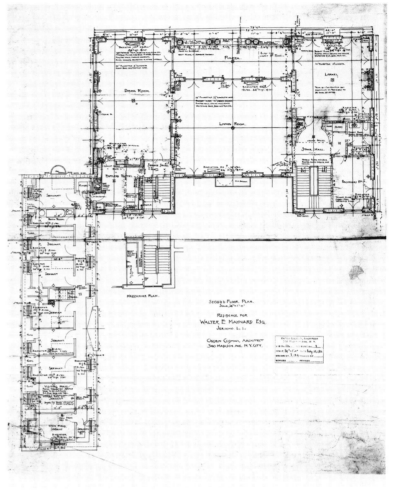

Below, left: Library, Hautbois

Below, right: Drawing room, Hautbois

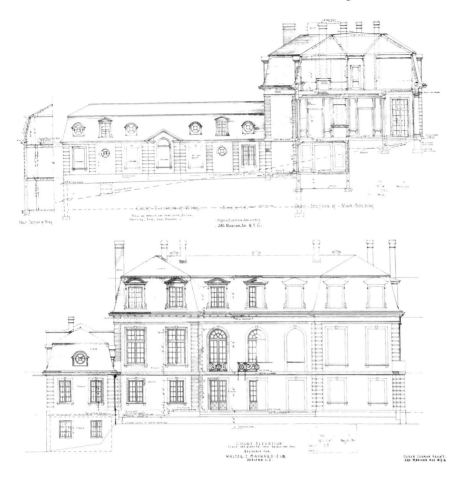

Cross section, Hautbois

Court elevation, Hautbois

Codman rooms as a device for balancing the lines of door and window heights. The pale tinted walls, probably a soft gray, with the moldings painted a lighter shade, and simple curtain treatment (a reminder that their primary function is to control light and drafts) completed the basic formula of Codman's style of interior decoration. The library was paneled in black and gold Directoire boiserie, which came from a château in France, and the recessed shelves filled with leather-bound books provided an important element of color and texture. To balance the door and window openings, Codman placed mirror panes above the door opening on the left.

Both of these rooms bear the qualities of timeless elegance and taste for which Codman's interiors are remembered. They show the "sense of interrelation of parts, of unity of the whole."[42] Finally, what gives the decoration of these rooms the "crowning touch of distinction" are the "good objects of art."[43] As stated in *The Decoration of Houses*, "a room should depend for its adornment on general harmony of parts, and on the artistic quality of such necessities as lamps, screens, bindings, and furniture."[44]

The ultimate expression of Codman's philosophy of design and decoration was La Leopolda (plates 13, 14). Few architects have had an opportunity to demonstrate their taste and ideas in such grand fashion. Codman wrote that La Leopolda was, in fact, designed to show "how a house can be built exactly on the lines laid down in that book," meaning *The Decoration*

Ogden Codman, principal elevation, La Leopolda, Villefranche-sur-Mer, France, 1929–31

of Houses.[45] As Edith Wharton had done thirty years before at The Mount, Codman wanted to create his own "laboratory" for the ideas and taste which they had expressed in their collaborative venture. Whereas The Mount compressed the concepts of plan and arrangement into a well-conceived, succinct statement, La Leopolda was much more elaborate and expansive, containing the full complement of rooms and anterooms outlined in the book.

The two houses have several important similarities in form and concept which clearly demonstrate key principles of design emphasized in *The Decoration of Houses*. Each house reflected aspects of the European tradition combined with American practicality. Both were situated on a hillside and featured a balustraded terrace and double staircase, a device with numerous Italian precedents, which extended the house into the landscape. Inside, following the French tradition, both had plans that emphasized the importance of privacy and distinctly articulated spaces. This was carried out by the arrangement of the stair hall in a subsidiary space off the vestibule and the separation of bedroom from boudoir or private sitting room; on the first floor, the principal rooms were arranged enfilade, each opening onto the terrace.

In 1939 Codman published a handsomely illustrated booklet about La Leopolda that serves as a guide to the rooms and grounds of the estate.[46] Each detail of its design and decoration was carefully thought out to enhance the total classical ambience, but it also incorporates the "most modern developments in plumbing, heating, and lighting such as are used . . . in America." Similar in form to several of his other country houses, La Leopolda has a hip roofline, central block with modified projecting wings, and two side extensions connecting the main block to two octagonal towers, one a water tower, the other used for a small apartment. As in other houses of his design, Codman borrowed elements and details from eighteenth-century sources — here the Château Borelli in Marseilles, the "magnificent" Villa Belgiojoso at Milan, and the "superb" Villa Melzi at Bellagio — which he then adapted to his taste for a more suitable scale and less formal decoration.

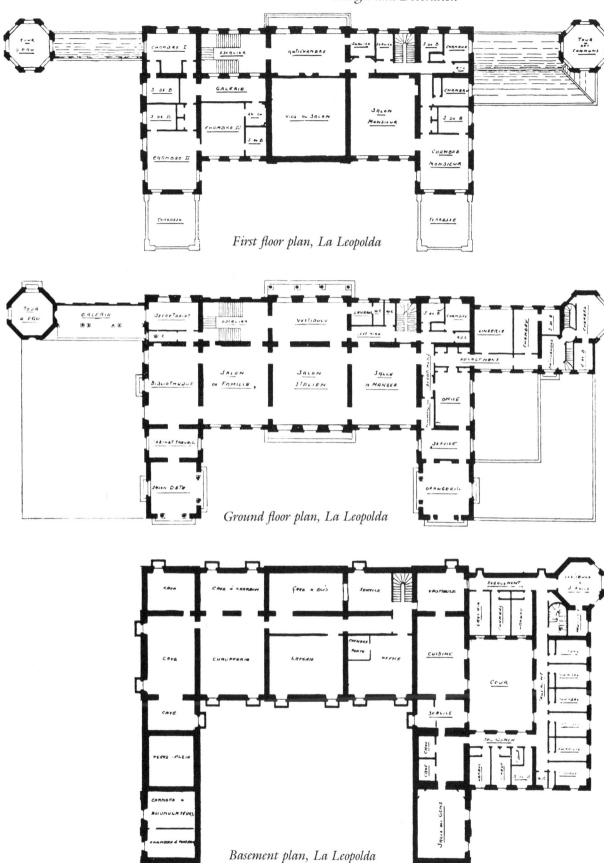

First floor plan, La Leopolda

Ground floor plan, La Leopolda

Basement plan, La Leopolda

*Stair hall, with statue
representing Spring,
La Leopolda*

*Opposite: Italian salon, La
Leopolda*

Approaching La Leopolda up the steep winding road of the Moyenne
Corniche rising above Villefranche, the visitor first glimpses its pedimented
facade through the iron gates of the grand staircase, each level of which is
decorated with stone urns (plate 13). "One enters the house through an
austere simili-stone vaulted vestibule, which," according to Codman, "makes
an agreeable contrast in its sober simplicity, to the gay colouring of the Gala
apartments that lie beyond." The staircase was modeled on that of the Château Borelli, but is "somewhat smaller and simpler," with the black wrought-
iron stair rail picked out with bronze green, "somewhat less pretentious than
the gilding at Château Borelli." A statue of Spring stood in the well of the
staircase, and a stone console table with an urn from a nearby faience factory
completed the decoration of the stair hall.

Dining room, La Leopolda

The decoration of the "Gala apartments"—the *salon de famille*, Italian salon, and dining room "is very characteristic of the eighteenth century in Italy." The walls of all three were "stucco, called by the Italians *Scagliola*." While the *salon de famille* or sitting room was decorated in three shades of green, closely following designs from the Château Borelli, the design for the Italian salon, or ballroom, a cube of thirty feet, was drawn from the works of Albertolli, with walls "very like *Bleu-turquin* marble, with yellow, Sienna, and Breche violette trimmings." Over the mantelpiece (which was "copied exactly from that of the principal salon at the Château Borelli") was a mirror with a semicircular top, which reflected a window of similar shape leading out to the terrace. "Two similar mirrors placed in the middle of the side walls . . . reflect an endless vista, of immense decorative value. The over-doors and over-windows are exquisitely modelled in plaster and painted in soft shades of blue and white." Concealed lighting in the cornice threw a soft light on the coved, painted, and domed ceiling, and from the center hung a chandelier of bronze and gilded wood with crystal drops ("equipped for using candles as well as electric lights"). Six pairs of double doors, painted with designs by Albertolli, connected the gala rooms. When the doors were thrown open, a mirror outside the dining room reflected "a magnificent enfilade with a view of the garden, seen through a window in the library, the fourth room of the suite."

In the dining room, the *scagliola* walls were in three shades of soft-toned red, and the ceiling was painted to represent a blue sky with white clouds. Placed in two semicircular niches were the life-sized plaster groups of figures holding garlands of fruit that Codman brought from the dining room of his New York house. They were copies of Clodion originals in the

Codman's bedroom, La Leopolda

Musée des Arts Décoratifs and had once formed part of the decoration of what Codman claimed was "no doubt the most beautiful dining room in Paris."

Codman stated that no wood was used "where its use could possibly be avoided, as the heat in summer makes wood panelling most inadvisable." The floors throughout the house were of *terrazzo* and mosaic, in marbles of several shades, and several of them were laid in designs taken from Albertolli. They were designed to be "very cool in summer, but covered in winter with . . . eighteenth-century Aubusson carpet[s]."

The upstairs was given over to Codman's extensive private quarters and three guest suites. Codman's apartment included an anteroom, shaped like a long gallery, which was used as a private dining room, plus a private sitting room, bedroom, dressing and bath rooms, valet's room, housemaid's closet, and a small room for a trained nurse in case of illness. Each room was precisely furnished with the requisite pieces of predominantly French or Italian eighteenth-century furniture and with carefully selected decorative objects and pictures whose color and shape would suit the theme of each room. In his own bedroom, Codman had a Louis XVI four-post bed, hung with a French glazed chintz of Louis XVI design, with window curtains to match. While the overmantle was also of Louis XVI design, the mantelpiece was Louis XV, reflecting Codman's characteristic combination of mismatched but complementary objects. "As is often the case in old châteaux," he reminds us, "the changes made by successive owners often result in unexpected harmonies, that some professional decorators would never permit." It was an effect he tried to achieve throughout his career—to create a room that looked like its decoration had evolved over the years.

Servant's hall with marble dining table, La Leopolda

Another important aspect of La Leopolda's design was the careful incorporation of service conveniences, from the concealment of closets to the pleasant surrounding of the servants' quarters. There were eleven servants' bedrooms on the basement level and a large servants' hall complete with marble dining table.

The grounds and gardens of La Leopolda were as magnificent as the house. At every level, terraces and gardens provided a variety of visual sensations. Outside the library and secretary's office on the ground floor was a loggia that linked the house with the water tower. Stone benches, a stone

Terrace and steps, La Leopolda

console table, and several terra-cotta pieces made this space a sheltered spot for a private winter garden. Outside the bachelor wing and first-floor bedrooms were terraces from which to view the panorama of Cap Ferrat, Villefranche, and the Mediterranean. Monumental flower pots similar to ones used by Catherine the Great decorated the main terrace, which was paved in a pattern with brick, slate, and marble. Down the steps from the wide staircases of the main terrace was a grotto, paved with pebbles of many colors laid in patterns. On one side of the grotto was the rose garden, treated in a formal architectural manner *à la Française* with a trellis and niches making "a suitable transition from the villa itself to the wildness and make-believe naturalness of the park itself." On the right of the grotto was a garden in the Hispano Mauresque style, laid out by the previous owner of the property, which was considered by Codman to be "too exotic, yet by contrast making all the rest of the garden seem more harmonious." On the terrace below this were two small enclosed gardens followed by other terraces with orange trees and many kinds of flowering shrubs. On the other side of the house, parallel to the entrance with columned portico and gravel courtyard, ran the great pool, 257 feet long by 40 feet wide. Codman took obvious pride that the four fountains of water flowing from vases held by the River Gods could be controlled from the vestibule of the villa: "this means that one may have the pleasure, while still in the villa, of operating the fountains from a distance." Additional landscape features of the property included the kitchen garden, orange grove, King Leopold's rock garden, as well as numerous outbuildings, including garages, gardeners' cottages, greenhouses, and guest cottages.

No detail that added to its luxury or splendor was overlooked by its creator. Named for a property once owned by a king, Codman valued its reputation among members of royalty. He was especially pleased with the compliment given by the Duke of Connaught, who said that La Leopolda was "by far the most magnificent house on the whole Riviera."[47]

Built as a showpiece, La Leopolda has often been used as a stage set for many types of gala occasions, from charitable *fête de nuits* and fancy-dress balls to the rousing parties held during its occupancy by American soldiers. The grand staircase was memorialized for filmgoers in *The Red Shoes*, when in a climactic scene Moira Shearer, who plays the role of an aspiring ballerina, ascends the stairs in a flowing green silk cape.

At La Leopolda, Codman fulfilled his artistic ambitions in every way. It was the culmination of his approach to design, as outlined in his booklet on his masterpiece:

> *He had reached the conclusion that in order to arrive at a really harmonious result, one should carefully study local tradition and local conditions and avoid everything exotic, it being his belief that the more restraint was exercised, the more harmony was certain to result. He had collected a large library of books about the buildings that had been erected in the various countries of Europe, as well as in the United States during the eighteenth*

Garden in Hispano Mauresque
style, La Leopolda

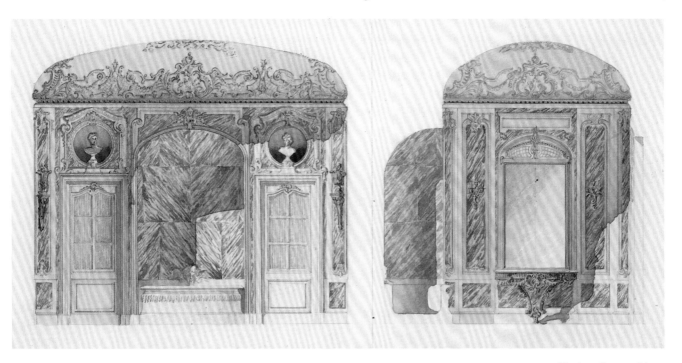

PLATE 18. *Design for marble bathroom, Frederick W. Vanderbilt house, Hyde Park, New York, 1898*

PLATE 19. *Design for marble bathroom, Vanderbilt house*

PLATE 20. *Design for music
room, Eben Howard Gay house,
170 Beacon Street, Boston, 1900*

PLATE 21. *Wall decoration in
neoclassical style*

century. He had travelled extensively in France and Italy in order to study the actual buildings wherever possible, and thus acquire the art of building with the greatest simplicity, of avoiding unnecessary ornament, of depending almost entirely upon the proportions of voids and masses, and of searching always for a tradition or precedent.

NOTES

1. Edith Wharton and Ogden Codman, Jr., *The Decoration of Houses* (New York: Charles Scribner's Sons, 1897), introduction.
2. Ibid., 17.
3. Ibid., 18, 22.
4. Ibid., 22.
5. Ibid., introduction.
6. Ibid.
7. Two well-known contemporaries, representative of opposite ends of the architectural spectrum, who also felt as he did were Stanford White and Frank Lloyd Wright.
8. The only contemporary architect whose work Codman liked was Horace Trumbauer, who had attended the Ecole des Beaux-Arts.
9. Richard Chafee, "The Atelier Vaudremer and the Ecole des Beaux-Arts," *A Continental Eye: The Art & Architecture of Arthur Rotch* (Boston: The Boston Athenæum, 1985), 35.
10. Ogden Codman to Fiske Kimball, 17 March 1935, BA.
11. Ogden Codman to William Sumner Appleton, 12 August 1931, BA.
12. Rudolf Wittkower, *Architectural Principles in the Age of Humanism* (New York: Random House, 1962), 95.
13. *Decoration of Houses*, 11.
14. Ogden Codman to Russell Page, 31 August 1936, BA.
15. Ibid.
16. Ogden Codman to Robert Tritton, 23 December 1936, BA.
17. Ibid.
18. Ibid.
19. One American collector was Egerton Winthrop, a cosmopolitan lawyer in New York whose taste for French furniture and objects was an important early influence on Edith Wharton.
20. Ogden Codman to Robert Tritton, 28 June 1936, BA.
21. Edith Wharton to Ogden Codman, 28 May 1897, SPNEA.
22. Steven Ruttenbaum, *Mansions in the Clouds* (New York: Balsam Press, Inc., 1897), 34–35.
23. Codman was hired to complete the exterior shell structures of three town houses built by a developer at 16–20 East 84th Street. He added window and door details and provided the interior detailing and decoration for two of the three connecting town houses. Extant are the working drawings of the houses, the specifications for their interior finishes, and the renderings of the drawing room at 20 East 84th Street and the bills for its contents. The bills and drawing are in the possession of Nicholas King, grandson of Ethel Rhinelander King. Architectural drawings for 16–20 East 89th Street are at the Avery Library, Columbia University.
24. Two others who worked in Codman's office from 1912 to 1914 were Chester Griswold Burden, a nephew of Codman's wife, and James D. Geddes. The hourly wage for a draftsman in 1917 was $1.90. For actual construction work, subcontracts were made with the contractor and other major tradesmen for such items as heating, plumbing, iron work, marble, and cabinetry. The client was charged ten percent of the total cost.

    The locations of Codman's New York office were 281 Fourth Avenue (1896–1903); Windsor Arcade, 571 Fifth Avenue (1903–10); and 340 Madison Avenue (1910–20).

25. In the summer of 1909 he was able to have the assistance of Geoffrey Scott, who was given a leave of absence from his position of secretary-librarian with Bernard Berenson. No doubt Mary Berenson, who suggested the arrangement, thought the exchange would be beneficial to both the young scholar interested in classical architecture and to Codman. Among others who held the position were Robert Tritton and Ronald Hadow. Francis White came in 1931 and remained with Codman for the remainder of his life.

26. A notation made by the late David McKibbin, former art librarian of The Boston Athenæum, who catalogued the Ogden Codman Collection.

27. Barr Ferree, "Notable American Houses," *American Homes and Gardens* (February 1906).

28. Ogden Codman to Sarah Codman, 8 October 1902, SPNEA.

29. Elizabeth Odgers, "Villa Rosa, A Newport Home," *Town & Country* (August 1904).

30. Ogden Codman to Martha Codman, 8 August 1909, BA.

31. *Das Ornamentwerk des Daniel Marot* (Berlin: Ernst Wasmuth, 1892). This particular edition was in Codman's library.

32. Peter Thornten, *Authentic Decoration* (New York: Viking, 1984), 353; see figure 472, A Smart Parisian Drawing Room, 1887. The illustration shows a drawing room in Louis XVI style with an adjoining garden room decorated with trelliswork.

33. The drawings of Beatrix Jones Farrand are in the Reef Point Archive at University of California, Berkeley.

34. R. Curtis Chapin, "Excavating an Italian Garden in America," *Horticulture Magazine* (19 November 1975).

35. Interview with Mrs. John Auchincloss, daughter of Walter Maynard, August 1977.

36. James T. Maher, *The Twilight of Splendor* (Boston: Little, Brown and Company, 1975), 191, 358.

37. Ogden Codman to Fiske Kimball, 30 April 1917, BA.

38. In a 1910 letter to Martha Codman, Codman said that the inspiration for her circular hall was Thornden Hall, illustrated in James Paine's *Plans, Elevations, and Sections of Noblemen's and Gentlemen's Houses*, vol. 2. Thornden Hall does not have a circular hall, but Wardour House, also illustrated in the book, does.

39. Ogden Codman to Charles Wulff, 15 August 1910, BA.

40. Sarah Coffin, "Francis Henry Lenygon and His Role in 20th Century Georgianism," unpublished manuscript, Columbia University, 1975.

41. Walter Maynard to Ogden Codman, 16 August 1916, SPNEA.

42. *Decoration of Houses*, 198.

43. Ibid., 187.

44. Ibid., 195.

45. Ogden Codman to Julian Sampson, 14 April 1938, BA.

46. Ogden Codman, *La Leopolda* (Paris: N. R. Money, 1939), n.p. No longer able to afford living at La Leopolda, Codman wrote the booklet "to help in letting the place." It illustrates and describes the contents and decoration of each room. As he notes in the booklet, "Mrs. Wharton would have made a literary achievement out of it as she did out of *The Decoration of Houses*, but [mine] will be a sort of suite to that." Except where noted, all the following quotations are from this text.

47. Ogden Codman to Julian Sampson, 14 April 1938, BA.

The Town Houses of Ogden Codman: A Brief Tour

HENRY HOPE REED

NCE A WEEK CERTAINLY, AND POSSI-
BLY MORE WITH SYNDICATION, AN ENTER-
taining and very popular situation comedy appears on
television. The opening frames show a handsome brick
mansion, which we subsequently discover to be in Boston.
Anyone familiar with the city can place the building; it is
at the corner of Beacon and Brimmer streets across from the Public Gardens.
Now called Hampshire House, it was originally the Bayard Thayer residence,
built in 1912 on the designs of Ogden Codman, Jr.

The comedy? *Cheers.* No doubt Codman would have resigned himself
to a sardonic smile at the knowledge that, unknown to occupied professionals
and eager art historians, a sample of his work was on prime time, seen by
millions of his countrymen wholly ignorant of his name.

"Wholly" may be an exaggeration, as his name is being recognized,
both here and in England, by those in the interior decorating business. After
all, the best work on the subject remains *The Decoration of Houses*, which he
wrote with Edith Wharton in 1897. Now for a number of years in the Classical
America Series in Art and Architecture (Norton/Classical America), as well
as in the Leisure Class in America Series (Ayer), the book is reaching a new
public, one bored with Modern and Postmodern architecture and turning
to America's classical heritage. And it is reaching the interior decorators,
who, unlike architects, never quite deserted our heritage and who now find
the volume a solid resource.

Beyond the book Codman's reputation has not fared as well as that of
other residential architects of his era, such as William Adams Delano and
David Adler. But then he was never keyed into the profession, and not much
admiration was lost between him and his colleagues. That he had no professional training and was best known as coauthor of a book on interior decoration placed him in a lower professional category in their eyes. It also
meant that they never looked beyond his work as an interior decorator, a
curious limitation when his house designs are so successful. There was a
third count against him—his devotion to the classicism of eighteenth-century
France. Such was his fealty that, of all his contemporaries among architects,
only Horace Trumbauer of Philadelphia, another devotee, received his praise.
Most of Codman's houses–the Boston ones are the exception—bespeak the
inclination.

The French influence in America is interesting. In the case of David Adler, it is filtered as we see it in his stately residences in Lake Forest, Illinois. Then there is Carrère & Hastings, a firm which, like Codman, found Ange-Jacques Gabriel an inspiration, as we know well from the New York Public Library. Yet how different is the interpretation. Nor should we overlook Warren & Wetmore and Bakewell & Brown. The latter's San Francisco City Hall and the former's Grand Central Terminal and New York Yacht Club show the France of the seventeenth as well as the eighteenth century.

Ogden Codman, elevation, Archer M. Huntington house, 1083 Fifth Avenue, New York, 1913–15, now the National Academy of Design

Fashion, however, leaned heavily to the American Colonial and the English Georgian, not just in the work of Delano, but also in that of Charles Adams Platt and, later, Mott Schmidt. We have to remember that Delano once observed that he was satisfied with the Georgian "because there is no limit to its possibilities."

The first building we shall examine is the one that houses the National Academy of Design at 1083 Fifth Avenue in New York. In 1913 Codman was commissioned by the maecenas Archer M. Huntington to convert and enlarge an existing mansion. (The stepson of Collis P. Huntington, one of the Big Four of California, Huntington is chiefly remembered as a Spanish scholar and the founder of the Hispanic Society of America. It was he who developed Audubon Terrace at 155th Street and Broadway, which included the Hispanic Society's building. His wife was the sculptor Anna Hyatt, who is best known for the group *El Cid* on the Terrace.) Only the facade with its bow front was saved, and, even here, Codman removed the original ornament with its opulent overtones and replaced it with something of late-eighteenth-century sobriety, seen in the brackets of the second-floor balcony, the carved panel beneath the round pediment of the central window of the second floor, and the block keystones of the dormer pediments. In addition, he built a wing facing 89th Street to form an L-shaped plan with the Fifth Avenue structure. Essentially, he created a new building.

With the conversion of the building to the National Academy's use, changes have occurred, but enough remains to provide the visitor with the leitmotifs of the Codman style. The restraint of the facades on Fifth Avenue and 89th Street reveals the man. In the wing, for example, there is the rustication of the ground floor, the plain curved brackets with channeling of the second-floor balcony, and the round-arch second-story French windows descending to the floor. The wing, curiously, is also faced with yellow brick above the first floor. Why a client of Huntington's wealth did not call for an all-limestone front, much like that of the Fifth Avenue facade, is hard to explain, unless client and architect agreed that this front, belonging to a subsidiary part of the house, deserved no distinction.

After entering the building, the visitor has to go beyond the entrance hall (now a bookshop) to come to Codman's work. The black-and-white and beige marble tile is the first sign. We are in the reception hall with its floor-to-ceiling niche, reserved for the bust of Samuel F. B. Morse, the Academy's first president. The walls here, painted a solid gray, were once in plaster imitating limestone and even had false mortar joints in white. Doric columns guard the hall's two entrances. Now painted to imitate marble, they were originally in imitation limestone like the neighboring walls. Such false stone, very much a French device, is best seen in the catalog and reading rooms of the New York Public Library, the Grand Central Terminal, and in Horace Trumbauer's Duke mansion at 1 East 78th Street.

The circular stairwell, with its saucer dome set on a cove, or concave curve of the ceiling, is a pure Codman touch. It had several purposes. One was to join the house to its new wing. Another was to provide a setting for

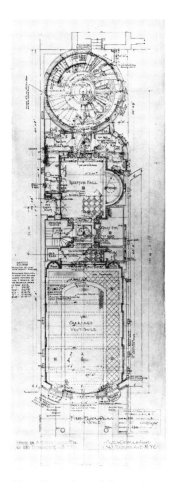

First floor plan of the main wing, Huntington house

a grand staircase. This last was an important distinction of the larger residences built at the time; the one in the Duke mansion is a good example. The lower part of the stairwell has false stone rustication and false mortar joints, which convey the sense of supporting the paired pilasters above. Such use of imitation materials, anathema to John Ruskin, Viollet-le-Duc, and their Modern heirs, is in line with the advice in *The Decoration of Houses*—"if the effect be satisfactory to the eye, the substance used is a matter of indifference."

View of staircase from the second-floor landing, Huntington house

The staircase itself is of a creamy beige marble, a real stone this time. A particular feature of the staircase, and very much a device of eighteenth-century France, is the black wrought-iron railing. The main element, which is set in a frame, consists of several swirling bars shaped in a Vitruvian wave. The bars have acanthus leaves, which look like foam on a wave.

Ascending to the second floor, we can appreciate the skill with which Codman treated the upper wall and its openings. The wall is divided by the paired Corinthian pilasters, which frame six round-arch bays, three with windows, two with doorways, and one a blank wall; that is, a blind bay. The aim is to achieve symmetry while admitting daylight and permitting doorways to house and wing. Here we are reminded of the third-floor landing (McGraw Rotunda) of the New York Public Library where Carrère & Hastings made use of similar devices to achieve a similar balance. Both are perfect examples of the functional being subsumed into a beautiful symmetrical interior, wholly foreign to today's conventional theories of architecture.

Opposite: Staircase with sculpture of Diana *by Anna Hyatt Huntington, Huntington house*

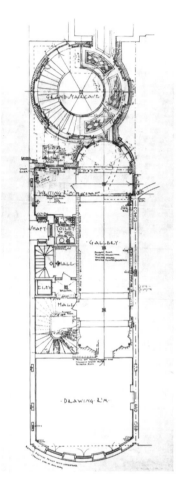

Second floor plan of the main wing, Huntington house

Overhead, from the center of the saucer dome, hangs a bronze lantern with four curved glass sides. It is a *lanterne d'escalier*, descendant of the famous one by Ange-Jacques Gabriel in the Petit Trianon. Again, the New York Public Library provides several examples for comparison. And looking down we discover a floor of several marbles set in a pattern of circle and star, much like that of a compass, framed by a pattern derived from a Palladian window.

To the right, on reaching the second-floor landing, a doorway opens to what was, and is still, a gallery. Its distinctive feature is the segmental vault of the ceiling with a saucer semi-dome at either end. "A ceiling is the largest uninterrupted surface in any room," wrote the late John Barrington Bayley in *Letarouilly on Renaissance Rome*, "and presently the greatest of all opportunities for decoration." Here Codman recognized the fact by having enrichment in the manner of Robert Adam. This shift in allegiance by Codman is understandable, as decorated ceilings were not part of French residential architecture in the eighteenth century. The parquet floor repeats, in outline, the basic ceiling pattern.

The gallery led to what was the drawing room, now another gallery, overlooking the avenue. Codman handled the room with the care and thoroughness that characterize all his designs, simple as they may often appear. It was too small for pilasters, so he placed vertical panels in the upper portion and horizontal panels in the lower. *The Decoration of Houses* explains the function of such paneling:

> *In well-finished rooms the order is usually imagined as resting, not on the floor, but on pedestals, or rather on a continuous pedestal. This continuous pedestal, or "dado" as it is usually called, is represented by a plinth surmounted by mouldings, by an intermediate member often decorated with tablets or sunk panels [as here] with moulded margins, and by a cornice. The use of the dado raises the chief wall-decoration of the room to a level with the eye and prevents its being interrupted or concealed by the furniture which may be placed against the walls. This makes it clear that in all well-designed rooms there should be a dado about two and a half feet high. If lower than this, it does not serve its purpose of raising the wall-decoration to a line above the furniture; while the high dado often seen in modern American rooms throws all the rest of the paneling out of scale and loses its own significance as the pedestal supporting an order.*

The entablature, very much modified, has the cornice resting on volute modillions; the enrichment consists of egg-and-leaf below and anthemion and acanthus above.

The room presents another lesson in symmetry, although on a humbler scale than in the stairwell. Three square-headed windows face the avenue; across from them is the square-headed door through which we entered. Having just one door set in one side of a wall would throw the scheme askew, so Codman simply added a false door to balance the real one, and symmetry was achieved. He and Mrs. Wharton offer this eloquent passage on symmetry:

> *If proportion is the good breeding of architecture, symmetry, or the answer-*
> *ing of one part to another, may be defined as the sanity of decoration. The*
> *desire for symmetry, for balance, for rhythm in form as well as in sound, is*
> *one of the most inveterate of human instincts. Yet for years Anglo-Saxons*
> *have been taught that to pay any regard to symmetry in architecture or*
> *decoration is to truckle to one of the meanest forms of artistic hypocrisy.*
> *The master who has taught this strange creed, in words magical enough to*
> *win acceptance for any doctrine, has also revealed to his generation so*
> *many of the forgotten beauties of early art that it is hard to dispute his*
> *principles of aesthetics. As a guide through the byways of art, Mr. Ruskin*
> *is entitled to the reverence and gratitude of all; but as a logical exponent*
> *of the causes and effects of the beauty he discovers, his authority is certainly*
> *open to question. For years he has spent the full force of his unmatched*
> *prose in denouncing the enormity of putting a door or a window in a cer-*
> *tain place in order that it may correspond to another; nor has he scrupled*
> *to declare to the victim of this practice that it leads to abysses of moral as*
> *well as of artistic degradation.*

I would not cite this passage at length were it not for the fact that Ruskin's influence radiates as strongly as ever. Asymmetry remains fashionable to a degree unknown even in the last century. At the National Academy we have, again and again, evidence of how right Wharton and Codman were in their observations.

We return to explore the wing. On the landing, directly opposite the head of the stairs, a doorway opens on a small foyer which once led to the salon. As small as the foyer is, Codman achieved a monumental interior. The walls of imitation stone are rusticated. Set in the four walls are four round-arch openings, three for doorways and one for a window, whose shape is dictated by the arch bays of the stairwell. They rise to a groin vault, from the center of which hangs another cylindrical lantern.

The visitor will notice two lesser, square-headed doorways set in the east wall to either side of the high central one. Both are for elevators, while the center one opens on a secondary stairwell. The foyer, besides serving as a link between stairwell and salon, was a discreet link between the public rooms and the private.

Nothing of the original salon remains. It had, on the east wall, three round-arch French windows looking out on an open shaft; on the east there was one window to the left, a fireplace at the center with a mirror set in a round-arch bay, and a false window. At either end were pairs of real and false doors. Symmetry, as always, had to be achieved.

Beyond the salon is the former dining room, which faces 89th Street. False stone, with incised mortar joints, sets the tone. Doric pilasters with partially fluted shafts rest on a shared plinth of red griotto marble. The wall

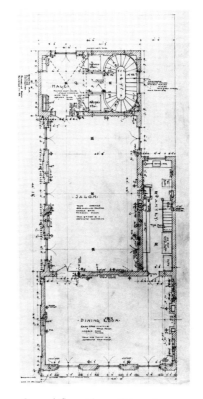

Second floor plan of the wing facing East 89th Street, Huntington house

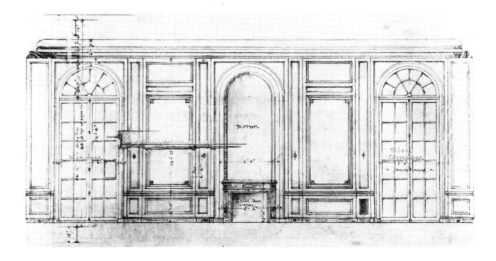

Elevation of the east wall of the salon, East 89th Street wing, Huntington house

opposite the windows contains not just the entrance doorway, but also a blind doorway recessed from the wall. In it is a small door, real this time, which led to a pantry. Between the two doorways is a blind-arch bay reflecting the center window on the street side. In this way Codman both gained symmetry and kept an essential door unobtrusive.

The dining room has two unusual decorative elements. The walls at the narrow ends are broken up in a different way, with center niches for statues set between the pilasters. And Codman, for once, turned to painted panels. The six panels might be seen as two-dimensional versions of early reliefs by the sculptor Gaston Lachaise (compare, for example, Codman's

Gallery, National Academy of Design, formerly the dining room in the Huntington house

panels to Lachaise's reliefs over the elevator doors in 195 Broadway, the former AT & T Building).

A brief note on the utility and service rooms. The servants' entrance and the kitchen were in the wing below the dining room and the salon.

What Codman did for the Huntingtons was to adapt the Paris, and Bordeaux, town house to a New York lot. Here, to be sure, he had two lots; but, as we shall see, he handled the single lot with equal felicity. What strikes us, first of all, at the Huntington residence is the use of the stairwell to join the old and new buildings. Second, he was able to do so and obtain symmetry, ever paramount in his designs. He achieved in a modest way what Carrère & Hastings accomplished in a large public building, the New York Public Library, both equally monumental. He stamped symmetry on his rooms, making use of the false door, if need be, much as Carrère & Hastings did in the library's Trustees' Room. Then he concealed the secondary private facilities from the *chambres d'apparat* or public rooms.

Codman always thought in artistic terms. This did not mean that he neglected the structural or the functional, as is testified by his use of steel framing and elevators. But he never let these lesser, if important, elements obtrude on the artistic. In addition he was able to give each room its own, often monumental, identity. All this is to be seen and studied in the Huntington residence which, as the National Academy of Design, is open to the public. The visitor can return again and again to explore the triumph of Ogden Codman.

Only ten blocks south, at 18 East 79 Street, is another house by Ogden Codman. Built in 1911 for J. Woodward Haven, it is today the Aquavella Gallery. The facade immediately signals something different from its neighbors. The treatment of the wall, the dimensions of the windows, just the use of rustication at the first floor tell the observer that, again, the French influence rules. It appears as well in the brackets of the second-floor balcony and in two panels beneath the fourth-floor windows, with their relief of fruits, swags, and rosettes. Bordeaux houses were the source. "Houses there," he wrote to Mrs. Woodward Haven, are "more the size of our N.Y. houses than any town I know." He found the Parisian *hôtels particuliers*, with their courts and gardens, too big to serve, but "I felt as if I must have built Bordeaux myself in some previous existence," he concluded. "Everything [is] so thoroughly as I like it."

Codman did not, however, always confine himself to the favored model. A Bordeaux house would not have had either a stoop or an area. A New York house had to, for the basement was where the kitchen and other service rooms were customarily placed. Codman could have adopted the New York stoop, area, and basement, but he chose a London version.

The visitor to the Woodward Haven house is admitted through a wrought-iron door with plate glass into a square vestibule with walls of pronounced rustication. Four bays are set in the walls; two have doorways, and two are blind. Overhead is a saucer dome. A second wrought-iron door with plate

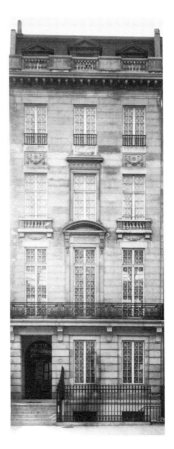

Ogden Codman, J. Woodward Haven house, 18 East 79th Street, New York, 1911

glass leads to a short hall, where the rustication is repeated and where—
something of a surprise—there is a barrel vault with coffers.

The visitor then enters yet another square space. Here the rusticated
wall on the left has a blind bay; opposite is another, but, instead of a wall,
there is a niche. On the right a third bay opens on the stairway hall. The
ceiling has its saucer dome. Both this space and the vestibule are treated in
much the same way as the foyer on the second floor of the National Academy
outside the former salon.

What Codman has done, as he did with all the semipublic parts of a
residence, is to convey a sense of the monumental. Here we have an entrance
hall divided into three parts with rusticated walls. He has made use of the
two saucer domes and a barrel vault. It is rare to find such devices in so
small a corridor, and so succesfully adopted.

It is only a step into the stairway hall. The rustication is continued
effectively around the walls and doorways are set in round-arch bays. The
north and south ones balance, with the north one enclosing a square-headed
doorway opening on the reception room. The other leads to the former
dining room. This last has been converted to gallery use, but the renovations
have preserved a miniature vestibule which, in addition to rusticated walls,
has a barrel vault. In the former dining room a cornice with modillions in
double volutes with acanthus remains, as does the fireplace and its mantel.

The reception room opposite, now also a gallery, has its original fireplace of marble and cast-iron fireback and three panels with fluttering ribbon
and flower swag. The ceiling has a cove, a device, *The Decoration of Houses*
reminds us, that "greatly increases the apparent height of a low-studded
room."

As in the National Academy, the lower portion of the stairwell wall
is rusticated, while the upper part has pilasters, here Scamozzi Ionic, not
Corinthian. On the long wall the pilasters frame a panel reserved for a
tapestry. On the short walls they frame round-arch bays, the south one for
a window, the north one blind. The same bays are repeated in the second-
floor landing. The floor here, as in the entrance and stairway halls, is of black
and white marble tile.

To the right at the head of the stairs is a gallery in wood paneling. The
characteristic round-arch bay is repeated in the room. Five bays on one side
have windows looking out on the backyard; opposite are five more bays. Of
these the center one has a fireplace and mantel and the two on either side
have walls for pictures. The narrow ends of the room have two bays, one
of which contains the doorway to the landing. Inside the round arches are
niches with busts; the niches have, at the top, cartouches with elaborate
scroll frames from which extend fluttering ribbons and swags of husks.

Codman considered the gallery the most interesting room in the house,
in part because of the wall of windows and the special handling he gave it.
The tall rectangular panels between the windows are framed by recessed
molding, then a raised molding consisting of a bead, an ovolo, and a fillet.

Such a profile both pushes the panel forward visually and lends a visual rhythm to the wall.

The door from the landing to the drawing room, like the one from the gallery to the landing, consists of two leaves, which Codman preferred to a single leaf, and has his characteristic box lock. The room itself, though altered, has paneling similar to that of the drawing room of the National Academy. Large vertical rectangular panels surmount a dado of small horizontal rectangular panels. Beneath the frieze are rectangular panels with fluttering ribbons and bay leaf in wreath and swag. The cornice rests on paired modillions.

The three windows, so tall on the outside, have been lowered with interior panels. Between the paneling and the window is space for curtains. This is a device of classical architecture which the late John Barrington Bayley called *doublure*, the French word for lining. There is no need for an exterior to reflect an interior, and here the interior fenestration was more effective when reduced to fit the room's design.

Codman, of course, did not confine his study of French architecture and decoration to visits to Paris, Bordeaux, and elsewhere. Like many architects of his time, his office had a first-class library with books such as César Daly's *Motifs historiques d'architecture et de sculpture: Décorations intérieures empruntés à des edifices français*. They served to buttress his detailed knowledge of eighteenth-century architecture. One can savor here the result, handled with his wonderful skill. What he achieved was a sense of well being and of visual repose, in large part the reward of proper symmetry and proportion throughout.

By now the Codman student in New York can easily spot his work. The search for it is bound to lead to 96th Street between Fifth and Madison avenues. Numbers 7, 12, and 15 are his. Number 7 was his own house; it is now a school. Number 15, built in 1914 for Mrs. Lucy Drexel Dahlgren of Philadelphia, houses the Paul Singer Foundation and contains an art gallery. For that reason, like 18 East 79 Street, it is open to an interested public.

The inspiration for the facade of the Dahlgren house is to be found on Bordeaux's rue Sainte-Catherine, but Codman, as always, recast it to his own end. One must be careful in attributions because the architect, no different from others in the profession, drew on a number of sources and offered some of his own interpretations as well. To be sure the Bordeaux house has a rusticated ground story, but Codman carried the rustication in four vertical bands up the facade. Where the Bordeaux example has a square-headed doorway and square-headed windows on the ground floor, he adopted segmental arches. He further added a round pediment at the center window of the second floor, two carved panels, and, under the lintels of the third floor, bay leaf swags. We have seen these devices before; only the segmental arches of the ground floor are unfamiliar. A final difference between the Dahlgren house and any Bordeaux house is the pitch roof with dormers.

The aspect that most distinguishes the Dahlgren house is the first floor

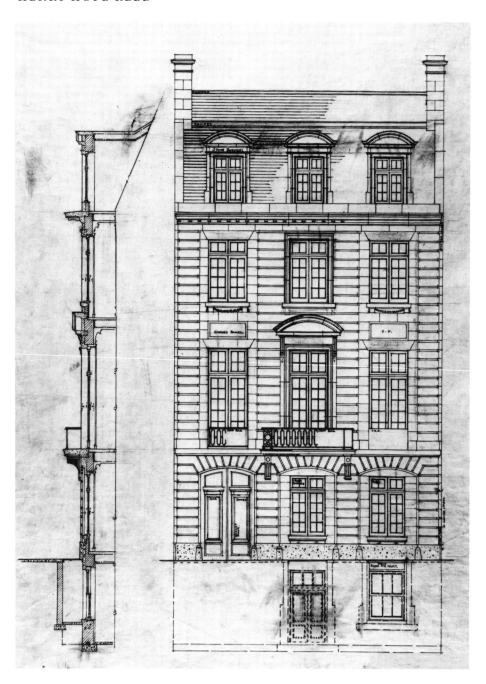

Ogden Codman, elevation,
Lucy Drexel Dahlgren house,
15 East 96th Street, 1915

plan, also seen at number 7. The doorway opens to a porte-cochère, a short entrance drive leading to a narrow court and carriage house (later a garage) instead of to a backyard. The carriage house has a turntable for rotating the carriage to an elevator which descends to the cellar, with its stable and carriage house. Codman said that he first saw such a porte-cochère at Depau Row on Bleecker Street, built around 1830. (The houses stood on the site of 160 Bleecker Street, now occupied by a former Mills Hotel designed by Ernest Flagg.)

The pivoting wood doors of the porte-cochère are closed except when the driveway is in use. The visitor on foot steps through a small door cut in the right leaf of the door to stand in the driveway. The entrance leading to the main hall is on the right.

In contrast to the Woodward Haven house, there is no elaborate corridor to the stairway hall; it has been replaced by the porte-cochère. Instead, the visitor enters a shallow vestibule; but even here Codman found space for niches in the side walls. One enters the main north-south hall abutting the stairway through a set of brass-framed, single-pane glass door leaves, with a transom with an interlocking *C* at its center. The second set of door leaves are glazed gates in wrought and cast iron, which also have an interlocking *C* in the ornate ironwork of the transom. The monograms were placed there by Pierre Cartier of the jewelry family, who owned the house for a number of years; the railings of the full-height casement windows on the second floor also have them.

On the right is the reception room. The walls treated with framed panels and dado have been met with before. One modern touch is the presence of three mirrors, one opposite the doorway between the windows, one between the closets, and one in the middle of the western wall. Plaster bas-relief panels surmount the mirrors and entrance doors.

At the opposite end of the hall was once a shallow closet behind which was the servants' dining room and, beyond it, the kitchen. The door to the servants' dining room was the small one hidden directly left of the closet, invisible from the hall. Again Codman, you might say, is up to his tricks. The closet door has been replaced with wood-paneled doors matching those of the reception room, and the area of the servants' dining room and kitchen is now a wood-paneled octagonal study that replicates the details of the reception room.

Above the stairs, at the second floor, a large, framed portion of the wall was set aside for a tapestry. Curiously, this wall does not repeat the round-arch bays on the opposite wall, which serve to frame a doorway and a window. At the narrow ends one bay leads to a library/drawing room and, opposite, the other is for the dining room doorway.

Preceding the dining room is a small foyer with a barrel-vaulted ceiling. The dining room is an octagon, unlike the circular rooms of French eighteenth-century town houses. The three sides to the left have three round-arch bays with three French casement windows, surmounted by lunette transoms overlooking the driveway. On the right there are three similar bays, two with niches for elaborate marble fountains and the middle one left blind as a place for a server. The ceiling is flat with a plaster cornice of simple square brackets.

Opposite on the landing a two-leaf door with a box lock serves the library. The English oak walls are designed much as those in the gallery of the Woodward Haven house: the panels are slightly projected within an elaborate profile, part sunk and part raised. The cornice is of elaborate plaster brackets grained to resemble wood. The original Estey organ has been restored to the west wall opposite the fireplace with overmantel mirror.

On the library's inner wall are two doors, one opening on the hall by which the visitor entered, and the other presumably to a room. Instead, this second one is part false. If its right leaf opens to a secondary stairwell, its left is permanently closed, concealing a wall. The false or partly false door is a common eighteenth-century device.

Much of the effectiveness of the second floor stems from the ceiling height of sixteen feet and the twelve-foot-high bay arches. In fact, the entire house has a stateliness unexpected in one with so modest an exterior.

We abandon New York to see the one residence Codman built in Washington. It is at 2145 Decatur Place, in the quarter known as Kalorama. Designed in 1908–10 for his cousin, Martha Codman, it is a substantial building on an irregular plot, and it is set against a hillside. Rather than having an open lot, like so many mansions in Washington, it is approached through a courtyard formed by two advancing wings. A high wrought-iron fence guards the entrance to the courtyard. The closed court is reminiscent of that of The Mount, Edith Wharton's house in Lenox, Massachusetts, for which Codman did the first set of plans.

What the viewer beholds is a large eighteenth-century English manor house in brick with limestone trim. The stone is particularly effective in its use as quoins at the wings' corners. It is also to be seen in the ground floor of the center wing, where the doorways are in a wall with courses alternatively recessed.

The French influence reasserts itself on the interior. As at The Mount, the ground floor has a low ceiling. Here the entrance hall almost forms part of the square stairwell, which rises to the full height of the house. To have the principal stairway serve all the floors is an exception in a Codman house,

Ogden Codman, Martha Codman house, 2145 Decatur Place, Washington, D.C., 1908–10

PLATE 22. Design for dining
room wall, Nathaniel Thayer
house, Edgemere, Newport,
Rhode Island, c. 1896–97

PLATE 23. *Walter Gay,*
drawing room, Egerton
Winthrop house, 23 East 33rd
Street, New York, c. 1900

as he preferred a secondary master stairway going to the bedrooms from the second floor. The major rooms, all with fourteen-foot ceilings, are in the wing on the left. First comes the drawing room overlooking the court, then a music room, and, in the rear, a dining room. All three have doors opening on a terrace that wraps around one side of the house from the back; Achille Duchêne, the great classical landscape architect of the turn of the century, advised Codman on the terrace. The round arch of the second-floor windows is repeated throughout the interior in round-arch bays, attesting to Codman's belief that they, like the high ceilings, underscored the importance of the *bel étage*.

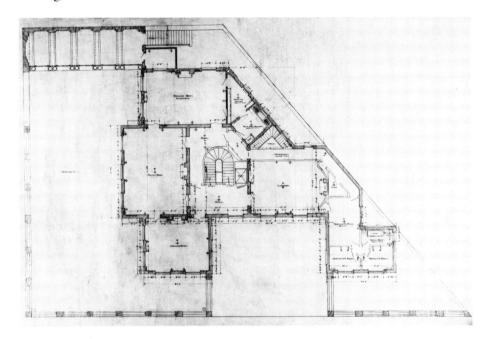

First floor plan, Martha Codman house

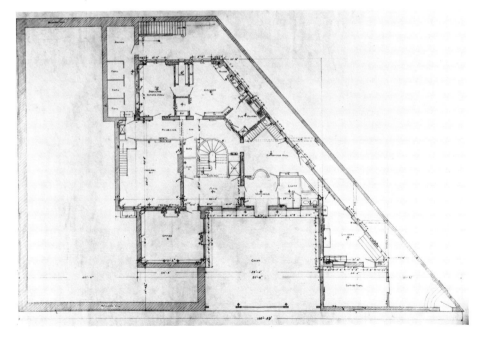

Ground floor plan, Martha Codman house

Achille Duchêne and Ogden Codman, terrace, Martha Codman house

Though the French influence dominated Codman's New York houses, he did have other inspiration, as we already know from the Washington house and the Robert Adam gallery in the Huntington house. When we turn to his Boston houses, we discover his allegiance to the young Republic and to Georgian England.

170 Beacon Street, now the Goethe Institute, was decorated and refronted in 1901 for the financier Eben Howard Gay. The round-arch bays of the first floor, set in rustication, recall the work of Charles Bulfinch and Robert Adam, as does the use of a round-arch window framed by a recessed surround within the bay. We are reminded that Codman, at the start of his career, drew and measured old houses in and around Boston. The same fenestration is repeated in the flat wall of the second floor. Another touch from the same source is the balustrade parapet with urns set on posts.

The entrance hall is similar to that of the Woodward Haven house in being divided into square vestibule and lobby. From the lobby the visitor goes into the hall with stairs rising to the full height of the building.

Inevitably, with several changes in ownership, there have been alterations, but the principal rooms are relatively intact. Off the hall we stand in what appears to be one large room; originally there were two, a salon in front and a music room to the back, separated in part by a wall with a large doorway and sliding doors (plate 20). Today wall and doorway are gone, creating the large room. (In view of the fact that Wharton and Codman condemned the sliding door, it is surprising to learn that this house once had one.)

What is most striking about the two rooms is not the planning, but the abundant decoration. The ceiling frieze, chimneypiece, and wall panel have masks, garlands, trophies, and swags. Codman was evidently cued to this enrichment by being able to obtain paneling and marble mantelpieces from England. The variety of the ornament is to be warmly praised. The

Opposite: Music room, Martha Codman house

Ogden Codman, salon and music room, Eben Howard Gay house, 170 Beacon Street, Boston, 1900

music room, for example, has several roundels with playing cherubs, while the wall panels have trophies of musical instruments. The general style stems from William Kent, James Gibbs, and William Chambers; what had to be made in 1900 is beautifully executed to match the antique parts.

The last house on our Codman tour is the first one met with, now Hampshire House, the setting for *Cheers*. Originally the Bayard Thayer residence (1912) at 84 Beacon Street, it is the largest of Codman's town houses and it sits on a lot fifty by eighty feet. Here Codman turned to Boston materials, to Quincy granite and red brick. He made use of the first in the ground floor and the second in the upper floors, both most suitable for a site near Beacon Hill. And the fenestration of the first story, like that of the Gay residence, is of Boston inspiration, largely via Charles Bulfinch. It has the same round-arch windows set in a recessed surround within a round-arch bay. Above, the three stories are divided vertically by shallow buttresses. The third floor is interrupted by a strong course. Over the fourth is a stone cornice with modillions. On the Beacon Street front a parapet completes the whole with — it is a nice touch — urns on the parapet posts. On the Brimmer Street side the parapet becomes an attic wall for a fifth story, which has four round windows.

The staircase on the right end of the Beacon Street front is above a narrow area guarded by a wrought-iron fence. The visitor finds himself in much the same kind of entrance hall as at the Woodward Haven house. First comes the vestibule with rusticated walls of false limestone, then a lobby. The setting is familiar: round-arch bays for the doorways and the same bays, only blind, set in rusticated walls. Overhead are groined vaults.

The center hallway and stairwell are combined and are lined with rusticated walls. Immediately to the left was the living room, which is now a bar. Wood walls remain, treated as Wharton and Codman urged with panels apportioned above and below a dado rail. The overmantel of the fireplace, also of wood, has side panels beautifully carved with doves, flowers, and fruit in the manner of Grinling Gibbons, the famous eighteenth-century English sculptor of ornament.

A doorway to the left side of the fireplace leads to the former dining room. Now the main dining room of Hampshire House, it has been reduced in size. The walls that remain are divided by round-arch bays, repeating the shape of the exterior bays of the first floor, and they are framed by Corinthian pilasters with fluted shafts. In the spandrels of the arches are cloth swags. The cornice is plain with block modillions. The beautiful crystal chandelier and the sconces were originally in the ballroom directly above on the second floor.

From the dining room the visitor steps into the stairway hall. The chandelier here, like that of the dining room, came from the ballroom. It will be noted that the rustication of the wall is confined to the first floor, as is customary. Over the stairwell is a circular skylight, now painted over by

Second floor plan, Bayard Thayer house

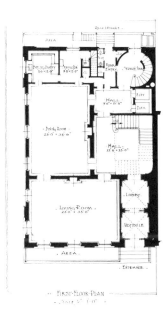

First floor plan, Bayard Thayer house

Ogden Codman, Bayard Thayer house, 84 Beacon Street, Boston, 1912

orders of the Building Department; originally the light came from a round airshaft above it.

The second-floor rooms, especially the former ballroom, have undergone considerable change. Still, there are details worth seeing if permission be granted to visit them. The library has a very fine white marble fireplace with beautiful ornament, possibly antique. The ballroom, now cut in half and with plaster walls stained to resemble wood, has little to show of its first state except for the decoration of the frieze. To envision what it was like when the Bayard Thayers were in residence, we have to see it in white and gold with the two crystal chandeliers and sconces.

Considering that Codman's town houses are nearly a century old, it is astonishing that so many have survived and that, on the whole, so many of the interiors remain.

Of course, they should be explored with *The Decoration of Houses* in hand. And one should not dwell too much on the inspiration but rather on the skill of Ogden Codman in giving the traditional doorways and wall bays the proportions required by a New York or Boston house. They should be measured and studied, as should the profiles of the panel frames and the channeling of the rustication. If anything, Codman often improved on the model. It was his skill in planning and creating a monumental presence on a domestic scale that places Codman in the ranks of outstanding American architects.

ACKNOWLEDGMENTS

The author wishes to thank the following for their help. In New York, Luis E. Rodriguez of Thompson, Robinson & Toraby; William Butler of the National Academy of Design; William Acquavella of Acquavella Gallery; Janet Parks and Lisa Rosenthal of the Drawings Collection, Avery Library, Columbia University; and David Kiehl of the Prints and Photographs Collection, Metropolitan Museum of Art. In Washington, Michael Baker. In Boston, Jean Kole, and Paul Marx of the Boston Architectural Center.

The author is particularly grateful to Pauline Metcalf for suggestions and for the citations from the letters of Ogden Codman in the Codman Family Manuscripts Collection, Society for the Preservation of New England Antiquities.

Edith and Ogden: Writing, Decoration, and Architecture

RICHARD GUY WILSON

ETWEEN EDITH WHARTON AND OGDEN CODMAN, JR., LAY A VITAL RELATIONSHIP stretching over nearly fifty years. They were not just client and architect, but collaborators on several important houses, and they coauthored the pathbreaking book *The Decoration of Houses*. As close friends they had to suffer each other's idiosyncrasies. In a sense they were characters right out of her fiction: Ogden the ever-pretentious architect finically obsessed with social niceties and status, and Edith the artful arranger of chairs or tapestries calculated to create an impression upon the innocent visitor, whom she would carefully observe. The roles they played in the friendship come through in their names for each other: Ogden called her "Puss" or "Pussy" informally, but his letters always used the proper "Mrs. Wharton." For Edith he was always "Coddy" or that "clever young Boston architect."[1]

During her projected visit in June 1937 to Ogden's Château de Grégy, they intended to discuss a new edition of *The Decoration of Houses*, an inexpensive one that would put the book within everybody's reach.[2] Edith arrived and collapsed; the doctor diagnosed a stroke and ordered an ambulance to take her back to her Pavillon Colombe at Saint-Brice, where she died on August 11. Ogden was of course "alarmed" by her illness, but initially he was also miffed, for he had to cancel the carefully orchestrated lunches and dinners.[3] Edith would have understood: meals, the conversation, and the setting were key elements of her world and her fiction. And Ogden's petulance could have become an amusing incident—complete with an architectural setting—for a story, especially since she had used him before. But Ogden was more than a character to Edith; he had assisted in revealing to her the world of architecture and decoration, which became a controlling element of her fiction. And for Ogden, Edith was equally important. Her analytical eye was crucial to his development as a decorator and architect, and without her writing skills he would have hardly been remembered. Their friendship had testy and rivalrous moments, but ultimately it helped create the characters of Edith Wharton and Ogden Codman we know today.

Background

The efforts of Edith Wharton and Ogden Codman in literature, architecture, and decoration provide an excellent introduction to the American Renais-

133

sance. The term American Renaissance was used at the turn of the century to mean the identification of many Americans with the Renaissance, in particular Italy of the fifteenth and sixteenth centuries and France and England of the seventeenth and eighteenth centuries.[4] Bernard Berenson, who would become a friend of both Edith and Ogden, prefaced his first book on Italian painting of 1894 by noting the great affinity of America for the Renaissance: "The spirit which animates us was anticipated by the spirit of the Renaissance. . . . That spirit seems like the small rough model after which ours is being fashioned."[5] The American Renaissance spirit meant the appropriation, as background for the new American wealth, of Italian palazzos, Georgian country houses, French tapestries and furniture, and old master paintings. It also meant the training of American painters, sculptors, and architects abroad at such schools as the Ecole des Beaux-Arts or at home in imitations of European schools. As the architect Charles Follen McKim explained, "As many European countries had gone to Rome to understand the splendid standards of Classic and Renaissance art, so must we become students, and delve, bring back and adapt to conditions here, a ground work on which to build."[6] The American Renaissance reordered culture, and a shift occurred in visual and physical form: the brown and ponderous decades of the 1860s, 1870s, and 1880s gave way to the light colors and classical forms of the 1890s and 1900s. The dark, overly elaborate, and ahistorical furniture of Belter or Herter Brothers—and of the parlors of Edith and Ogden's youth—was replaced by simple and gracefully curving reproductions of Louis XVI or American Georgian.

Edith and Ogden came from similar backgrounds. They were born scarcely a year apart into genteel, patrician families who traced their lineage to the seventeenth-century beginnings of America. She was born Edith Newbold Jones on 24 January 1862 in New York City. Though she had New England origins, her immediate family was "Old New York," which became a background for many of her writings. Her youth was sheltered and, combined with a homely appearance and a mother who seemed not to care for her, a time of trial.[7] In her fiction mothers frequently appear as cold and manipulative. Her father, who died in 1882, was more caring, and she adored him. But she also recognized his ineffectual and indecisive characteristics, and he became a model for many of her male characters, such as Lawrence Selden of *The House of Mirth* and Newland Archer of *The Age of Innocence*. Edith and her family spent the years 1866–72 and 1880–82 in Europe. They also owned a Newport house, and she spent many summers tediously driving up and down Bellevue Avenue, making calls, and attending picnics, archery matches, and dances. After several unsuccessful courtships, Edith met Edward (Teddy) Wharton, a socially prominent and handsome Bostonian, in 1883. They were married in 1885. Incompatible intellectually and sexually, the couple was not happy. Edith experienced recurring bouts of headaches and depressions, and then in 1902 Teddy began suffering breakdowns. They were divorced in 1913. Henry James called their marriage "an almost—or rather an utterly—inconceivable thing."[8]

Opposite: Publicity portrait of Edith Wharton at her desk, The Mount, Lenox, Massachusetts, c. 1904

Teddy and Edith Wharton were "comfortable" but not wealthy. He never worked but existed on an allowance from his mother and on Edith's money. Edith inherited money in a series of trusts that accumulated over time. In the 1880s she was gaining about $9,000 per year, and in 1901, after the death of her mother, she was getting over $22,000 from trusts alone.[9] Initially Edith and Teddy set up housekeeping in Newport in Pencraig Cottage, a wooden, gingerbread festooned house across the street from her mother's, where they lived from June to February before traveling abroad. Beginning in 1889 they spent part of the winter in New York. Travels abroad would continue; they were important for her. Italy became her favorite escape, and she acquired the knowledge which would later appear in print. Teddy liked to travel and he certainly gained something from Edith's various enthusiasms, but he never had her consuming interests; in time he would fall far behind.[10] Hence when the young Ogden Codman appeared around 1890, one can sense a sigh of relief from Edith: her life began to gain some focus.

That children reject the taste of their elders is almost an axiom of the last two centuries, so it is not surprising that visually and intellectually Edith rejected the architecture, decoration, and art of her parents. Later in her life she would look back with a certain fondness at the taste of her parents, but she saw their era as innocent, not one for emulation. In her autobiography she contrasts "the shameless squalor of the purlieus of the New York dock in the seventies" with "the glories of Rome and the architectural majesty of Paris."[11] She discovered in her father's library a respite from New York's "mean monotonous streets without architecture, without great churches or palaces, or any visible memorials of an historic past." When she was past seventy she still remembered the "intolerable ugliness of New York, of its untended streets and narrow houses so lacking in external dignity, so crammed with smug and suffocating upholstery."[12] Certainly it was her parents' house on West 23rd Street she recalled: a town house with a "universal chocolate-coloured coating of the most hideous stone ever quarried"[13] and decorated with overstuffed furniture, flocked wallpaper, and printed upholstery. The brownstone was a virtual archive of everything Edith would dismiss in *The Decoration of Houses*. Her mother, whom she characterized as a "born shopper," filled the drawing room with bric-a-brac and stuffed the gilded cabinets with old lace and painted fans.[14]

Her father gave her John Ruskin's *The Stones of Venice* and Walter Pater's *Renaissance Studies*, and in his library and her time abroad, she glimpsed the possibility of a different environment. In *A Backward Glance* she recalls the appearance in that "stagnant air of Old New York . . . the dust of new ideas" and attributes it in part to "men of exceptional intelligence": Charles McKim, Stanford White, and Ogden Codman.[15] Another of these bright lights was a man nearly twice her age, Egerton Winthrop, a widower, lawyer, cosmopolitan, and connoisseur of paintings, furniture, and literature. Winthrop traced his lineage back to both Governor Peter Stuyvesant of New York and Governor John Winthrop of Massachusetts, and he had lived in Paris for

Living room, Jones house, West 23rd Street, New York

many years. He took Edith under his wing beginning in 1885 and introduced her to advanced French literary naturalism and to Darwin, Spencer, and Huxley.[16] Winthrop also was fascinated by society and may have subtly influenced Edith, who claimed an indifference to the pretense of society, to set her fiction within its realm. She acknowledged Winthrop in a characteristic way: he was the model for her fictional society gossip Sillerton Jackson, who appears in *The Age of Innocence* and in the novellas that make up the quartet known as *Old New York*.

Winthrop's New York house on East 33rd Street had been designed in 1878–79 by Richard Morris Hunt—the first American to attend the Ecole des Beaux-Arts—in an austere French Second Empire style (plate 23).[17] The interiors showed Winthrop's taste and involvement; he "had gone so far as to import from France every article of furniture used—even the *papier mâché* ornamentations of the walls and ceiling," along with mantels, tapestries, and paintings. These interiors were well known in stuffy New York; they appeared in that remarkable compendium of taste *Artistic Houses* as a rare example, in 1883–84, of Louis XVI style and a "persistent determination to reproduce in all respects the forms, color and feeling of a particular era." According to *Artistic Houses*, it looked as if Winthrop had said to himself,

"I will create a Louis Seize room that shall reproduce the impression of an absolute original. It is the kind of room that I prefer to all others, and neither diligence nor expense shall be spared in pursuit of my object."[18] Mixed in with this were a few well-selected examples of American antiques. For Edith, Winthrop's interiors were a revelation: "educated taste had replaced stuffy upholstery and rubbishy 'ornaments' with objects of real beauty in a simply designed setting." But she also noted his interests could become "trivial" and "frivolous," that an emptiness could yawn in the middle of such fastidious taste.[19]

By 1890 Edith had completed her initial aesthetic education. Unplanned at first, but with perhaps a subliminal purpose, Edith acquired through her father's library, her travels, and Winthrop an extensive background in architecture and decoration. Certainly she was escaping from an unsatisfying marriage and in a very real sense architecture and decoration became surrogates; but she also discovered an empathy with physical objects that became a central feature of her art and life. Through her writing and her houses Edith attempted in the best tradition of the American Renaissance to raise the country's aesthetic consciousness. She found America wanting; it lacked, as she later wrote about France, "a universal existence of taste, and of the standard it creates."[20]

Land's End

Ogden Codman personified "taste," and he had an air of cultivation that Edith found compelling. He was not like the usual men of wealth — the Gus Trenors of *The House of Mirth* — who knew art, architecture, furniture, and sometimes women as well, only as commodities. Not a belle or a flirt, she preferred the company of sexually neutral men like Ogden, Berkeley Updike, and Henry James to that of the game-playing businessmen.

In 1892 – 93, Edith purchased for $80,000 her own house, Land's End. Located on the southernmost part of Aquidneck Island, Land's End was several miles from her mother's Newport house. Edith loved the site, with the building's "windows framing the endlessly changing moods of the misty Atlantic and the night-long sound of the surges against the cliffs."[21] Originally designed for Samuel G. Ward in 1864 by John Hubbard Sturgis — Ogden's uncle — Land's End was described by Edith as "incurably ugly." Constructed of wood in the so-called Stick Style with lots of surface ornament and massive ill-proportioned mansard roofs, it was exactly the sort of house Edith and Ogden would loathe.

Codman was encouraged by Edith and Teddy to remodel the house. This involved extensive interior alterations, some minor exterior changes such as stripping away some of the extraneous ornament, and extensive work on the grounds. The work went on between 1892 and 1897, with the majority of the interior and forecourt done in 1892 – 93 and the garden and minor interior work done in the next few years.[22] Though the exterior of the house remained awkward, a circular forecourt and hedge added formality to the

*John Hubbard Sturgis,
Wharton house, Land's End,
Newport, Rhode Island, 1864*

main approach and masked the service wing. On the garden side terraces and paths were graded. Wooden trellises, pergolas, columns, and lath niches—drawn from Daniel Marot's book *Das Ornamentwerk*,[23] and also recalling stone niches Edith had recently seen at Vicobello in Siena—masked the rambling house from the formal garden. Edith's niece, Beatrix Jones Farrand, possibly assisted on some of the trellis design; a rendering attributed to her survives (plate 24). As the work proceeded, Edith pointed out the issues to "Coddy": "it will perhaps be a rather nice question how to 'marry' the pergola with the hedge on the one side and the veranda columns on the other."[24]

*Daniel Marot, design for a
fountain and trellis, from* Das
Ornamentwerk *(1892)*

Certainly both Edith and Ogden intended for the interior to be a showpiece in the manner of the much-admired rooms of Egerton Winthrop. Land's End is also the starting point for *The Decoration of Houses*; yet seen from the perspective of the book and of Edith's later lambasting of "curtains, lambrequins, jardinieres of artificial plants, wobbly velvet-covered tables littered with silver gew-gaws and festoons of lace on mantelpieces and dressing-tables," the rooms at Land's End retreat into the overdone Rococo scroll work and still-cluttered interiors of the early 1890s.[25] Constrained by the existing shell, some rooms, such as the drawing room, appear too low for their breadth; the proportions are mean. The library (plate 25) has delicate Louis XVI paneling, medallion scroll work, and leafage but was set off with the overstuffed furniture and dark bookcases that would be attacked in *The Decoration of Houses*. A too heavy and large clock and urns overpower the mantel and the room. Simple eighteenth-century French and Italian furniture occupied the dining and sitting rooms, but the wall covering of damask—which Wharton and Codman would soon announce as unsanitary—had a heavy and bold pattern resembling flock. In both rooms the plaster ceiling lacked any relation to the room below and asserted too much weight.

Other portions of the interior were more successful. Codman enclosed a former porch off the sitting room, making a glass veranda. With its plain floor covering and elegant wooden furniture, this sitting room was the most relaxed and inviting space in the house. Photographed with "clutter" on the reading table, it exhibits vestiges of the taste of earlier decades. When Edith was unable to purchase a suitable ceiling in Italy, Codman designed, probably in 1897, an Adamesque or Pompeiian "tent" ceiling for the glass veranda. With its pattern of ropes and colored sky and clouds, the space would have

Ogden Codman, drawing room, Land's End, 1893

become even more intentionally an ambiguously indoors-outdoors room; but it was never installed.

The vestibule and entrance hall came very close to what Edith and Ogden would advocate in *The Decoration of Houses*: "The vestibule is the introduction to the hall, so the hall is the introduction of the living-rooms

Library with ornamental patchwork, Land's End

Dining room, Land's End

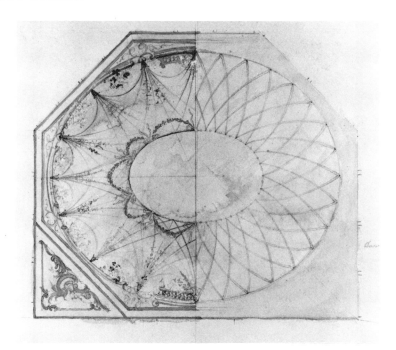

Design for a ceiling in the glass veranda, Land's End

Glass veranda, Land's End

PLATE 24. *Trellis design, Wharton house, Land's End, Newport, Rhode Island, c. 1893, watercolor rendering attributed to Beatrix Farrand*

PLATE 25. *Design for fireplace wall, library, Land's End, 1893*

PLATE 26. *Design for master bedroom, J. Randolph Coolidge house, 147 Beacon Street, Boston, 1895*

Staircase, Land's End

Stair hall, Pencraig, house of Edith Wharton's mother in Newport, Rhode Island

of the house; and it follows that the hall must be much more formal than the living rooms." What they especially deplored was the "tendency of recent English and American decoration . . . to treat the hall, not as a hall, but as a living room."[26] Not for Edith and Ogden were the vast informal halls of the shingled cottages of McKim or Richardson further up Bellevue Avenue or of her mother's house. As they later outlined in *The Decoration of Houses*, the hall at Land's End had white plaster moldings simulating reeds—a popular eighteenth-century motif. The applied cornice and dado gave it an architectural order, while the furniture was sparse and elegant, a prelude to the rooms beyond.

Edith's involvement with the remodeling of Land's End was total. Codman's fee schedule stirred her wrath, and she told him that she felt betrayed because his charges were too high. Codman's twenty-five percent commission brought forth "suckers," Edith claimed, "who would pay any price because you are 'the fashion', [but] you would not have found such in the beginning."[27]

She also admonished Codman about the colors of the library in one of his elegant renderings (plate 25): "Room will suffer *very much* unless the draughtsman can take off that dark red from the upper part of the panels & make them a uniform pink." The library as constructed followed her colors. Much of the furniture, such as the eighteenth-century Italian chairs in the dining room, came from purchases she made abroad in the next few years. In a sense the house was never finished, as she constantly introduced new ideas, changed colors, altered the garden, or purchased new toile fabrics.[28]

Boudoir with toile fabric, Land's End. The furnishings were later transferred to The Mount, where Codman added large floral bouquet panel paintings.

The Book

Ogden and the Whartons visited constantly, dining together at least once and frequently several times a week when in New York or in Newport. Ogden also remodeled the Whartons' New York town house at 884 Park Avenue, a very small house with only fifteen feet of street frontage. They purchased it in 1891 and then a few years later purchased the house next door. The exact extent of Codman's involvement is unclear. Drawings exist for integrating the two houses, but apparently the project was never completely carried out. Codman's hand is evident in the French wallpaper and architectural fittings on the interior.[29]

    Finding they shared similar views about architecture and interior decoration "we drifted," Edith later wrote, "I hardly know how, toward the notion of putting them into a book."[30] They quickly discovered that books are different from houses, and while Edith noted in her autobiography "that

Ogden Codman, dining room, Wharton house, 884 Park Avenue, New York

neither of us knew how to write," other problems existed as well. Edith was certainly the person who took the lead; when they began work in late 1896 she had already published a few short stories, poems, and travel pieces. Codman was not a writer and undoubtedly thought (as many nonwriters —especially architects—do) that a book would be easy: he would tell Edith and she would write it down. Later they differed on who contributed what, with Ogden at one time claiming that it was his work and that Edith had simply polished up his sentences.[31] Yet the unalphabetical arrangement of the authors' names on the published book and the surviving correspondence indicate that Edith not only wrote most of the book, but also contributed many of the ideas. *The Decoration of Houses* reflects both Edith's and Ogden's extensive European travel and study. Codman drew upon his European background from his youth in France and his travels in Italy during 1893– 94. He certainly knew the technical elements of architecture and decoration far better than she, and he could draw. But Edith also had something to contribute. Her yearly trips to Europe and especially to Italy brought her into contact with the examples of architecture and decoration they were seeking. Through the French novelist Paul Bourget, whom she entertained at Land's End during his American tour of 1893, she met Vernon Lee (Violet Paget) in 1894. Vernon Lee was the center of the Anglo-American colony located in the hills around Florence. Bernard Berenson would join this colony and later become a friend of Edith. Vernon Lee, a noted author and aesthete, would be very important in introducing Edith to the concept of empathy in art and also to the special genius of the Italian eighteenth century.[32] Edith's purchases of Italian *settecento* furniture began at this time, as did her explorations of villas, gardens, and monasteries. These adventures would result in her first novel, *The Valley of Decision* (1902), which was set in the eighteenth century, and also the book *Italian Villas and Their Gardens* (1904) and *Italian Backgrounds* (1905), which was composed of sketches from the mid and later 1890s.

Her letters to Codman from Italy were those of the delighted discoverer and serious student. From Parma in 1896 she wrote, "Alas, however, there is apparently no 'call' for anything in architecture later than the 16th century, and all the lovely barocco [sic] fountains, palaces, staircases, and etc. remain unphotographed."[33] From Turin she writes over five pages on Juvarra's Stupinigi Castle or Royal Hunting Lodge, noting the "curious" lack of "stucchi" and moldings on the exterior and interior. She adds, "There are no tapestries, either, & no boiseries, & even the doors & shutters are almost without mouldings, & depend entirely for their effect on the exquisitely varied paintings which adorn them." And from Mantua come pages on the Palazzo del Te.[34] Many of the photographs used in the book were acquired by Edith and Teddy during their European travels.

Edith also turned her pen on contemporary architecture and design. A visit to Paris brought forth, "it is so full of horrible modern Whitney-Warren architecture that I was glad to get away from it."[35] Neither Edith nor Ogden liked the overcooked, frothy "Beaux-Arts" manner into which even Stanford

White could fall. Teddy, she wrote, had problems recovering from White's remodeling of William C. Whitney's New York town house: "It must indeed be a ghoul's lair." A theme of *The Decoration of Houses* would be that wealth did not guarantee good taste, and she pronounced: "I wish the Vanderbilts didn't retard culture so very thoroughly. They are entrenched in a sort of *thermopylae* of bad taste, from which apparently no force on earth can dislodge them."[36] She kidded Ogden by telling him that if she found his work incomplete at Land's End, she would spread the word that he had done some of the most garish work in Newport.

Architects and their work also appear in her fiction of this period, and Ogden is the subject of some thinly veiled satire. Her short story of 1896, "The Valley of Childish Things, and other Emblems," contains ten short fables that reveal her increasing dissatisfaction with Newport and her marriage. Two of the fables focus on architects. One concerns a lady who needs her house turned around; she engages an architect who tells her that "anything could be done for money." Edith expresses some of her anger at Codman's fees, for in the fable, the lady, "who enjoyed a handsome income, was obliged to reduce her way of living and sell her securities at a sacrifice to raise money enough for the purpose." Another fable pokes at architects' egos. When a "successful architect" appears at heaven's gate, he is told that "either we can let the world go on thinking your temple a masterpiece and you the greatest architect that ever lived, or we can send to earth a young fellow we've got here who will discover your mistake at a glance and point it out so clearly to posterity that you'll be the laughing-stock of all succeeding generations of architects." The architect answers, "Oh well, if it comes to that, you know—as long as it suits my clients as it is, I really don't see the use of making such a fuss." This fable points directly to Codman: he had just finished his first house, for Mrs. Charles Coolidge Pomeroy in Newport, a small classically pedimented house of stucco that local wags christened the "mud palace." Edith's architect wanted to build a temple but could produce only "a mud hut thatched with straw." She ends her fable with a passerby observing: "There are two worse plights than yours. One is to have no god; the other is to build a mud hut and mistake it for the Parthenon."[37]

Some conflicts of ego no doubt occurred during the writing of *The Decoration of Houses*. The project lasted for nearly a year, from late fall 1896 to September 1897, and the book appeared on 3 December 1897. In her autobiography Edith acknowledged the help of a distant relative, Walter Van Rensselaer Berry. The year before she met Teddy, Edith had fallen in love with Berry, and he probably with her, but then he retreated, scared. Now he reappeared in Newport, a man of "sensitive literary instincts," who with a shout of laughter at the lump of the manuscript replied: " 'Come, let's see what can be done.' "[38]

The search for a publisher had its setbacks. Edith's sister-in-law got them an entry at Macmillan's in early 1897, and the editor, Mr. Brett, received the work positively. Brett found the title "not ambitious enough," and wanted to call it *The Philosophy of House-decoration*.[39] But there were other concerns, as apparently Codman was not upholding his end. Before a meeting between Ogden and Brett, Edith warned, "I don't wish to seem peremptory, but I think a good deal depends on the impression produced during that visit."[40] What exactly transpired is unclear, but in *A Backward Glance* Edith claims that Macmillan's showed the manuscript to an architect who rejected it with "cries of derision."[41] This was patently false, since Edith already had in hand Charles McKim's warm praise of the manuscript. Instead she was probably covering up the vexing problem of Codman's incompetence. Apparently he so offended Brett that the project was called off, for in May 1897 Edith wrote to Ogden, "Before we embark on any other experiments with the book, I am going to make it a condition that you leave the transaction entirely to me."[42]

Edith then turned to Edward Burlingame, senior editor of *Scribner's*, who had published several of her short stories and poems. He in turn passed it on to William Crary Brownell of Scribner's book publishing arm, and after some hesitation over the expected audience and sales, they accepted it. Charles Scribner, the owner of the firm, felt it lacked potential, but Burlingame and Brownell wanted to encourage Edith; she claimed they "liked my poetry."[43] She showered Brownell with ideas for the book and convinced him that

Walter Berry and dog standing in the trellis niche designed by Ogden Codman for Land's End, here in the Red Garden, The Mount, photographed c. 1905–11

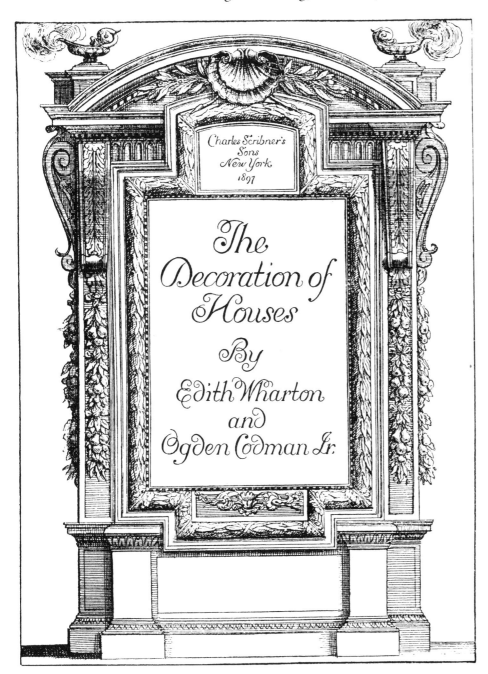

Charles Scribner's
Sons
New York
1897

The
Decoration of
Houses
By
Edith Wharton
and
Ogden Codman Jr.

Daniel Berkeley Updike,
frontispiece for The Decoration
of Houses *(1897)*

thirty-two plates would not be enough illustrations. In fact, she accosted him at his Newport summer home and successfully argued for fifty-six half-tone plates.[44] And she convinced him to have Daniel Berkeley Updike, the Boston Arts and Crafts printer, both design and print the book. Updike, an old friend of Ogden's and a new acquaintance of hers, also designed the title page, drawing inspiration from Ogden's favorite source book, Marot's *Das Ornamentwerk*.[45]

Edith's letters to Ogden reveal the struggle of writing and the problems of collaboration: "I think I have mastered hall & stairs at last, & I should like to see all the French & English Renaissance house plans you have."[46]

Later she writes, "I have finished *walls* (which will have to be a chapter by themselves preceding the Chps. on openings) & I should like you to read it at once."[47] And in a peevish tone she complains about his failure to produce:

> *Anytime in the last three months you could have made the whole bibliography in your office in an hour—I suppose now that will have to be left out too. [Edith wanted plans in the book, but none appeared.] I regret very much that I undertook the book. I certainly should not have done so if I had not understood that you were willing to do half, & that the illustrations & all the work that had to be done with the help of your books were to be included in your half. I hate to put my name to anything so badly turned out.*[48]

There are many more letters attesting to the trial of collaboration, but by November 1897 Edith's letters reveal a renewed warmth, as she was correcting galleys, compiling the index, and anticipating reviews. She hoped that *The Nation* would review it using Thomas Hastings, the architect of the New York Public Library, and she adds that "in any case Russell Sturgis is not to touch it."[49]

Already Charles McKim had given the book his approval. As the senior partner of the New York firm of McKim, Mead & White, the designer of the Boston Public Library and the Agriculture Building at the 1893 Chicago World's Columbian Exposition, and the founder of the American Academy in Rome, McKim represented what Edith called, " 'the high-water mark' of criticism in that line in America."[50] McKim knew Codman only slightly when he reviewed the manuscript, but the contact would lead to several decorating commissions and to McKim's unsuccessful attempt to gain membership for Codman in the American Institute of Architects.[51] McKim knew Edith both socially and through her fund-raising activities for his American Academy in Rome.[52] She wrote to McKim probably in January 1897 asking him to read what they had written:

> *I should not have troubled you about the matter at all, if I had not fancied from some talks we have had together that you felt that there were things which needed saying on this very subject, and had I not hoped that, if Mr. Codman and I could say them in the right way we might, in a slight degree, cooperate with the work you are doing in your Roman academy.*[53]

McKim reacted enthusiastically to the manuscript, and offered specific advice about the introduction. Edith noted to Ogden that "I think it would be well in some respects to remodel the Introduction. . . . The other chapters he entirely agrees to, which is nice."[54] McKim argued that Italian Renaissance architecture and its progeny in other countries should be the basis of modern architecture. He quibbled with their assertion that the Italian villa was unsuitable for northern climates and claimed that it could "easily be adapted to modern uses as the type of French and English country houses built after 1600." He cites as an example Wheatleigh, the H. H. Cook house in Lenox by Peabody and Stearns.[55] He agreed that France had a "present superiority" in architecture; he had been a student at the Ecole de Beaux-Arts. He concurred with Edith and Ogden that originality lay not in a "willful rejection of what have been accepted as the necessary laws of the various forms of art . . . but in using them to express new . . . conceptions."[56] McKim more explicitly stated the prospect:

> *The designer should not be too slavish, whether in the composition of a building or a room, in his adherence to the letter of tradition. By conscientious study of the best examples of classic periods, including those of antiquity, it is possible to conceive a perfect result suggestive of a particular period . . . but inspired by the study of them all.*[57]

McKim, Edith, and Ogden concurred that specific styles should rule and that the foundation of modern design is the study of the past. Given McKim's encouragement, *The Decoration of Houses* emerges as one of the most important texts from the period and a key to understanding the eclectic methodology of the American Renaissance.

The message of the book comes from the belief—common to the American Renaissance—that the level of civilization of a nation or a people could be read through its arts and, especially, architecture. Edith and Ogden argue that interior decoration should be considered a branch of architecture. This is a claim that each generation seems to assert anew, and while Edith and Ogden rather pretentiously cite in support C. A. d'Aviler's *Cours d'Architecture* (1760) and Isaac Ware's *A Complete Body of Architecture* (1756), essentially similar views had been expressed by Andrew Jackson Downing and Marianna Griswold Van Rensselaer.[58] The difference is in the models chosen, for Edith and Ogden reject the medieval and turn to the Renaissance. Renaissance Italy, while seen as approaching "modern civilization," was unsuited for northern climates; it returned to the "Roman ideal of civic life: the life of the street, the forum and the baths." Instead, Edith and Ogden cite as models "the French and English styles later developed from it," and particularly the French. The reign of Louis XIV was the great divide: "it is to the school of art founded by Louis XIV and to his magnificent patronage of architects and decorators trained in these schools that we owe the preservation, in northern Europe, of that sense of form and spirit of moderation which mark the great classical tradition." English classic taste they describe as less sure, being "perpetually modified by a passion for . . . 'conveniences' which instead of simplifying life not infrequently tend to complicate it." America had little to offer except the Colonial, which was "simply a modest copy of Georgian models."[59]

The opening premise of *The Decoration of Houses* is that room decoration has to be considered as part of the total design of a building. Architectural elements rule the interior as much as they determine the exterior. The authors

Antechamber in the Palazzo Durazzo, plate 29 in The Decoration of Houses

equate superficial application of ornament derived independently of the structure with the unsettled medieval period and barbarianism.[60] High civilization appeared when room decoration became architecture; the Renaissance and the return to classicism comprised an academic tradition that offered consistency. The book is not just a historical study, but a philosophy and a handbook of dos and don'ts. The chapters follow a seemingly practical bent — first the elements of rooms and then the totality. Actually their outline also follows that of both Charles Locke Eastlake's *Hints on Household Taste* (1868) and Clarence Cook's *House Beautiful* (1877), two books which Edith and Ogden despised and whose influence *The Decoration of Houses* was an attempt to correct. After a historical survey come chapters on parts of rooms such as walls, doors, windows, fireplaces, and ceilings and floors, and then specific rooms are treated: entrance and vestibule, hall and stairs, and the others. After a chapter on bric-a-brac, a conclusion calls for a return to architectural principles "based upon common sense and regulated by the laws of harmony and proportion."[61]

While part of their argument is based on the environmental suitability of French architecture, furniture also plays a role. The Italians, unlike the French, did not have a furniture tradition adaptable to modern conditions. Edith collected Italian eighteenth-century furniture because it was cheap and a variation on the French. The book shows examples of medieval furniture and describes them as born of an "unsettled state" of "warfare and brigandage" and as "stiff and angular." They were designed to be transported from castle to castle on mule back. Compared to the medieval chairs are the comfortable and civilized armchairs and bergères of Louis XIV, XV, and XVI.[62] Ironically, the tall medieval chairs became the predecessors for Arts and Crafts furniture and for chairs by designers such as Gustav Stickley and

Frank Lloyd Wright. Throughout *The Decoration of Houses*, photographs of rooms and furniture support the thesis that there are constants or laws of good taste that govern the proportion of rooms and the forms of furniture. This law and the language in which it is couched make the book a prime example of scientific eclecticism.

The term "scientific eclecticism" recognizes both the wide-ranging selection from past models and also the methodology by which models are studied and used. Scientific methodology or the selection of samples, the identification of types, and the arrangement into groups, families, or hierarchies had a great influence on many areas of nineteenth-century thought: biology, archaeology, and history. In the decorative arts, architecture, painting, and sculpture, the identification, classification, cataloguing, filing, and recording of styles, motifs, and details became almost obsessive. The modern stylistic history of art, architecture, and decoration were products of this nineteenth-century activity. From such classification, its proponents argued, come standards, laws of taste, or, a key word of the period, "authority." Accuracy in replication was a prime object of scientific eclecticism. Ornamental details on buildings and furniture would be replicated with great fidelity. Necessary to the development of scientific eclecticism were reliable methods of recording the original models. Measured drawings were one method, but photography, which came into widespread use after the mid-1870s, and the invention of the dry-plate process finally allowed Americans to study old-world models with a great degree of accuracy.[63]

Codman's designs, with his notations of specific sources, illustrate the methodology of scientific eclecticism. His interiors and houses were never

Louis XVI dining chair, plate 53 in The Decoration of Houses

Medieval chairs, plate 2 in The Decoration of Houses

an exact copy of a single historic building, but a composite of specific elements he drew from on-site investigation or, more frequently, from works in his vast library and photographic collection.[64] The rendering for the J. Randolph Coolidge drawing room in Boston (plate 26) is particularly illuminating since working and tracing paper drawings for the project list specific sources.[65] Some of the notations, such as for the ornament over the mirror, list only a number (in this case, "#266"), which refers to a supplier stock number. Similarly, the egg-and-dart molding and large boiserie on the left are identified as adaptations from a catalogue as well, in this case "#434." Other notes refer to the cornice and list the "Black book our designs Wharton house interior" and specific references in books, such as "F. Boucher [*Ornements*] A-3, B-3, C-2," and "*Portefeuilles des arts décoratifs*" by Champeaux. The molding for the mirror and the two vertical decorated panels are identified as coming from César Daly, *Motifs historiques d'architecture* (1870). Such exact and specific usage of elements drawn from a variety of sources was the hallmark of scientific eclecticism.

The Decoration of Houses reflects the impact of scientific eclecticism. Wharton and Codman write that the nadir of American taste came in the period 1840 to 1890, which they describe as a "confusion resulting from . . . unscientific methods" of "piling up of heterogeneous ornament, [and] a multiplication of incongruous effects." This is known as High Victorian, or what the historian Carroll Meeks has labeled "synthetic eclecticism," in which agitated picturesqueness in buildings and furniture was at its height. Wharton and Codman call modern overstuffed furniture padding fit for a "lunatic's cell" or "dubious eclecticism." These bulbous pieces dominated American furniture design in the period 1840–90. American architects had led the way in returning to Renaissance models; now if only American decorators and furniture designers would follow in a "study of the best models" and "true principles," the "notable development" would continue.[66]

The close and scientific observation of interiors and furniture was primarily Edith's contribution and came from her travels and studies in Italy. She had digested as soon as they came out Bernard Berenson's studies of Renaissance painting, which introduced her to the "scientific accuracy" of Giovanni Morelli's methods. "A Tuscan Shrine" of 1895 recounts her discovery at an obscure monastery of an unknown Giovanni della Robbia terra cotta, which she identified through close observation and comparison of small details. Proudly she parades her knowledge of the Morelli-Berenson method: "The perception of differences in style is a recently-developed faculty." She aspired to replace the "cultured dilettante" type of art and architectural writing of Symonds and Pater; she wanted to become a "scientific critic" and combine "scholarly standards" with "aesthetic sensibility."[67]

A spirit of rediscovered classicism pervades *The Decoration of Houses*. Ruskin and other medievalists are attacked for their promotion of asymmetry. Calling upon the acknowledgment of "all students of sociology," Wharton and Codman claim the "instinct for symmetry . . . is more strongly developed in those races which have reached the highest artistic civilization." The effect

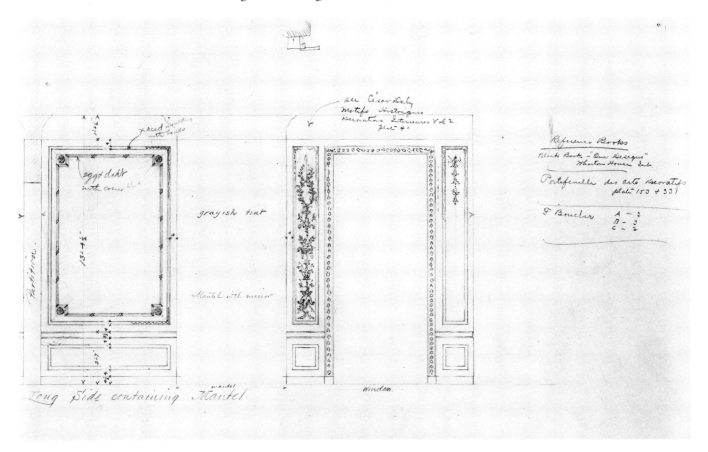

of a room is largely the result of proportions and the "distributions of openings." This concern with the impact of form was a direct result of Vernon Lee's influence and the notion of empathy; forms, shapes, and spaces have an impact on people. Through "mathematical calculation" and "scientific adjustment of voids and masses," good proportions result, which are "good breeding in architecture." Wharton and Codman advance their arguments through a discussion of principles and then of specific examples, such as the hall in the Durazzo Palace in Genoa or a drawing room at Berkeley Square, London.[68]

The Decoration of Houses gained a somewhat notorious reputation as a decorating manual for the very rich robber barons in their "cottages" at Newport. But obviously neither Edith nor Ogden liked, and indeed they parodied, such high caloric excesses as the dining rooms at the Vanderbilts' Marble House and The Breakers, designed by Richard Morris Hunt and Allard et Fils. Their conclusion attacks the "gilded age," and they claim "the supreme excellence is simplicity." Also, since neither author had children, their chapter "The School-Room and Nurseries" has been laughed at. But here is also a clue to their outlook and especially to Edith's modern literary naturalism, which would shortly come to the fore in *The House of Mirth* and *Ethan Frome*. People, as she demonstrates in these books, are creatures of their environment; they are formed by it and cannot escape it. In *The Decoration of Houses* the child's room, where education takes place, is one of the

Ogden Codman, design for wall, J. Randolph Coolidge house, 147 Beacon Street, Boston, 1895

most important, for here the sense of beauty is developed. "Beauty," the authors note, "needs as careful cultivation as the other civic virtues." Art should not be regarded as a thing apart from life, and "the daily intercourse with poor pictures, trashy 'ornaments,' and badly designed furniture may, indeed, be fittingly compared with a mental diet of silly and ungrammatical story-books."[69] Perhaps Edith also remembered her education in her father's library and the importance of that environment.[70]

The reviews were generally positive, although Edith's fears were warranted, as *The Nation*'s critic, probably Russell Sturgis, while claiming the book was "handsome, interesting, and well-written," criticized their reliance upon beauty as the guide.[71] One reviewer found the collaboration of a man and woman noteworthy: "Many details are discussed which would not have been included if there had been but one author, or two authors of one sex."[72] Several reviewers highly praised the book but felt the illustrations were a disservice as they were too ornate and "not . . . examples of that simplicity which the text preaches."[73] The reviewer for the *New York Herald* recounted at length the contents of the book in positive terms and noted that the authors "also condemn in sweeping terms the glaring faults in decorative art shown in many American houses."[74] Walter Berry, who had helped Edith rewrite the book, contributed a review claiming the book began to repair the damage of Eastlake's *Hints on Household Taste*.[75] The reviewer in *The American Architect and Building News* chided their severe condemnation of current American design, but claimed that "on the whole, the volume is far ahead of anything of the kind we know of within the last half-century."[76]

The book, which sold very well and was reprinted in England and later in America,[77] helped change taste in decoration on both sides of the Atlantic. Edith astutely sent copies to English architects and critics she felt might be sympathetic and received friendly replies from W. J. Loftie and Reginald Blomfield. They praised her condemnation of "excessive & unmeaning ornament" and hoped her views would prevail in England as in America.[78] For years the book was the bible of classical decoration, and it exercised a substantial influence on succeeding books.

Codman's protégé Elsie de Wolfe replayed many of the book's themes in her own book (though really largely ghostwritten by Ruby Ross Wood), *The House in Good Taste* (1913). As the title indicates, her house was less rigorous and philosophical than *The Decoration of Houses*. It was also far more personal than either Edith or Ogden would ever allow themselves to be; Elsie describes in intimate detail with gossipy chatter her own houses and apartments. Decorating in Elsie's hands becomes fashion design; architecture is not the controlling element. The book has a lighthearted air and is filled with such pronouncements as "The effect is the thing you are after, isn't it," which would be unthinkable to Wharton and Codman. However, in essentials, *The House in Good Taste* follows the outline of *The Decoration of Houses*. First appears a historical outline, then a treatment of the architectural elements, and then chapters devoted to individual rooms. Many phrases, such as the title of Elsie's second chapter, "Suitability, Simplicity and Proportion," directly echo lines in *The Decoration of Houses*. *The House in Good Taste* is a lesser book than Edith and Ogden's, but as de Wolfe notes on the opening page, it contributes to an "awakening, development, American Renaissance" to "a most startling and promising condition of affairs."[79]

The Decoration of Houses had a substantial impact on both authors. Codman's stature as a decorator grew and his career as an architect blossomed after 1897 with a series of important city and country house commissions. The philosophy he and Edith developed and expounded in the book had an effect on his work. The lingering synthetic eclecticism drops away, and he becomes more rigorous and pure in his use of architectural elements.

While Edith would later discount *The Decoration of Houses* as unrelated to her literary career, the experience did give her a surer sense of herself as a writer.[80] Edith's main *métier* would be fiction; however, after *The Decoration of Houses* she found herself in demand as an architectural writer. Charles McKim, involved in remodeling the White House for Theodore Roosevelt, to whom Edith was distantly related by marriage, wanted her to write it up.[81] Edith's interest in architecture and decoration grew, and trips abroad,

Left: Maxfield Parrish, Vicobello, Siena, from Italian Villas and Their Gardens *by Edith Wharton (1904)*

Right: Maxfield Parrish, Villa Gamberaia, near Florence, from Italian Villas and Their Gardens

whether to Italy or England, and a tour of Wilton were reported in great detail to Ogden. Though she at one point proposed to Ogden that they write a book on "Garden-architecture," it never came to pass.[82]

She did, however, bring her interest in houses and gardens to another collaboration. In August 1900 she wrote to Ogden and asked him to read her new story in *Scribner's*: "See how you like my description of a Palladian villa, & whether you don't think that Maxfield Parrish's illustrations are delightful."[83] Parrish's photographic, magical realism fit well with Edith's descriptions of Venetian palaces, villas, and gardens planned in "all manner of agreeable surprises in the way of water-jets that drenched you unexpectedly, and hermits in caves, and wild men that jumped at you out of thickets."[84] The result would be a collaboration with Parrish on a series of articles published in *The Century* in 1903–4 and then as a book, *Italian Villas and Their Gardens*. The result of Edith's years of travels in Italy, the book was a natural successor to *The Decoration of Houses* and contained many of the same themes: principles could be extracted from the gardens abroad and applied at home. The book is not about horticulture — "The Italian garden does not exist for its flowers, its flowers exist for it" — but a treatment of gardens as architectural assemblages. Though Charles Adams Platt had published *Italian Gardens* in 1894, Edith's book was longer, more comprehensive, and more knowledgeable; it helped to fuel the rage for Italian gardens in America and led her to her own creation at The Mount.[85]

The Mount

While the tensions between Edith and Ogden generated by the collaboration on *The Decoration of Houses* were temporarily alleviated by its success, they arose anew with Edith's new project, a complete house and garden for Teddy and herself at Lenox, Massachusetts. As she could create worlds on paper and describe the ideal house, now she would try to create a complete physical world. Here Edith would build a country estate that would consume much of her interest and provide a setting for her novels. And in the countryside she observed another scene, the rural poverty of New England, which would result in *Ethan Frome*.

For the fall of 1899, Edith and Teddy took over his mother's summer house at Lenox, in the Berkshire mountains. Edith became entranced with the area. A return for part of the summer and fall of 1900 brought rapture in a letter to Ogden: "The truth is that I am in love with the place, climate, scenery, life & all."[86] Negotiations to purchase 113 acres of land began in February 1901; later she would add 13 more acres. The deed was signed by her in June, and shortly thereafter both Land's End and the New York house were sold to help pay for the new home and garden. The property was in her name, though Teddy later did sign a guarantee for the mortgage as "husband of said grantor." Edith had the funds, though not unlimited, to design and construct a house and setting that would meet her discriminating eye.[87]

View of The Mount from the
Red Garden, c. 1905

Much later Edith explained that she had never cared for the "flat frivolity," the "trivialities," the "depressing climate, . . . and the vapid watering-place amusements" of Newport. Several of her stories from this period —including "The Line of Least Resistance" and "The Twilight of the God"—were scathing portraits of Newport society.[88] But Lenox and the Berkshires were also part of a summer colony, known in fact as the "inland Newport," with many of the same excesses. When Edith arrived, Carrère & Hastings had just completed Bellefontaine for Giraud Foster at a cost reported in excess of a million dollars, and Elm Court by Peabody and Stearns for George W. and Emily Vanderbilt Sloane was a gigantic "cottage" that rambled for over a hundred yards along a mountainside. Yet Edith changed her home for several very good reasons. First, Lenox was not Newport and lacked associations with her mother, who had left Newport several years earlier to live in Paris. Symbolically and providentially, since now she could afford The Mount, her mother died only a few days before Edith purchased the property. Second, Edith could be dismissive of society, but she was a member, and in the Berkshires it existed alongside a more intellectual and artistic, and hence appealing, group, which included Charles Eliot Norton, Owen Wister, Thomas Shields Clarke, I. N. P. Stokes, Daniel Chester French, Richard Watson Gilder, and others. Third, here she could import—and control—her friends: Henry James, Clyde Fitch, Egerton Winthrop, Walter Berry, and Daniel Updike. Finally, instead of the ocean, the Berkshires offered the mountains and varieties of scenery that Edith genuinely liked better, for as she wrote, "I was to know the joys of six or seven months a year among fields and woods of my own, and . . . the deep joy of communion with the earth."[89] Henry James arrived in 1904 and, while noting the "injury" of the "summer people," still felt the Berkshires was "that heart of New England which makes so pretty a phrase for print and so stern a fact, as yet, for feeling."[90]

As soon as negotiations began on the property, Edith turned to Ogden to design the house. Immediately disputes broke out. To his mother Ogden wrote, "I fully realize what an idiot Teddy is," and he recounted a shouting match with Teddy over who was the most disliked.[91] The conflict involved several issues. Edith and Teddy felt that as both an old friend and collaborator, Ogden should reduce his fee of twenty-five percent; he refused. Ogden worried about the time the Whartons would demand; he wrote to his mother, "I told them that I was so busy and my work was so scattered I could not be coming up to Lenox all the time."[92] He also worried about his social standing, convincing himself that Edith's story "The Line of Least Resistance," which had appeared the past summer, had alienated those who mattered: "Mrs. Wally Sloane did not like the story . . . and Mrs. Wharton wrote and apologized for it. Mrs. Sloane is the social queen of Lenox." Filled with infidelity, greed, ignorance, and selfish and shallow characters, the story evidently hit too close to home, for, Ogden claimed, "her story about the Sloanes finished her with all the Sloane Vanderbilt hangers on who are now barking at her like a lot of yellow dogs." Ogden fancied "their [the Wharton's] day of usefulness is over," and in a later letter coldly noted that "poor Miss Pusscod must be replaced while she is still stunned." But he also admitted he wished they had been more upset about his declining to do their house.[93]

Edith resolved the imbroglio by hiring another architect. She then wrote to Ogden:

> *It is of much more importance to me that we should maintain our old relation as good friends than risk it by entering on the new and precarious one of architect and client. We are in such close sympathy in things architectural that it would have been a pleasure for me to work with you, but perhaps after all we know each other too well, and are disqualified by that very fact for professional collaboration.*

She added, "Now that you need not be on your guard against me as a client, perhaps I shall be all the more useful as a friend. . . . for it has been a great interest to me to follow your work and try to make people understand what it represents." Ogden wrote his mother that she "will be glad to hear that peace has been declared by the Whartons," and he later remarked, "I shall continue to stand up for her as she was kind and helpful to me long ago."[94] Between the lines one can sense Ogden's surprise that Edith hired another architect; perhaps he realized the chance to do a house with a fully sympathetic client had been lost. But he was busy in 1901 with three of his most important commissions—the Morse, Coats, and Bryce houses were either under contract or on the horizon—and he knew the Whartons could be demanding and that Edith's ideas could conflict with his. Trouble and hurt feelings were a certainty.

The new architect was Francis (Frank) L. V. Hoppin, of Providence and New York, whom Edith had known for several years. Hoppin had attended Brown, studied architecture at MIT, and then spent time in Paris

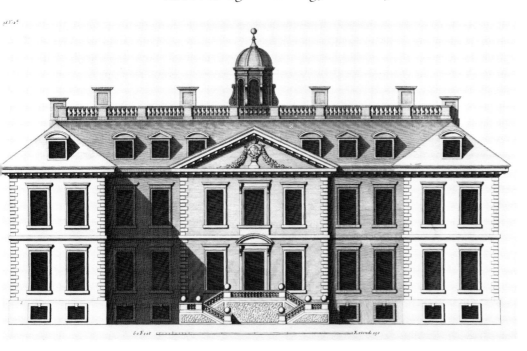

Colin Campbell, elevation of Belton House, plate 38 in Vitruvius Britannicus

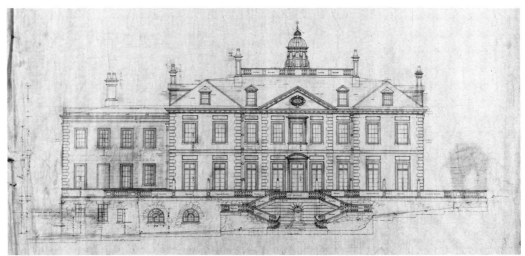

Hoppin & Koen, east elevation, The Mount, 1901

Hoppin & Koen, west elevation, The Mount, 1901

(possibly at the Ecole) before entering the McKim, Mead & White office, where he became known for his splashy renderings. With Terrance A. Koen he had recently set up an office, and the Wharton commission was an important job, though he undoubtedly knew that Edith's knowledge and proclivities would not allow him a free hand. Ogden gleefully reported to his mother that Hoppin "is having an awful time with the house, which she telegraphs him every day or two and fusses terribly over every detail." Hoppin, according to Ogden, had "been cut down in every way" and had been forced to change the house from brick to stucco over wood and make three sets of plans. "Poor Pussy," he concluded, "is of course very unpopular. . . . She has gone out of her way to be rude."[95]

Edith was completely involved in the building of The Mount, which she named after the Long Island home of her great-grandfather. She was so absorbed in the project—from site to design, construction, and furnishings—that she found writing and reading a distraction.[96] Ultimately the house is Edith's own creation, though she was assisted by her niece Beatrix Farrand on the drive and gardens, Frank Hoppin designed—or drew up—the house and gardens, and Ogden returned to help on the interiors. After long walks on the property, she decided to site the house on a small hill with a marble rock outcropping near the center of her acreage, with a view of Laurel Lake about a mile away. The completed house, gardens, and grounds show Edith's architectural enthusiasms and are a perfect example of the American Renaissance impulse. The approach to the house through the long *allée* and the dense woods is reminiscent of French country estates near Compiègne or Versailles. The opening onto a broad green lawn, upon which the house sits, is American suburban. The form of the house is usually called Georgian, though the English label "Wrenaissance" would be more accurate. Of course the ultimate source for the English model was the Italian villa made serviceable for northern climates, as Charles McKim had noted in his memorandum to Edith and as she and Ogden had argued in *The Decoration of Houses*.[97] The plan, however, was French, while the interior was American in convenience and mechanics though the decor recalled French, English, and Italian sources. The terrace and garden were Italian in inspiration, and beyond an English-style meadow lay the American landscape.

Set into the hillside, the house has three full stories on the west or approach front and only two stories on the east or garden side. Belton House in Lincolnshire (1684–86) is the most identifiable source for the east facade. Edith had visited Belton, and apparently she and Ogden had decided to use it as a model before their blowup.[98] Ogden favored Belton and had used it for other houses; Hoppin had also designed or had on the drawing board houses derived from the Belton prototype.[99] A great house of the Carolinian period, Belton had recently been published in the English magazine *Country Life* and attributed to Christopher Wren, with carvings by Grinling Gibbons. Belton's elevations were also available through Colin Campbell's *Vitruvius Britannicus*.[100] Yet The Mount is not a copy; it is smaller than Belton and not of stone but white stucco. It also meets the ground differently; while

Belton sits on a half basement on a flat site, The Mount sits on a hillside. The east front of The Mount rises from the hill like a white temple, and terraces and stairs support it and also tie it back to the land.

The plan of The Mount, by which one enters at the basement level on the west front, progresses up to the piano nobile, and then exits onto the terrace on the east front, is ingenious. Its origin was undoubtedly French, possibly the Petit Trianon at Versailles (1762–68) by Ange-Jacques Gabriel, where the same spatial sequence takes place with entry from a forecourt into a three-story block. Codman had very hastily drawn up some floor plans which show this circulation in embryo. Codman's plans also have some relation to Belton, especially the H shape and the main staircase pushed into a separate space beside the entry hall. It is doubtful that Codman had visited the site, for his orientation is backward.[101] Also Ogden had projected the basement entry continuing through the rock and becoming a grotto on the east side, which would have necessitated expensive rock blasting. Codman's main floor or piano nobile plan was awkward in circulation and had a clumsy, L-shaped hall.

Hoppin and Edith revised this scheme. The house became a series of spaces at right angles to the main entrance axis. Through a high-walled forecourt, one enters the basement entrance hall, turns to the right, and progresses to the stairhall. The main floor is a series of enfilade spaces. Across the west front is the cross-axial gallery, which opens at one end onto the stair hall and at the other end onto the den. In placement and function the gallery is unique in American country houses of the period. Parallel to the hall and opening from its spatial slot is the enfilade of the main living apartments, dining room, drawing room, and library. The same layering of perpendicular spaces occurs on the east front: the terraces as well as the gardens lie across the house's central axis. The service spaces are located in the basement and a wing to the south. On the north and east side the house rests on the marble rock, and the basement remains unexcavated; directly

Left: Ogden Codman, basement plan, The Mount, c. 1901

Right: Ogden Codman, first floor plan, The Mount, c. 1901

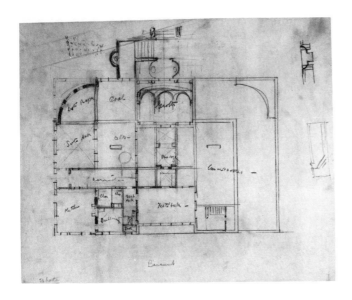

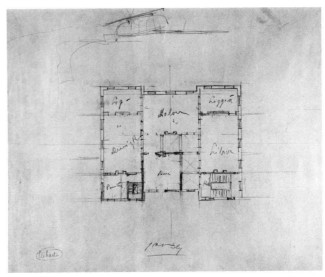

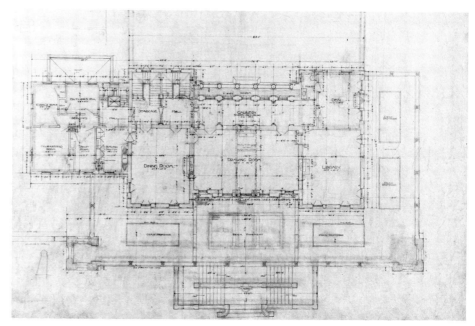

Hoppin & Koen, first floor plan, The Mount, 1901

Hoppin & Koen, basement plan, The Mount, 1901

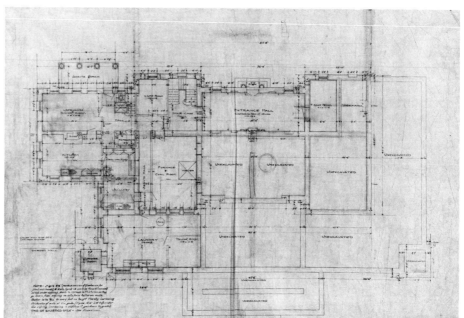

above are the den and library, and on the second floor was Edith's boudoir and bedroom. She did most of her writing from the bedroom and would not be bothered by noise from below. The plan can be interpreted as a series of barriers to protect Edith at her work and yet allow the house to function with visitors and guests. Whatever questions might be raised about the awkwardness of the exterior, the plan carefully met the Whartons' requirements, and as formal design it is impressive—a high point of country house organization from the period.

The exterior of The Mount also adds American touches to the European models. The white color and green shutters recall early New England houses.[102]

The east elevation, or garden facade, while drawn from Belton, is transformed. The relationship of The Mount's end and central pavilions are different, for at The Mount they are all of the same size and the hyphens are reduced, giving the central pavilion a pinched quality. Hoppin also projected twin belvedere pavilions on the terrace, which were never built. On the approach, or west front, Hoppin designed a large and elaborate forecourt with French-styled wrought-iron gates.[103] This was modified into a small and somewhat cramped space with a small verge of turf and two statues in niches. Hoppin also projected for the gallery five round-headed, loggia-type windows. They would have more truthfully revealed the gallery, but they would have appeared incongruous and cramped on the facade; Edith had them changed to three openings. Ornamental detailing, while simple, has an insistent—almost scientific—quality typical of American design of the period. The quoins, bell courses, dentils, and the roof balustrade and cupola appear a little too obvious, too prominent. Symmetry is emphatic; window frames with no openings were inserted to balance real windows. The shutters covered the blank openings.

For the interior Edith and Hoppin had hired a French firm, but Edith grew dissatisfied with the designs and turned to Ogden again. At dinner on New Year's Eve, 1901, Edith broached the subject of decorating the house; and, as he wrote to his mother, "I am much pleased as it will put a stop to all talk about our having quarrelled." He, with Edith's questions and advice, did most of the interior.[104] Her letters show the usual problems: "Please do it today, if you haven't already, for I know that there will be pretexts for

Ogden Codman, entrance hall, The Mount, with Pan of Rohallion *and furniture belonging to subsequent owners, photographed c. 1942*

delay." They argued about tapestries and chimney breasts, with Edith citing alternative precedents.[105] Edith "edited" her furniture—some came from Land's End and New York—and there were some new pieces. The decoration of several of The Mount's rooms, especially the den and her boudoir, closely followed Codman's designs at Land's End.

In her autobiography Edith recalls being "taxed by my friends with not applying to the arrangements of my own rooms the rigorous rules laid down in *The Decoration of Houses*."[106] The interior at The Mount both followed and departed. Each room was designed for a particular purpose and personality, so that "it must be not 'a library,' or 'a drawing room,' but the library or the drawing-room best suited to the master or mistress of the house which is being decorated."[107] The entrance vestibule on the basement level retains the air of the proposed grotto: Frederick MacMonnies's garden statue *Pan of Rohallion* greets the visitor, the walls are finished in a rusticated stucco, and the floor has a reddish and white terra-cotta tile pattern.[108] The stair hall, appropriately separate as dictated by *The Decoration of Houses*, recalls eighteenth-century Parisian *hôtels*, with their smooth masonry courses imitated in stucco and their wrought-iron balustrades. The guest progresses upward toward light and into the bright gallery, with its terrazzo floor

Detail of plasterwork fruit and foliage, dining room, The Mount

Gallery, The Mount, photographed c. 1905

dominated by the vaulted ceiling. Intended as a space for passage and not lingering, the forms and lines are bold; the ceiling compels attention as Edith and Ogden claimed it should. They also stated that the gallery should "display the art-treasures of the house," but that spaces people use only for passage should have "forcible simple lines, with vigorous massing of light and shade."[109] Consequently, the furnishings were sparse, three "highly-prized Italian console tables," marble columns, vases, and some terra-cotta statues.[110]

Symmetry as a guiding principle is evident throughout the main floor. False doors or paneling balance real openings in rooms. All the main floor rooms have a luminous quality, as ten-foot-high windows open from all the rooms and provide access to the terrace. The drawing room, "decorated in English XVII century style," as claimed by a local writer, is the blandest and most mixed room; Edith appears to have tried to combine the functions of both a *salon de compagnie* and a *salon de famille*, which she and Ogden had argued must be rigorously separated.[111] The furniture could be easily moved for conversation, and tapestries dominated. The dining room is the brightest in the house, as natural light is important to digestion. To assist the artificial illumination at night, the dining room was painted in white, as they had proposed in the book, and it was decorated with appropriate symbols. Imitation Grinling Gibbons stucco-and wood carvings of fruit and foliage, perhaps in memory of Belton, were installed along with two Italian painted fruit-and-flower panels set into the fireplace breast and the opposite wall. The dining room chairs, with "wide deep seats so that the long banquets of the day might be endured without constraint or fatigue," were eighteenth-century Italian from Land's End.[112] The table was a nineteenth-century pedestal type that could be extended. Edith disliked such tables but admitted their convenience. A Louis XV styled china cabinet and two serving tables made up the rest of the room.

The library received perhaps the most attention. Louis XVI style dark oak cases filled with leather-bound sets of books reach to the ceiling on three sides, while a tapestry dominates the other. The carving in the overdoor panels and bookcases is more elaborate than suggested in *The Decoration of Houses*. A portrait of Edith's great-grandfather Stevens hung over the mantel. The furniture, such as a *lit de repos* or Louis XVI chairs brought from Newport and two new Regency-styled writing tables, were background—as stated in *The Decoration*—to the books and the conversation that would take place.[113]

At the end of September 1902 Edith wrote to Sally Norton, "*Finalmente!*" They had moved in. The gossipy newspaper *Lenox Life* reported a "house warming" party attended by, among others, Egerton Winthrop, Reginald Vanderbilt, and the Sloanes, with whom peace had been restored.[114] Edith's haste in getting the house done and her economy with money left problems which would constantly reappear. The guest rooms and servants' quarters were not adequate, and Hoppin began to plan an enlargement, which was never built. Also the house suffered from poor construction.[115] Ogden visited a few days after the Whartons moved in and utterly disapproved; he claimed "the place looks *forlorn* beyond my powers of description," with marble floors half finished, the courtyard all out of proportion, and the furniture looking "awful." He called Hoppin "superficial," and with some glee he claimed the Whartons were unhappy. While he expressed some satisfaction with his work, Codman also realized he had made a mistake in not taking the job: "They got in too deeply over their heads, and I am almost sorry I did not come."[116] He had passed up perhaps his best chance to create the ultimate country house according to his tastes.

The landscaping was unfinished, and Codman noted that it would "take years and a small fortune . . . to make it even look decent." Part of the landscaping had been designed, but it needed to be planted and mature. In 1901 Edith's niece, Beatrix Jones Farrand, designed the kitchen garden behind the stables near the entrance and gate lodge and also the sugar-maple-lined *allée* and drive.[117] This work is French in feeling and opens to the broad grass lawn—typical of American country houses—that leads to the house. The rock outcroppings to the north of the house and elsewhere were retained as part of the landscape. The east front terraces (which had been graded and

Library, The Mount

Hoppin & Koen, entrance gate, showing the allée *designed by Beatrix Farrand, The Mount*

planted) recall Edith's contemporary collaboration with Maxfield Parrish on Italian gardens. The broad terrace off the main rooms, delineated by balustrades; the terrace steps; the views to the gardens; and in the distance the lake and hills have sources in the Villa Gamberaia, the Villa Chigi, and the Villa Campi—all illustrated in *Italian Villas and Their Gardens.*

Below the terraces and on the layered cross axis, were two gardens laid out in 1903 and 1905. On the north was a flower garden with a rectangular pool and a dolphin fountain, which was designed in 1903. Beatrix Farrand spent that summer at The Mount and certainly gave advice.[118] Laid out in 1905 on the southern axis was a sunken, stone-walled garden with a circular pool. Edith's diary for late October 1905 records, "F. Hoppin came about garden" next to the entry "H. of M. [*House of Mirth*] best-selling book in New York." Hoppin drew up the plan for the southern garden with the advice of Edith.[119] The trellis niche of laths by Ogden from Land's End occupies the northern garden, while statues stood in niches in the southern garden. A pergola projects from the walled garden into the meadow. A clipped hemlock hedge and a double row of lindens line the limestone gravel walk between the two gardens. The meadow opening below the gardens ties the formal portion of the house to the middle distance of natural forest and the lake. Through paths cut in the woods and the meadow lay the sparkling glint of Laurel Lake, which provides a transition to the far distance of the Berkshire Hills. A visitor to The Mount in 1911 recorded the splendor of the scene:

> *Looking down upon these two gardens, separated from each other by the terraced lawns, as you stand on the broad veranda of the villa, the glory of their coloring actually vibrates in the sunlight; yet framed as they are in spacious green, they do not clash with the distant prospect.*[120]

Carolina Palermo Schulze, measured drawing of The Mount and gardens, 1984

Afterword

The Mount was Edith's most complete realization of a total environment. It was, as Henry James noted, "an exquisite and marvelous place, a delicate French château mirrored in a Massachusetts pond (repeat not this formula), a monument to the almost too impeccable taste of its so accomplished mistress. Every comfort prevails."[121] Edith loved her gardens and wrote to Sara Norton about the "mass of bloom," her ten varieties of phlox, snapdragons, lilacs, and the profusion of pinks, blues, purples, and whites. She entered her flowers in the Lenox Horticultural Society annual exhibits and received numerous prizes.[122] Edith wrote a number of stories as well as *The House of Mirth* (1905) while at The Mount; and gardens at the Trenor's estate, Bellomont, in that novel reflect the view from Edith's bedroom window:

> *The windows stood open to the sparkling freshness of the September morning, and between the yellow boughs she caught a perspective of hedges and parterres leading by degrees of lessening formality to the free undulations of the park.*

Later in the novel, Lily Bart and Lawrence Selden escape from one *tableau* into another:

> *Gravel grated beneath their feet, and about them was the transparent dimness of a midsummer night. . . . The magic place was deserted: there was not sound but the splash of the water on the lily-pads, and a distant drift of music that might have been blown across a sleeping lake.*[123]

But The Mount and the Berkshires also gave her insight into an entirely different life: the hard rural poverty which infuse *Ethan Frome* (1911) and *Summer* (1917). In her various drives through the countryside with visitors such as Henry James, she spied the "forlorn and stunted" farmhouses with "their worn coat of paint" and their occupants, "my *granite outcroppings*; but half emerged from the soil, and scarcely more articulate."[124]

The Mount was for Edith "my first real home," but also an interlude, for it would all quickly change. A close friend of Edith's claimed that "she was absorbed in the study of houses, furniture and of course gardens, . . . but once the house in hand was finished her interest ceased."[125] At this time, Edith and Teddy reversed roles: he began to suffer nervous breakdowns, and the always-strained marriage began to unravel. They each had an affair and then sought new settings abroad. By 1911 the marriage was over; The Mount was sold in 1912; and Edith and Teddy were divorced the following year.

After The Mount Edith and Ogden drifted on separate yet parallel paths toward Europe and France, where they would live for the remainder of their lives. Their strained friendship had suffered further in a dispute over bills that lingered until 1905. Lawyers were contacted, but it was settled out of court.[126] In France they both found the taste and cultivation they had tried to create, but ultimately despaired of making, in America. Each had left contemporary America and moved toward a romanticized view of America's past.

Edith traveled frequently and established several homes in France, the best known of which were the Château Sainte-Claire at Hyères, and the Pavillon Colombe at Saint-Brice. Her interest in architecture and decoration did not vanish, and all of her residences were lovingly decorated. She crossed the Atlantic again in 1923 to receive an honorary Doctorate of Letters from Yale. On Long Island she stayed with old friends, Eunice and Walter Maynard, in Hautbois, a house designed by Codman. The house reminded her in its plan of The Mount, as did its French atmosphere.[127]

Among American writers of fiction, Edith Wharton's knowledge of architecture and decoration stands out. R. W. B. Lewis notes that her nearly professional competence in this area is not "entirely explicable"; her New York background seems hardly an adequate preparation. Quite consciously Edith appears to have set out to become an expert in architecture and decoration. The "scientific analysis" and acute perception learned in Italy and shown in *The Decoration of Houses* and her own houses would stand her in good stead in her novels. In this she was assisted by "my photographic memory of rooms and houses — even those seen but briefly, or at long intervals." Sixty years later she could recall the "terror," the "intolerable ugliness," of the "Hudson River Gothic" house of her aunt at Rhinecliff, which became the Willows in *Hudson River Bracketed* (1929).[128] She knew her architectural history; and even among American historians she is outstanding in the 1920s for her recognition of Andrew Jackson Downing or Charles Eastlake, as shown in *Hudson River Bracketed* and *Old New York*. At the end of her life she still remembered the Pompeiian red and the frieze of stenciled lotus leaves, taken from Owen Jones's *Grammar of Ornament*, in the vestibules of old New York houses.[129]

Edith was obsessively concerned with foreground and background. She found Italy "divided, not in *partes tres*, but in two: a foreground and a background." The foreground she defined as that of the guidebook: it must be understood before one can know the background, which is that of the "dawdler, the dreamer, and the serious student."[130] This she hoped to find in America and did not, for "the American landscape has no foreground, and the American mind no background."[131] This was also the lament of the architects and artists of the American Renaissance: they found the American models of the nineteenth century poor; consequently there was no background worthy of emulation. This cosmopolitan view was in a sense typically American, especially for those who had seen the riches of the old world. What did America have to offer? Land's End, The Mount, and her writing were Edith's attempts to fill this emptiness in both the American landscape and the American mind. As she explains in the *Writing of Fiction*, "The impression produced by a landscape, a street or a house should always, to the novelist, be an event in the history of a soul."[132]

Her residency in France after 1912 both confirmed her earlier proclivities and provided an escape from the social ostracism of her divorce. But also it indicates her despair of ever creating, much less finding, cultivation and taste in America. She attempted to explain that culture could not be predicated upon pragmatism and usefulness; rather, "the deeper civilisation of a country may . . . be measured by the care she gives to her flower-garden — the corner

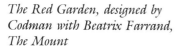

The Red Garden, designed by Codman with Beatrix Farrand, The Mount

of her life where the supposedly 'useless' arts and graces flourish." The French, she found, saw art in everything, from the curve of a woman's hat brim to the droop of curtains and the branches of avenues laid out by Le Nôtre. Puritanism was the problem with America: art became "something apart from life." For Americans art belonged only in museums, poets — as in Plato — were banished to remote and boring reaches that resembled death.[133] This is the lament of "The Spark" in *Old New York*: men of property are vacuous, empty shells sitting in bookless libraries, who cannot even understand Walt Whitman. In "False Dawn," also part of *Old New York*, she laments that paintings (in this case Italian primitives) that depart from society's accepted notions of how art should look are rejected. The American background was weak, and Americans seemed determined to reject any foreground.

Edith disliked the architecture and decoration of her youth, though as she grew older she found it valuable for her fiction. There is an air of reconciliation with what she had earlier despised; the brown stain and Eastlake gewgaws of her youth populate *The Age of Innocence* and *Old New York*. But as is clear in both the title and the resolution of *The Age of Innocence*, the high point of American design comes around 1900. Newland Archer's son, Dallas, becomes an architect and works for a firm like McKim, Mead & White or Charles Adams Platt. Dallas Archer is part of the classicism of the American Renaissance; he is designing a "Lakeside palace" for a young Chicago millionaire and thinks nothing of nipping abroad "to look at some Italian gardens." Newland Archer's library, which in the 1870s had been decorated in the "brown decade" style, has by 1907 been done over by his

View from the terrace, The Mount

son with "English mezzotints, Chippendale cabinets, [and] bits of blue-and-white." Sitting incongruously midst this high style was a memory of past innocence, an "old Eastlake writing table."[134]

Edith Wharton is perhaps the most purely visual writer America has produced. Even when the setting of a scene is not openly described, the reader has a strong sense of place. In building and furnishing the house of fiction, Edith had to reenact the collecting of materials or sources and had to imagine the rooms populated with characters. To Edith the descriptive elements of a building or a room's furnishings, and the impact of form, color, and setting, reveal character. She even asserted that "character and scenic detail are in fact one to the novelist who has fully assimilated his material."[135] Ellen Olenska and Undine Sprague, to take characters from two very different novels, *The Age of Innocence* and *The Custom of the Country*, respectively, are revealed through the rooms they inhabit. The discerning observer could understand them from just their rooms and furnishings. Certainly this is one of the reasons why Edith liked the interior scenes of Walter Gay, a fellow expatriate and old friend. Gay's paintings of unpeopled rooms are more than just renditions of elegant furnishings; they are psychological portraits of the society of rooms and the people who arranged and inhabited them. Critics at the time seemed to find in the inanimate objects he painted "memories, . . . a little soul of their own," for as one critic remarked, "He [Gay] has felt that a cracked wall of the past, a period table, an armchair worn out from use, seem to possess certain features similar to those of the human face, that change according to the time and the hour." They were rooms not unoccupied, but filled with personality and meaning.[136]

On one level Edith's interest in architecture, decoration, and furniture provided her with a wealth of detail for her novels, but there were deeper resonances, as an empathy existed between people and forms and space. In her short story "The Fullness of Life," contemporary with the work at Land's End in 1893, she writes:

> *I have sometimes thought that a woman's nature is like a great house full of rooms: there is the hall, through which everyone passes in going in and out; the drawing room, where one receives formal visits; the sitting room, where the members of the family come and go as they list; but beyond that, far beyond, are other rooms . . . and in the innermost room, the holy of holies, the soul sits alone and waits for a footstep that never comes.*[137]

Certainly a commentary on her marriage, the passage also shows that architecture as a metaphor had distinctly physical connotations and a sexual or erotic dimension.

The belief in the sensuous aspect of architecture, furniture, and decoration found a number of adherents at the turn of the century with whom Edith was well acquainted. Through Vernon Lee and also Bernard Berenson she came in contact with the German philosopher Theodor Lipps and the concept of *Einfühlung*, or empathy, and the belief that between objects and people a sympathy can exist.[138] Empathy had a strong following in the Anglo-American expatriate community; its strongest statement came from Berenson's secretary, Geoffrey Scott, in his book *The Architecture of Humanism*. For Scott, the goal of classical architecture was "to transcribe in stone the body's favorable states." The center of the classical tradition and the source of its greatness was this relationship to the human body, and it could therefore only be understood through empathy.[139]

Edith's fiction is filled with correspondences between people and the rooms they inhabit, and often they take on sexual meanings. In the novella *New Year's Day* Edith observes, "The most perilous coquetry may not be in a woman's way of arranging her dress but in her way of arranging her drawing-room." Here the subject is one of "those women" — a middle aged, striking though not beautiful, but vivacious woman who lives just on the edge of polite society. She is not *declassée*, but she creates a salon of male admirers of all ages and types. "Those women" attract men not with raw sexual power but rather through the aura they create: "The difference of atmosphere is felt on the very threshold." Their flowers even grow differently, and their "lamps and easy-chairs have found a clever way of coming together."[140] In *The Age of Innocence* Newland Archer is sexually aroused when he surveys Ellen Olenska's drawing room, which, through "the skilful use of a few properties, [had] been transformed into something intimate, 'foreign,' subtly suggestive of old romantic scenes and sentiments." A stretch of red damask, a delicate little Greek bronze, "bits of wreckage," thin-legged art furniture, and two Jacqueminot roses in a slender vase leave Newland Archer flat-footed, tongue-tied, and desperately in love with the Countess Olenska.[141]

Architecture, decoration, and furniture served as many purposes in Edith Wharton's life as in her fiction. The low state of American culture, and hence of architecture and the visual arts, were a great concern, and she worked hard to create an American Renaissance. Throughout her long and sexless marriage to Teddy, architecture and decoration acted as not just a diversion, but as erotic surrogates. Her passions and loves were poured into them, at Land's End, in New York, The Mount, and finally in France. But also in her travels and her writings, from *The Decoration of Houses* to *Old New York*, architecture and decoration are not simply settings for characters, but *are* character and a guide to action. Without an understanding of Edith's architectural enthusiasms, much of her fiction remains mute, only half understood. Here the role played by Ogden Codman is of central importance, for without their friendship both their lives and accomplishments would be very different.

Ogden and Edith maintained contact in France, and as the years passed some of the old tensions lessened and their rapport returned. They had apartments near each other on the rue de Varenne in Paris. Their social circuits coincided and letters continued to flow. In the 1930s Ogden had to admit that Edith achieved real successes with her gardens in both Lenox and France and wrote for advice. Surprisingly, he not only sought technical advice, such as how to keep lawns from being burned during the hot summer, but also asked questions about color and massing.[142] The Mount's plan and formal gardens would have an impact on Ogden's own La Leopolda. And *The Decoration of Houses* remained a real bond, and they considered reissuing it in an inexpensive edition.

But some things could never change between them. Old rivalries resurfaced when Walter Gay painted several silent portraits of the rooms at Edith's Pavillon Colombe (plate 12). Apparently Ogden was miffed that she received such attention, for to a friend he described her salon as "cold and Louis Philippe gray" and the furniture as "covered with quite the ugliest cretonne I ever saw, Chinese but much Europeanized flowers and hideous colour." Gossipy as ever, he reported, "[People] do not think she has much taste, no eye for colour. Alas I must agree to both." They are the words of a wounded ego, for he added, "And she is not clever enough to get some one to help her."[143] If Edith had known of the letter—which she apparently did not—she probably would have smiled. Ogden never changes: what a wonderful idea for a story!

NOTES

1. Edith Wharton, *A Backward Glance* (New York: D. Appleton-Century, 1934), 106.

2. Ogden Codman to Wharton, 18 April 1937, SPNEA.

3. Ogden Codman to Julian Sampson, 4 June 1937, BA.

4. For background, see Richard Guy Wilson, Dianne Pilgrim, and Richard Murray, *The American Renaissance, 1876–1917* (Brooklyn: The Brooklyn Museum and New York: Pantheon, 1979).

5. Bernard Berenson, "Preface to the First Edition of *Venetian Painters*," in his *Italian Painters of the Renaissance* (New York: Meridian, 1957 [1894]), v.

6. Charles Moore, *The Life and Times of Charles Follen McKim* (New York, 1929), 260.

7. For background I have relied primarily on R. W. B. Lewis, *Edith Wharton, A Biography* (New York: Harper & Row, 1975).

8. Henry James, letter to Howard Sturgis, 22 February 1912, quoted in Millicent Bell, *Edith Wharton & Henry James* (New York: Braziller, 1965), 180.

9. Lewis, *Wharton*, 47–48, 59–60, 101.

10. Ibid., 57.

11. Wharton, *Backward Glance*, 44.

12. Ibid., 54, 55.

13. Wharton, *Backward Glance*, 55.

14. Edith Wharton, "A Little Girl's New York," *Harper's* 176 (March 1938): 361, 358.

15. Wharton, *Backward Glance*, 8, 149, 70–71, 91; Lewis, *Wharton*, 43.

16. Wharton, *Backward Glance*, 149, 92–95; Lewis, *Wharton*, 56.

17. Paul R. Baker, *Richard Morris Hunt* (Cambridge: The MIT Press, 1980), 230.

18. [George William Sheldon], *Artistic Houses* (New York: D. Appleton, 1883–84), vol. 1 pt. 2, 135. See also Arnold Lewis, James Turner, and Steven McQuillin, *The Opulent Interiors of the Gilded Age: All 203 Photographs from "Artistic Houses" with New Text* (New York: Dover, 1987), 70–71.

19. Wharton, *Backward Glance*, 92–94.

20. Edith Wharton, *French Ways and Their Meaning* (New York: D. Appleton, 1919), 43.

21. Wharton, *Backward Glance*, 106; see also Lewis, *Wharton*, 68.

22. Edith Wharton to Ogden Codman, 8 May [1895], SPNEA, notes interior work still going on at Land's End. Lewis, *Wharton*, 68, claims Edith purchased Land's End in March 1893; however, Codman's account books indicate he was working there in 1892. Additionally, Ogden Codman to Arthur Little, 27 July 1891, SPNEA, mentions work at "the Wharton house." This could be reference to some work at Pencraig Cottage. The problems of dating exactly the work Codman did for the Whartons is difficult since he did not date his drawings and his account books are garbled and do not identify specific projects. The account books in the Codman Collection at the Metropolitan Museum of Art, New York, offer the following information:

[Extracted from accounts pertaining to individual clients]

| 1892 | Mr. E. R. Wharton | $5121.78 |
| 1892 | Mrs. E. R. Wharton | 1670.45 |

[extracted from fiscal year receipts]

1892	Mr. E. R. Wharton	$ 25.00
1893	"	726.00
1894	[no entry]	
1895	Mr. E. R. Wharton	117.86
1896	"	57.61
1897	"	99.00
1898	"	100.00
1899	"	133.25
1900	[no entry]	
1901	[no entry]	
1902	Mr. E. R. Wharton	2116.46
1903	"	1402.60
	[no further entries]	

From these entries, it is obvious that Codman did extensive work for the Whartons in 1892–93 at Land's End. The billing of most of the accounts to the husband was common practice at the time. The entries for 1895–99 probably relate to both Land's End and the Whartons' New York house. The last entries are for The Mount.

23. Daniel Marot, *Das Ornamentwerk des Daniel Marot* (Berlin: Ernst Wasmuth, 1892), pl. 71. Marot (c. 1663–1752) was a French designer whose work, originally published in a variety of editions in the eighteenth century, was collected and republished by Wasmuth in 1892. Codman's copy of Marot was a German edition which he evidently just purchased; it is currently owned by Pauline Metcalf.

24. Edith Wharton to Ogden Codman, 30 April 1897, SPNEA. Land's End has been drastically altered over the years and only small traces of the Wharton tenure remain; hence most of my analysis comes from contemporary photographs and a few surviving drawings.

25. Wharton, *Backward Glance*, 106.

26. Edith Wharton and Ogden Codman, Jr., *The Decoration of Houses* (New York: Charles Scribner's Sons, 1897, 115.

27. Edith Wharton to Ogden Codman, 24 May 1897, SPNEA.

28. Edith Wharton to Ogden Codman, n.d. [c. 1893]; Edward Wharton to Ogden Codman, May 1896; Jansen et Cie to Edith Wharton, 23 February 1895; all in SPNEA. The identification of the furniture purchased abroad comes from *Lenox Life*, 9 August 1902, 1.

29. For a summary of Codman's billings to the Whartons, see note 22 above. Photographs of the interior are in Edith Wharton Collection, Yale University, New Haven. Drawings are at Avery. Relevant yet unrevealing letters are: Wharton, letters to Codman, 29 June 1896, and 20 November 1896, SPNEA. From these letters it is apparent that no work had begun. See also, Lewis, *Wharton*, 67.

30. Wharton, *Backward Glance*, 107. Some of this material appeared in my essay " 'The Decoration of Houses' and Scientific Eclecticism," *Victorian Furniture*, ed. Kenneth L. Ames (Philadelphia: The Victorian Society, 1982), 193–204.

31. Florence Codman, *The Clever Young Boston Architect* (Augusta, ME: Privately printed, 1970), 2.

32. Vernon Lee, *Studies of the Eighteenth Century in Italy* (London: T. F. Unwin, 1880).

33. Edith Wharton to Ogden Codman, 17 April 1896, SPNEA.

34. Edith Wharton to Ogden Codman, 29 June and 23 August 1896, SPNEA.

35. Edith Wharton to Ogden Codman, 11 July 1899, SPNEA.

36. Edith Wharton to Ogden Codman, 2 May 1897, SPNEA.

37. Edith Wharton, "The Valley of Childish Things, And Other Emblems," *The Century* 52 (July 1896): 467–69.

38. Wharton, *Backward Glance*, 107–8.

39. Edith Wharton to Ogden Codman, 20 February 1897, SPNEA.

40. Edith Wharton to Ogden Codman, 15 March 1897, SPNEA.

41. Wharton, *Backward Glance*, 108.

42. Edith Wharton to Ogden Codman, 9 May 1897, SPNEA.

43. Wharton, *Backward Glance*, 110.

44. The fifty-six original plates were reproduced in all the reprintings of *The Decoration* except, unfortunately, the most recent one by W. W. Norton Company in the Classical American Series. See note 77 below.

45. Marot, *Das Ornamentwerk*, pl. 29; a statement by Updike about his participation is quoted in Percy Lubbock, *Portrait of Edith Wharton* (New York: A. Appleton-Century, 1947), 18; see also Lewis, *Wharton*, 77–79.

46. Edith Wharton to Ogden Codman, n.d. [1897 is written in], SPNEA.

47. Edith Wharton to Ogden Codman, n.d., SPNEA.

48. Edith Wharton to Ogden Codman, Thursday [June 1897], SPNEA.

49. Edith Wharton to Ogden Codman, 9 November 1897, SPNEA.

50. Edith Wharton to Ogden Codman, Saturday [c. 6 February 1897], SPNEA.

51. Charles McKim to Ogden Codman, 19 February, 31 March, and 9 April, 1897, McKim Collection, Library of Congress. See also Katherine Boyd Menz and Donald McTernan, "Decorating for the Frederick Vanderbilts," *Nineteenth Century* 3 (Winter 1977): 44–50.

52. Moore, *McKim*, 161, 168.

53. Edith Wharton to Charles McKim, Wednesday [January 1897], Edith Wharton Collection, Manuscripts Room, New York Public Library.

54. Edith Wharton to Ogden Codman, Saturday [February 1897], SPNEA.

55. McKim's reply is a three-page typed "Memoranda," with "to Mrs. Wharton" penciled in at the top. It is bound into his letter copy book, and the surrounding letters are dated 2 February and 5 February 1897. McKim Collection, Library of Congress. McKim apparently sent the typed "Memoranda" with a personal handwritten note that has not survived. See also "Wheatleigh, House of H. H. Cook, Esq., Lenox," *American Architect* 76 (5 April 1902):pl. 1371.

56. *Decoration of Houses*, 1, 9.

57. McKim, "Memoranda."

58. Andrew Jackson Downing, *The Architecture of Country Houses* (New York, 1850); and Marianna Griswold Van Rensselaer, "Recent Architecture in the United States, VI. City Dwellings, II," *The Century Magazine* 31 (March 1886): 685–86.

59. *Decoration of Houses*, 4, 77, 8, 49, 58, 82.

60. Ibid., xix.

61. Ibid., 198.

62. Ibid., 6–8, xix, pl. II and IV.

63. Scientific eclecticism is explored in greater detail in Wilson, et al., *The American Renaissance*, ch. 4. Some of my thinking has been influenced by Edgar Kaufmann, Jr., "Nineteenth-Century Design," *Perspecta* 6 (1960): 56–67.

64. Codman deposited part of his extensive library with the Curator of Prints at the Metropolitan Museum of Art. The "Temporary Receipt" dated 20 April 1920 is 39 pages long and lists over 500 separate volumes, many scrapbooks of photographs, along with "64 bundles" and "202 loose" photographs and books of drawings. A few books, such as Marot, are not listed; see note 24 above. All of the books noted in the Coolidge drawing are on the Metropolitan Museum list.

65. JBB [Draughtsman], "Drawing #7-Full Scale detail of woodwork in drawing room, House J. Randolph Coolidge, 147 Beacon Street, Ogden Codman, Jr., October 18, 1895," SPNEA.

66. *Decoration of Houses*, xx, 128, 117, 2, 9, 28. See Caroll L. V. Meeks, "Picturesque Eclecticism," *The Art Bulletin* 32 (September 1950): 226–35.

67. Wharton, *Backward Glance*, 140–41; Edith Wharton, "A Tuscan Shrine," *Scribner's* 17 (January 1895):22–32; reprinted in Wharton, *Italian Backgrounds* (New York: Scribner's, 1905), 83–104; Wharton, "The Pelican," in, Wharton, *The Greater Inclination* (New York: Scribner's, 1899), 23. See also Lewis, *Wharton*, 72–73; Denys Sutton, "The Sharp Eye of Edith Wharton," *Apollo* 103 (January 1976):2–12; Ernest Samuels, *Bernard Berenson: The Making of a Connoisseur* (Cambridge: Harvard University Press, 1979), 47, 72–75, 86–95, 125, 161, passim; and David Alan Brown, *Berenson and the Connoisseurship of Italian Painting* (Washington, D.C.: National Gallery of Art, 1979).

68. *Decoration of Houses*, 34, 31.

69. Ibid., 196, 198, 175.

70. Scott Marshall suggested this parallel to me.

71. *The Nation* 65 (16 December 1897): 485.

72. *Advertiser* (Boston, Mass.), 21 December 1897, clipping in Codman Files, SPNEA 75.

73. E. B. B., "A New Book on Interior Decoration," *Architectural Review* 5 (10 March 1898): 20; "Literature. Hints for home Decoration," *The Critic* (April 1898): 161; *Book Buyer* 16 (March 1898): 129.

74. "Have Art With Comfort at Home," *New York Herald*, 23 January 1898.

75. Walter Berry, "The Decoration of Houses," *The Bookman* 7 (April 1898): 161–63.

76. "Books and Papers," *The American Architect* 59 (22 January 1899): 28.

77. *The Decoration of Houses* was reprinted in London: B. T. Batsford, 1898; New York: Scribner's, 1902, 1919, and Norton, 1978. As noted in note 44 this last edition does not reprint the original plates. A note in the Codman paper at SPNEA reports that as of 13 March 1913, 3580 copies had been sold in the United States and 605 abroad. To which edition(s) this refers is unknown.

78. W. J. Loftie, letter to Wharton, 3 January 1898, SPNEA; Reginald Blomfield, letter to Wharton, 20 January 1898, SPNEA. See also John Fowler and John Cornforth, *English Decoration in the 18th Century* (Princeton: Pyne Press, 1974).

79. Elsie de Wolfe, *The House in Good Taste* (New York: The Century Co., 1913), 268, ch. 2. On the authorship of the book, see Jane S. Smith, *Elsie de Wolfe* (New York: Atheneum, 1982), 142.

80. Wharton, *Backward Glance*, 112.

81. McKim, letter to John Cadwalader, 12 December 1903; McKim, letter to Wharton, 16 December 1903, both in Library of Congress.

82. Edith Wharton to Ogden Codman, 17 December 1897, SPNEA. Codman claimed in 1898 that he had written a manuscript on gardens, but nothing ever came of it. See Edith Wharton to Ogden Codman, 6 December 1898, SPNEA: "I am anxious to see your m. s. you know I have always done that, and I will give you all the help I can."

83. Edith Wharton to Ogden Codman, 1 August 1900, SPNEA.

84. Edith Wharton, "The Duchess at Prayer," *Scribner's* 28 (August 1900): 155.

85. Edith Wharton, *Italian Villas and Their Gardens* (New York: The Century Company, 1904), 5. See also Coy Ludwig, *Maxfield Parrish* (New York: Watson-Guptill, 1973), 32, and 206, 208 for publishing history.

86. Edith Wharton to Ogden Codman, 1 August 1900, SPNEA.

87. Lewis, *Wharton*, 93, 100, 110. The initial 113 acres cost $40,600. In February 1902 a $50,000

mortgage for the house was taken out. The Hoppin and Koen Billbooks, Avery Library, Columbia University, New York, show the house's contract price as $41,000, the stables, $14,000, and the gate lodge, $4,580. The "extras" added to the price, and the cost of the house was about $57,000, the stables about $20,000, and the gate lodge about $5,200. The architect's commission was probably ten percent. What she paid Codman is indicated in note 22 above. The cost of the gardens is unknown.

88. Wharton, *Backward Glance*, 143, 124, 106; Edith Wharton, "The Line of Least Resistance," *Lippincott's Magazine* 66 (October 1900): 559–70; and "The Twilight of the God," in Edith Wharton, *The Greater Inclination* (New York: Scribner's, 1899).

89. Wharton, *Backward Glance*, 124; Bell, *Edith Wharton & Henry James*, ch. 3. On the Berkshires as a summer resort, see Cleveland Amory, *The Last Resorts* (New York: Grosset & Dunlap, 1952), passim; Donald T. Oakes, ed., *A Pride of Palaces: Lenox Summer Cottages 1883–1933* (Lenox: Lenox Library Association, 1981); *Picturesque Berkshire* (Northampton, MA: Picturesque Berkshire Pub. Co., 1893); and Rollin H. Cooke, *Art Work of Berkshire County* (Pittsfield, MA: Gravure Illustration Co., 1900).

90. Henry James, *The American Scene* (New York: Harper, 1907), 40, 48.

91. Ogden Codman to Sarah B. F. Codman, 25 February 1901, SPNEA.

92. Ogden Codman to Sarah Codman, 9 March 1901, SPNEA.

93. Ogden Codman to Sarah Codman, 25 February 1901 and 19 March 1901, SPNEA.

94. Edith Wharton to Ogden Codman, 25 March 1901; Ogden Codman to Sarah Codman, 25 March 1901 and 1 July 1901, SPNEA.

95. Ogden Codman to Sarah Codman, 1 July 1901, SPNEA. For examples of Hoppin's renderings, see Wilson, et al., *The American Renaissance*, 6, 71, 206.

96. Wendy Baker, David Bennett, and Diane Dierkes, *A Landscape Architectural Analysis and Master Plan for The Mount* (Cambridge: Harvard Graduate School of Design, 1982), 54; Lewis, *Wharton*, 110.

97. See note 55 above and *Decoration of Houses*, 4.

98. Lewis, *Wharton*, 100, claims that she had visited Belton.

99. "Three Houses at Aiken, F. C. Hoppin & Koen, Architect," *Architectural Review* [Boston] 9 (September 1902): 114.

100. [H. Avary Tipping], "Belton House, Grantham," *Country Life* 4 (24 September and 1 October 1898): 368–72, 400–3; reprinted in [H. Avary Tipping], *In English Homes* (London: Country Life, 1904), vol. 1, 1–9. He claims Wren is the architect. Colin Campbell, *Vitruvius Britannicus, or The British Architect* (London, 1715), vol. 2, pl. 37, 38. Recent research has named William Winde as architect and William Stanton as contractor. Some of the carvings are still assigned to Gibbons. See John Cornforth, "Belton House, Lincolnshire," *Country Life* 136 (3, 10, 17 September 1964): 562–65, 620–24, 700–3.

101. Either Codman's sketch plans are backward or he was placing the house differently on the site.

102. James, *The American Scene*, 38–39, says the white painted houses are typically New England. While Hoppin's drawings do not show shutters, they were planned from the beginning.

103. Drawings for The Mount are in the Hoppin and Koen Collection, Avery Library, Columbia University, New York, New York, and also at The Mount.

104. Ogden Codman to Sarah Codman, 1 January 1902, SPNEA. At The Mount are Codman's drawings for the dining room, den, and library; presumably he is responsible for the other rooms.

105. Edith Wharton to Ogden Codman, 31 December 1901, SPNEA. For some of the following analysis of the interior, I have relied on Amelia Alexandra Peck, "Restoration Plan for the Interior of The Mount, Lenox, Massachusetts," M.A. Thesis, Columbia University, 1984.

106. Wharton, *Backward Glance*, 110.

107. *Decoration of Houses*, 17.

108. MacMonnies's *Pan* was originally done for the Edward D. Adams estate, Rohallion, in Seabright, New Jersey, 1889. McKim, Mead & White were the architects and commissioned the sculpture. It was then reproduced in copyrighted casts for wider sale.

109. *Decoration of Houses*, 138, 117.

110. " 'The Mount' in Lenox," *Berkshire Resort Topics*, 10 September 1904, 1, gives a description of the furnishings.

111. *Resort Topics*; *Decoration of Houses*, 123–26.

112. *Decoration of Houses*, 159.

113. Ibid., 150.

114. Lewis, *Wharton*, 111; *Lenox Life*, 20 September 1902, 5, and 27 September 1902, 1.

115. Hoppin's drawings for an extension at The Mount date from September 1907. The problems of the poor construction are evident to any visitor to The Mount today.

116. Ogden Codman to Sarah Codman, 8 October 1902, SPNEA.

117. Diana Balmori, Diane Kostial McGuire, and Eleanor M. McPeck, *Beatrix Farrand's American Landscapes* [Sagaponack, NY: Sagapress, 1985), 31, 198, fig. 11; and Baker, et al., *Landscape Architectural Analysis*, 49–50. Scott Marshall has discovered that Beatrix Jones Farrand was in Lenox in July 1901. See also Hildegarde Hawthorne, *The Lure of the Garden* (New York: Century, 1911), 135–36.

118. Information from Scott Marshall.

119. Edith Wharton, *Diary*, Edith Wharton Papers, Beinecke Library, Yale University, New Haven, CT.

120. Hawthorne, *The Lure of the Garden*, 135–36.

121. Henry James to Howard Sturgis, 17 October 1904. He repeated the "French château" description and added, "filled exclusively with old French and Italian furniture and decorations." In James to Jessie Allen, 22 October 1904. Both letters are reprinted in *Henry James Letters*, ed. Leon Edel (Cambridge: Harvard University Press, 1984), vol. 4, 325, 329. James also wrote, "I am very happy here, surrounded by every loveliness of nature & every luxury of art & treated with a benevolence that brings tears to my eyes." Quoted in Bell, *Edith Wharton & Henry James*, 92.

122. Quoted in Baker, et al., *Landscape Architectural Analysis*, 57; Mrs. Daniel Chester French, *Memoirs of a Sculptor's Wife* (Boston: Houghton, Mifflin, 1928), 205–6; and "The Lenox Cottagers," *Berkshire Resort Topics*, 23 July 1904, 6, and 6 August 1904, 6.

123. Edith Wharton, *The House of Mirth* (New York: Scribner's, 1905), 39, 137.

124. Edith Wharton, *Ethan Frome* (New York: Scribner's, 1911, 1922), 20, vi.

125. Wharton, *Backward Glance*, 125; Baker, et al., *Landscape Architectural Analysis*, 48.

126. Saunders, Webb & Worcester [Codman's lawyers] to Edward Wharton, 23 January 1905, and Edith Wharton to Saunders, Webb & Worcester, 2 February 1905, SPNEA.

127. Louis Auchincloss, *Edith Wharton* (New York: Viking, 1971), 141.

128. Lewis, *Wharton*, 78; Wharton, *Backward Glance*, 28.

129. Wharton, "A Little Girl's New York," 357.

130. Wharton, *Italian Backgrounds*, 177.

131. Edith Wharton to Sara Norton, quoted in Lewis, *Wharton*, 143.

132. Edith Wharton, *The Writing of Fiction* (New York: Scribner's, 1925), 85.

133. Wharton, *French Ways*, 38–40.

134. Edith Wharton, *The Age of Innocence* (New York: D. Appleton, 1920), 349, 347.

135. Wharton, *Writing of Fiction*, 84.

136. Henri Lavedan, *Paintings and Water Colors by Walter Gay* (New York: E. Gimpel & Wildenstein, 1920), n. p., quoted in Gary A. Reynolds, *Walter Gay* (New York: Gray Art Gallery, New York University, 1980), 67. See also, Albert Eugene Gallatin, ed. *Walter Gay* (New York: Dutton, 1920).

137. Wharton, "The Fullness of Life," *Scribner's* 14 (December 1893): 700; reprinted in *The Collected Short Stories of Edith Wharton*, 14.

138. Vernon Lee, *The Beautiful: An Introduction to Psychological Aesthetics* (Cambridge: Cambridge University Press, 1913); Vernon Lee with C. Anstruther Thomson, *Beauty*

and Ugliness (London: John Lane, 1912); and Theodor Lipps, *Asthetik; psychologie des Schonenund der Kunst* (Hamburg: L. Voxx, 1903–6).

139. Geoffrey Scott, *The Architecture of Humanism* (New York: Scribner's, [1914], 1969), 177. See also Iris Origo, *Images and Shadows, Part of a Life* (New York: Harcourt Brace Jovanovich, 1970), 103–4, passim.

140. Edith Wharton, *New Year's Day*, in *Old New York* (New York: Scribner's, 1924), 296.

141. Edith Wharton, *The Age of Innocence*, 71–72.

142. Ogden Codman to Edith Wharton, 25 February, 12 March 1934 and 15 July 1935, and Edith Wharton to Ogden Codman, 8 March 1934, 12 July 1935, BA.

143. Ogden Codman to ? [fragment], c. 10 August 1931, SPNEA.

Selected Bibliography

PRIMARY MATERIAL

ARCHIVAL SOURCES

Avery Architectural and Fine Arts Library, Columbia University, New York, New York
Architectural Plans and Drawings of Ogden Codman; The Hoppin & Koen Collection

Beinecke Rare Book Library, Yale University, New Haven, Connecticut
Edith Wharton Collection

The Boston Athenæum, Boston, Massachusetts
Ogden Codman Manuscript Collection

The Edith Wharton Restoration, Inc., Lenox, Massachusetts

The Grange, Lincoln, Massachusetts
Codman Family Residence, Property of the Society for the Preservation of New England Antiquities

Houghton Library, Harvard University, Cambridge, Massachusetts
Rare Books and Manuscripts, Norton Family Collection

The Lenox Library Photograph Archive, Lenox, Massachusetts

Library of Congress, Washington, D.C.
Charles Follen McKim Collection

The Metropolitan Museum of Art, Department of Prints and Photographs, New York, New York
The Ogden Codman Collection. Business Letters 1–5, 1894–1908; account books 1–2; office checkbook stubs #1–8; plans of country houses, eight boxes containing renderings, photographs, furniture designs, and miscellaneous material

The Nassau County Museum of Fine Art Photograph Archive, Roslyn, New York

The Preservation Society of Newport County, Newport, Rhode Island

The Society for the Preservation of New England Antiquities, Boston, Massachusetts
Ogden Codman Jr. Architectural Collection, Codman Family Manuscripts Collection and the Codman Family Photograph Collection

The University of California at Berkeley, Berkeley, California
College of Environmental Design
Reef Point Collection

INTERVIEWS

Audrey Maynard Auchincloss; interviewed at her house in Newport, Rhode Island, September 1977.

Curtis Chapin, interviewed at "The Grange," Lincoln, Massachusetts, March 1977, May 1977, April 1978.

Florence Codman, interviewed at her apartment, New York, New York, March 1977.

Stuart A. Drake, interviewed at his apartment, Boston, Massachusetts, May 1977.

Margaret Henderson Floyd, interviewed at The Grange, Lincoln, Massachusetts, April, 1978.

David McKibbin, interviewed at The Boston Athenæum, Boston, Massachusetts, May 1977.

William Pahlman, interviewed at the Plaza Hotel, New York, New York, November 1981.

SECONDARY MATERIAL

BOOKS

Amory, Cleveland. *The Last Resorts*. New York: Grosset & Dunlap, 1952.

Auchincloss, Louis. *Edith Wharton; a Woman in her Time*. New York: Viking Press, 1971.

Baker, Paul R. *Richard Morris Hunt*. Cambridge: The MIT Press, 1980.

Baker, Wendy, David Bennett and Diane Dierkes *A Landscape Architectural Analysis and Master Plan for The Mount*. Cambridge: Harvard Graduate School of Design, 1982.

Balmori, Diana, Diane Kostial McGuire and Eleanor M. McPeck. *Beatrix Farrand's American Landscapes*. Sagaponack, NY: Sagapress, 1985.

Bunting, Bainbridge. *Houses of Boston's Back Bay*. Cambridge: The Belknap Press of Harvard University, 1967.

Codman, Florence. *The Clever Young Boston Architect*. Augusta, ME: Privately printed, 1970.

Codman, Ogden. *Gravestone Insciptions and Records of Tomb Burials in the Granary Burying Ground, Boston*. Salem, MA: The Essex Institute, 1918.

———. *Index of Obituaries in Boston Newspapers, 1704– 1800*. Boston: G. K. Hall & Co., 1968.

———. *La Leopolda: A Description*. Paris: N. R. Money, 1939.

Codman, Richard. *Reminiscences of Richard Codman, 1923*. Boston: Privately printed, 1923.

De Wolfe, Elsie. *The House in Good Taste*. New York: The Century Co., 1913.

Downing, Andrew Jackson. *The Architecture of Country Houses*. New York, 1850.

Downing, Antoinette F. and Vincent Scully. *The Architectural Heritage of Newport, Rhode Island, 1640– 1915*. New York: Bramhall House, 1952.

Edel Leon. *The Life of Henry James, the Master: 1901– 1916*. New York: Avon Books, 1972.

Ferree, Barr. *American Estates and Gardens*. New York: Munn & Co., 1906.

Fowler, John and John Cornforth. *English Decoration in the 18th Century*. London: Barrie & Jenkins, 1974.

Gallatin, Albert Eugene (editor). *Walter Gay*. New York: Dutton, 1920.

Gay, E. Howard. *A Chippendale Romance*. New York: Longmans, Green & Co., 1915.

Hawthorne, Hildegarde. *The Lure of the Garden*. New York: Century, 1911.

James, Henry. *The American Scene*. New York: Harper, 1907.

Jourdain, Margaret. *English Interior Decoration 1500– 1830*. London: B. T. Batsford Ltd., 1950.

Kimball, Fiske. *Domestic Architecture of the American Colonies and the Early Republic*. New York: Charles Scribner's Sons, 1922 [Dover Publications, 1966].

Kirker, Harold. *Thee Architecture of Charles Bulfinch*. Cambridge: Harvard University Press, 1969.

Lewis, Arnold, James Turner and Steven McQuillin. *The Opulent Interiors of the Gilded Age: All 203 Photographs from "Artistic Houses" with New Text*. New York: Dover, 1987.

Lewis, R. W. B. *Edith Wharton, A Biography*. New York: Harper & Row, 1975.

Lowell, Guy. *American Gardens*. Boston: Bates & Guild Co. 1902.

Maher, James T. *The Twilight of Splendour*. Boston: Little, Brown & Company, 1975.

Marot, Daniel. *Das Ornamentwerk des Daniel Marot*. Berlin: Ernst Wasmuth, 1892.

Moore, Charles. *The Life and Times of Charles Follen McKim*. Boston and New York: Houghton Mifflin Company, 1929.

Oakes, Donald T. (editor). *A Pride of Palaces, Lenox Summer Cottages 1883–1933*. Lenox: Lenox Library Association, 1981.

Paine, James. *Plans, Elevations and Sections of Noblemen and Gentlemen's Houses*. Volume II. Farnsborough, England, 1793.

Percier, Charles and Pierre François Léonard Fontaine. *Recueil de décorations intérieures, comprenant tout ce qui à rapport à l'ameublement*. Paris: Privately printed, 1812.

Picturesque Berkshire. Northampton, MA: Picturesque Berkshire Publishing Co., 1893.

Reynolds, Gary A. *Walter Gay*. New York: Gray Art Gallery, New York University, 1980.

Richardson, A. E. and C. Lovett Gill. *London Houses from 1660 to 1820*. London: B. T. Batesford, 1911.

Schoy, Auguste. *L'Art architectural décoratif, industriel et somputaire de l'époque Louis XVI*. Paris, 1868.

Sheldon, George William. *Artistic Houses*. Volume I. New York: D. Appleton, 1883–84.

Smith, Jane S. *Elsie de Wolfe*. New York: Atheneum, 1982.

Thornton, Peter. *Authentic Decor: The Domestic Interior, 1620–1920*. New York: Viking, 1984.

[Tipping, H. Avary] *In English Homes*. Volume I. London: Country Life, 1904.

Wharton, Edith. *Italian Villas and Their Gardens*. New York: The Century Company, 1904.

———. *The House of Mirth*. New York: Charles Scribner's Sons, 1905.

———. *Italian Backgrounds*. New York: Charles Scribner's Sons, 1905.

———. *Ethan Frome*. New York: Charles Scribner's Sons, 1911, 1922.

———. *French Ways and Their Meaning*. New York: D. Appleton, 1919.

———. *The Age of Innocence*. New York: D. Appleton, 1920.

———. *A Backward Glance*. New York: D. Appleton-Century, 1934.

——— and Ogden Codman. *The Decoration of Houses*. New York: Charles Scribner's Sons, 1897.

Wilson, Richard Guy, Diane Pilgrim, and Richard Murray. *The American Renaissance, 1876–1917*. Brooklyn and New York: The Brooklyn Museum and Pantheon, 1979.

PERIODICALS

American Architect and Building News (18 October 1902).

Ames, Winslow. "The Transformation of Chateau-sur-Mer." *The Journal of the Society of Architectural Historians* 29:4 (December 1970):290–306.

Architectural Review 12 (1905).

Berry, Walter. "The Decoration of Houses." *The Bookman* 7 (April 1898):161–63.

Book Buyer 16 (March 1898):129.

"Books and Papers, Review of *The Decoration of Houses* by Edith Wharton and Ogden Codman." *American Architect and Building News* (22 January 1898):28–29.

Chapin, R. Curtis. "Excavating an Italian Garden in America." *Horticulture* (November 1975):39–44.

"The Country Home of John D. Rockefeller, Esq." *House Beautiful* (June 1909):1–9.

Country Life (19 January 1929).

E. B. B. "A New Book on Interior Decoration." *Architectural Review* 5 (10 March 1898):20.

Ferree, Barr. "Notable American Homes- The Summer House of Oliver Ames, Esq., Prides Crossing, Massachusetts." *American Homes and Gardens* (February 1906):83–87.

———. "Notable American Homes—'The Homestead'; The Home of Nathaniel Thayer, Esq. Lancaster, Massachusetts." *American Homes and Gardens* (May 1906):299–304.

" 'Hautbois'—The House of Mrs. Walter E. Maynard on Long Island." *Vogue* (13 October 1930):76–77.

"House for E. V. R. Thayer, Esq., Lancaster, Mass." *American Architect and Building News* 99 (20 September 1911):n.p.

Ivins, William Jr. "The Ogden Codman Library," *Bulletin of the Metropolitan Museum of Art* (November 1920):250–53.

Kaufman, Edgar Jr. "Nineteenth Century Design." *Perspecta* 6 (1960):56–67.

"The Lenox Cottagers." *Berkshire Resort Topics* (23 July 1904 and 6 August 1904).

"Literature. Hints for Home Decoration." *The Critic* (April 1898):161.

McGinty, Sarah M. "Houses and Interiors as Characters in Edith Wharton's Novels." *Nineteenth Century* 5:1 (Spring 1979):48–51.

Meeks, Carroll L. V. "Picturesque Electicism." *Art Bulletin* 32 (September 1950):226–35.

Menz, Katherine Boyd and Donald McTernan. "Decorating for the Frederick Vanderbilts." *Nineteenth Century* 3 (Winter 1977):44–50.

Metcalf, Pauline C. "The Interiors of Ogden Codman, Jr. in Newport." *Antiques* 108 (September 1980):486–97.

———. "Ogden Codman and The Grange." *Old Time New England* 71 (1981):68–83.

———. "Victorian Profile: Ogden Codman, Jr. A Clever Young Boston Architect." *Nineteenth Century* 7:1 (Spring 1981):45–47.

———. "The Bryce/Frick Estate: A Reflection of the English Country House on Long Island, 1900–1920." *The House and Garden*, with essays by Pauline C. Metcalf and Valencia Libby. Roslyn, NY: Nassau County Museum of Fine Art, 1986.

———. "Elegance without Excess." *Bulletin of The Preservation League of New York* (Winter 1986).

Monkhouse, Christopher. "Napoleon in Rhode Island." *Antiques* (January 1978):190–202.

" 'The Mount' in Lenox." *Berkshire Resort Topics* 2 (10 September 1904):1.

"Ogden Codman." *Proceedings of the American Antiquarian Society* 61 (1952):14–16.

Patterson, Augusta Owen. "American Architect's European Masterpiece." *Town and Country* (1 September 1947).

"Some Interesting Interiors." *Architectural Record* (July 1906):51–59.

Sturges, Walter Knight "Arthur Little and the Colonial Revival." *The Journal of the Society of Architectural Historians* 32:2 (May 1973):147–63.

Sutton, Denys. "The Sharp Eye of Edith Wharton." *Apollo* 103 (January 1976):2–12.

[Tipping, H. Avary]. "Belton House, Grantham." *Country Life* 4 (24 September and 1 October 1898):368–72, 400–3.

———. "Goodmersham Park, Kent, the Property of Lord Masham." *Country Life* 48 (6 November 1920):596–603.

Van Rensselaer, Marianna Griswold. "Recent Architecture in the United States, VI. City Dwellings, II." *The Century Magazine* 31 (March 1886):677–87.

Whitehill, Walter Muir. "Introduction" to *Index of Obituaries in Boston Newspapers, 1704–1800*. Compiled by Ogden Codman. Boston: G. K. Hall & Co., 1968.

"Wheatleigh, House of H. H. Cook, Esq., Lenox." *American Architect* 76 (5 April 1902):n.p.

Wilson, Richard Guy. " 'The Decoration of Houses' and Scientific Eclecticism." *Victorian Furniture*, edited by Kenneth L. Ames. Philadelphia: The Victorian Society, 1982.

UNPUBLISHED MATERIAL

Drake, Stuart, A. "Ogden Codman Jr. 1863–1951." Thesis, Harvard University, 1973.

Peck, Amelia Alexandra. "Restoration Plan for the Interior of The Mount, Lenox, Massachusetts." M.A. Thesis, Columbia University, 1984.

Appendixes

CHRONOLOGY

1862	Edith Wharton born

1863 January 19, Ogden Codman, Jr., is born to Ogden Codman, Sr., and Sarah Fletcher Bradlee Codman in the house of his maternal grandfather, James Bowdoin Bradlee, 34 Beacon Street, Boston

1867 Frank Lloyd Wright born

1872 November 9–10, the Great Fire of Boston destroys 770 buildings on 65 acres of land, including many Codman properties

1874–84 Having lost much of its financial investment in real estate, the Codman family moves to Dinard, France

1882 Apprentices in a banking firm in Bonn, Germany, then briefly returns to Boston, where he lives with his uncle, architect John Hubbard Sturgis

1883–84 Enrolls as a special student at the MIT School of Architecture

1884–86 McKim, Mead & White build the Henry A. C. Taylor house in Newport, considered the first full colonial revival structure

1886–87 Joins the architectural firm of Andrews, Jacques and Rantoul, where he meets fellow apprentice Herbert W. C. Browne and Browne's future partner, Arthur Little

1887–95 McKim, Mead & White build the new Boston Public Library at Copley Square

Begins to record many important eighteenth-century houses in Boston, New York, Philadelphia, and Washington, via photographs and measured drawings

1891 Opens first office at 100 Chestnut Street, Boston

1893 Edith Wharton purchases Land's End in Newport and commissions Codman to make alterations to the exterior and interior

1893 World's Columbian Exposition is held in Chicago, establishing a widespread revival of monumental classicism in planning, architecture, and painting in America

1894	Cornelius Vanderbilt II commissions Codman to design and decorate the second floor and third-floor bedrooms of The Breakers, Newport
1897	December 3, publication of *The Decoration of Houses* by Edith Wharton and Ogden Codman
	Opens an office in New York City at 5 West 16th Street and a branch at 18 Bellevue Avenue; also listed as an interior decorator at 53 State Street, Room 1036, Boston
1900	Rents house in Newport at 119 Gibbs Avenue for the summer
1904	October 8, marries Leila Howard Griswold of Troy, New York
1907	Begins compiling *A Catalogue Raisonné of French Châteaux*, eventually to reach 36,000 photographs and 400 notebooks containing illustrations and measured drawings
1908	Elected to the Colonial Society of Massachusetts
1909	Château Corbeil Cerf, Seine-et-Oise, near Paris, is rented for summer occupancy
1910	January 21, death of wife, Leila, at age 54
1911–12	Sells the 51st Street town house in New York
1912	Builds 7 East 96th Street, New York; leases an apartment at 60 rue de Varenne in Paris

1893	Charles Adams Platt publishes *Italian Gardens*
1902	MacMillan plan for Washington, D.C.
	Frank Lloyd Wright introduces Prairie style architecture with the Willard Willits house, Highland Park, Illinois
1903	Isabella Stewart Gardner Museum opens in Boston
1904	Edith Wharton publishes *Italian Villas and Their Gardens*
1905	Elsie de Wolfe, Elizabeth Marbury, and Annie Morgan purchase the Villa Trianon, Versailles
1908	The term "Cubism" is coined by Henri Matisse to describe developments in French abstract painting
1912	Elsie de Wolfe publishes *The House in Good Taste*
	The Titanic sinks off the coast of Newfoundland
1913	The Armory show is held in New York, introducing Cubism and Fauvism to an American audience
	Edith and Teddy Wharton divorce

1915–16	Resides in Ipswich, Massachusetts for the summer	1914–18	World War I
		1916	Henry James dies

1915–16 Resides in Ipswich, Massachusetts for the summer

1917 The Essex Institute, Salem, prints two hundred copies of his *Gravestone Inscriptions and Records of Tomb Burials in the Central Burying Ground, Boston Common and Inscriptions in the South Burying Ground, Boston*

1914–18 World War I

1916 Henry James dies

1920 Closes New York Office and moves to France

Arranges for The Grange estate in Lincoln to pass to the Society for the Preservation of New England Antiquities, founded by William Sumner Appleton, upon the death of the last Codman heir

1920 Museum of Modern Art under construction in New York

1920–29 Leases Villa Francesca, Cannes

1921 Edith Wharton awarded the Pulitzer Prize for her novel, *Age of Innocence*, granted to it instead of Sinclair Lewis's *Main Street*

1924 Occupies Château de Péthagny, Calvados

1925 First Exposition International des Arts Décoratifs et Industriels Modernes is held in Paris

1926 Purchases Château de Grégy at Brie-Comte-Robert, southwest of Paris

1927 Le Corbusier builds Les Terrasses, a villa at Garches, Seine-et-Oise, France based on abstract functionalism

1929–31 Builds La Leopolda at Villefranche-sur-Mer on the Riviera; domaine purchased from King Leopold of Belgium

1929 Wall Street stock market crash results in Great Depression of the 1930s

1934 Edith Wharton publishes her memoirs, *A Backward Glance*

1937 Edith Wharton dies at her home, Pavillon Colombe, France

1939–45 World War II

1951 January 8, dies at Château de Grégy

1968 The Grange is bequeathed to the Society for the Preservation of New England Antiquities, following the death of Dorothy Codman

1978 *The Decoration of Houses* is reprinted as a cornerstone in the Classical America series in Art and Architecture

MEASURED DRAWINGS BY OGDEN CODMAN

MASSACHUSETTS

James Bowdoin Bradlee house, Boston
Architect unknown

Thomas Amory (Ticknor) house, Park Street, Boston
Charles Bulfinch, 1803–4

Humphreys-Higginson houses, Boston
Charles Bulfinch, 1805–8

Harrison Gray Otis house, 45 Beacon Street, Boston
Charles Bulfinch, 1805–8

Old Tremont Street houses, Colonnade Row, Boston
Charles Bulfinch, 1810–12

David Sears house, Boston
Alexander Parris, 1819–22

Apthorpe house, Brighton
Architect unknown

Swan house, Dorchester
Charles Bulfinch, c. 1796

Codman Family house, The Grange, Lincoln
Architect unknown

Jeremiah Lee house, Marblehead
Architect unknown, 1768

Eben Crafts house, Elmwood, Roxbury
Peter Banner, 1805

Perez Morton house, Roxbury
Charles Bulfinch, 1796

Shirley-Eustis House, Roxbury
Attributed to Peter Harrison, after 1746

Joseph Barrell house, Somerville
Charles Bulfinch, 1792–93

Tyng house, Tyngsborough
Architect unknown

Lyman house, The Vale, Waltham
Samuel McIntire, c. 1793
Reconstruction of plan

OUTSIDE MASSACHUSETTS

Van Ness house, Washington, District of Columbia
Henry Benjamin Latrobe, 1813–19

Sparhawk house, Kittery, Maine
W. Pepperell

Woodlands, Philadelphia, Pennsylvania
1788

COMMISSIONS BY OGDEN CODMAN

The following list is based on the compilation of several items: Stuart A. Drake's 1973 compilation for his thesis for Harvard University, "Ogden Codman Jr., 1863–1951," and the revised version of Drake's list given in Pauline Metcalf's 1978 master's thesis for Columbia University, entitled "Ogden Codman, Jr., Architect, Decorator: Elegance without Excess." Materials from the principal Codman collections have been invaluable: The Avery Architectural and Fine Arts Library (AVERY), The Boston Athenæum (BA), especially Codman's correspondence collected in the "Green Book"; the Metropolitan Museum of Art (MMA) and the Society for the Preservation of New England Antiquities (SPNEA).

The list is arranged by location; commissions for which the extant information is incomplete are given following the list.

The present status of the commission, if known, is indicated as follows:

AL   Altered
DE   Demolished
EX   Extant, if known
E/A   Extant, but altered
NE   Not executed
UN   Nature of commission unspecified

CONNECTICUT

ISELIN, Adrian
Fairfield, Connecticut
Landscape design for cemetery plot
(AVERY)

DISTRICT OF COLUMBIA

1908–10
CODMAN, Martha
2145 Decatur Place
Washington, District of Columbia
Building design and interior decoration
(AVERY, BA, MMA, SPNEA); EX
Comments: Terrace designed by Achille Duchêne

ENGLAND

1936
TRITTON, Mr. and Mrs. Robert
Godmersham Park
Kent County, England
Consultation on alteration and decoration
(AVERY); EX
Comments: The working architect was Walter Sarel

FLORIDA

1913
ANDERSON & PRICE MEMORIAL LIBRARY
Anderson & Price Memorial Library
(Women's City Club)
Ormond, Florida
Building design
(AVERY); EX
Comments: Codman's single commission for a public building

c. 1911–12
PALMER, Berthe Honore (Mrs. Potter)
Sarasota, Florida
Building design
(BA, SPNEA); NE

FRANCE

1926–27
CODMAN, Ogden Jr.
Château de Grégy
Brie-Comte-Robert, France
Expansion, interior decoration and landscape design
(MMA, SPNEA); EX
Comments: Codman is buried in the garden at Château de Grégy

1929–31
CODMAN, Ogden Jr.
La Leopolda
Villefranche-sur-Mer, France
Building design and interior decoration
(AVERY, SPNEA); EX
Comments: Domaine once owned by King Leopold I of Belgium

MASSACHUSETTS

AMERICAN MUTUAL LIABILITY INSURANCE CO.
American Mutual Liability Insurance Co.
32 Beacon Street
Boston, Massachusetts
Building design
(SPNEA); NE

SOMERSET CLUB
Somerset Club
42 Beacon Street
Boston, Massachusetts
Interior decoration
(AVERY, BA, SPNEA); EX
Comments: Designed with Herbert W. C. Browne

THAYER, Nathaniel
22 Fairfield Street
Boston, Massachusetts
Interior decoration
(BA, MMA); E/A

THAYER, S. Van Renssalaer
1124 Tremont Street
Boston, Massachusetts
Alterations; interior decoration
(AVERY)
Comments: Residence built by A. W. Longfellow, Jr.

UPDIKE, Daniel Berkeley
Brimmer Chambers
122 Pinckney Street
Boston, Massachusetts
Interior decoration
(BA, MMA)

c. 1892–96
UPDIKE, Daniel Berkeley
Hotel Charlesgate

Charlesgate at Beacon Street
Boston, Massachusetts
Interior decoration
(MMA)

1893
THAYER, Eugene Van Renssalaer
1 Raleigh Street
Boston, Massachusetts
Interior decoration
(BA); E/A

1895
COOLIDGE, J. Randolph
147 Beacon Street
Boston, Massachusetts
Interior decoration
(BA, MMA, SPNEA); EX

1899
AMES, Oliver
15 Commonwealth Avenue
Boston, Massachusetts
Interior decoration
(AVERY, BA, MMA); EX

1900
GAY, Eben Howard
(Goethe Institute)
170 Beacon Street
Boston, Massachusetts
Refronting, alteration, interior
  decoration
(AVERY, MMA, SPNEA); EX

c. 1901
PAINE, Charles Jackson
(Archives of American Art)
87 Mount Vernon Street
Boston, Massachusetts
Interior decoration
(BA, SPNEA); EX

c. 1903−10
CROWNINSHIELD, Francis B.
164 Marlborough Street
Boston, Massachusetts
Interior decoration
(SPNEA); EX

c. 1903−10
SEARS, Herbert M.
287 Commonwealth Avenue
Boston, Massachusetts
Interior decoration
(SPNEA); EX

1909
DEXTER, Philip
65 Marlborough Street
Boston, Massachusetts
Interior decoration
(MMA)

1912
THAYER, Bayard
(Hampshire House)
84 Beacon Street
Boston, Massachusetts
Building design and interior
  decoration
(AVERY, BA, MMA, SPNEA); EX
Comments: Interior woodwork
  provided by Lenygon & Morant

1914−15
SAMPSON, Charles
111 Commonwealth Avenue
Boston, Massachusetts
Alterations and decoration
(BA, MMA, SPNEA); EX

BRYCE, Lloyd S.
Lancaster, Massachusetts
(AVERY) UN

THAYER, Bayard
Hawthorne Hill
Lancaster, Massachusetts
Interior decoration
(AVERY, BA); EX

THAYER, Eugene Van Renssalaer
Lancaster, Massachusetts
Interior decoration
(BA); EX

c. 1902−3
THAYER, Nathaniel
The Homestead
Lancaster, Massachusetts
Alteration and decoration
(BA, MMA, SPNEA); EX

CODMAN, Ogden Jr.
Lenox, Massachusetts
(AVERY); NE

1896−1903
KNEELAND, Adele
Fairlawn
Lenox, Massachusetts
Interior decoration
(AVERY, MMA, SPNEA); DE

1901
WHARTON, Edward R. and
  Edith
The Mount
Lenox, Massachusetts
Building conception and interior
  decoration
(BA, MMA); EX
Comments: Official architect was
  Francis Hoppin of Hoppin &
  Koen

1912−13
MORRIS, Newbold
Lenox, Massachusetts
Design of entrance courtyard
(MMA); CO
Comments: Design by Francis
  Hoppin of Hoppin & Koen

c. 1900−3
CODMAN, Ogden Sr.
The Grange
(Property of SPNEA)
Lincoln, Massachusetts
Alterations, interior decoration,
  landscape design
(BA, SPNEA); EX
Comments: Bequeathed to SPNEA
  by Dorothy Codman (1968)

1909
DEXTER, Philip
Boulderwood
Forest Street
Manchester, Massachusetts
(MMA); UN

1891−92
CODMAN, John
Nahant, Massachusetts
Alterations and interior decoration
(BA, SPNEA)

c. 1903−10
SEARS, Herbert M.
Hale Street
Prides Crossing, Massachusetts
Alterations and interior decoration
(BA, SPNEA); EX

1904
AMES, Oliver
High Wall
Prides Crossing, Massachusetts

Building design and interior
decoration
(BA, MMA, SPNEA); DE

after 1902
TENNY, Sanborn G.
123 Park Street
Williamstown, Massachusetts
Addition
NE

NEW JERSEY

1916
SCHLEY, Grant B.
Far Hills, New Jersey
Alterations and plans for
recreational facilities
(MMA, SPNEA)

1915
WINSTON, Owen
Gladstone, New Jersey
Alterations
(SPNEA)

NEW YORK

1898
VANDERBILT, Frederick W.
Hyde Park, New York
Interior decoration
(MMA)
Comments: Design by McKim,
Mead & White, 1896–99

c. 1901
BRYCE, Lloyd S.
(Nassau County Museum of Fine
Art)
Roslyn, New York
Building design and interior
decoration
(AVERY, BA, MMA, NASSAU COUNTY
MUSEUM OF FINE ART); E/A
Comments: Altered by Charles
Allom for Henry Clay Frick

before 1904
WEBB, Leila Howard Griswold
Beechwood
Scarborough, New York
Addition
(BA)

Comments: Building plans, also by
Codman, never executed

1905
CODMAN, Ogden Jr.
Valentine
Scarborough, New York
(AVERY, SPNEA); NE

1908
ROCKEFELLER, John D. Jr.
Kykuit
Pocantico Hills, New York
Interior decoration
(BA, MMA, SPNEA)
Comments; Rockefeller acted on
his father's behalf

CANFIELD, A. Cass
Cassleigh
Roslyn, New York
Interior decoration
(BA)

1911
LUDLOW, Mrs. M.M.
Oakdale, New York
Building and landscape design
(MMA, SPNEA)

SCHERER, Jacob
Hastings-on-Hudson, New York
Building design
(MMA, SPNEA)

1914
WEBB, J. Griswold
Hyde Park, New York
Building design
(SPNEA)
Comments: J. Griswold Webb was
the son of Leila Codman

1916–17
MAYNARD, Walter Effingham
Hautbois
Jericho, New York
Building design and interior
decoration
(AVERY, BA, SPNEA); EX

NEW YORK CITY

ATTERBURY, Anna D.
13 West 49th Street
New York, New York
Interior decoration (AVERY)

BLODGETT, Eleanor
46 East 65th Street
New York, New York
Building design and interior
decoration
(AVERY, BA); EX

BOWDOIN, Charles
281 Fourth Street
New York, New York
Alterations
(SPNEA)

BRYCE, Lloyd S.
1025 Fifth Avenue
New York, New York
Building design and interior
decoration
(AVERY, BA, MMA, SPNEA); DE
Comments: Purchased by Frederick
W. Vanderbilt before 1917; some
plans refer to 1024 Fifth Avenue

CANFIELD, A. Cass
40 Park Avenue
New York, New York
Interior decoration
(AVERY)

COOPER, Charles
113 East 21st Street
New York, New York
Interior decoration
(AVERY, BA, MMA)

CUTTING, R. Fulton
Madison Avenue at 67th Street
New York, New York
Alterations and interior decoration
(AVERY)

DAHLGREN, Eric
812 Madison Avenue
New York, New York
(AVERY)

GIMPEL AND WILDENSTEIN
ART GALLERY
Fifth Avenue and 28th Street
New York, New York
Alteration
(SPNEA)

GRISWOLD, F. G.
Park Avenue at 73rd Street
New York, New York
(SPNEA; UN)

HARRISON, Francis B.
576 Fifth Avenue
New York, New York
(AVERY); UN

HENRY, Seaton
32 Washington Square
New York, New York
Interior decoration
(BA)

HOME CLUB
11–15 East 89th Street
New York, New York
(AVERY); UN

ISELIN, Adrian
81 East 91st Street
New York, New York
(AVERY); UN

ISELIN, Adrian
Madison Avenue
New York, New York
Alterations
(AVERY)

LAWYER'S REALTY COMPANY
30 West 52nd Street
New York, New York
(AVERY); UN

MAYNARD, Walter Effingham
114 East 40th Street
New York, New York
(AVERY); UN

PENDLETON, Judge Francis Key
New York, New York
Interior decoration
(BA)

ROBBINS, Herbert Daniel
1034 Fifth Avenue
New York, New York
(AVERY); UN

VAN ALEN, J. J.
40 East 50th Street
New York, New York
Interior decoration
(BA)

VANDERBILT, Frederick
1025 Fifth Avenue
New York, New York
(AVERY); UN

WHITRIDGE, Frederick W.
16–18 East 11th Street
New York, New York
Interior decoration
(AVERY)

c. 1890s
WHARTON, Edward R.
882–884 Park Avenue
New York, New York
Interior decoration
(BA, MMA); DE

c. 1890s
FISH, Stuyvesant
Madison Avenue and 78th Street
New York, New York
Interior decoration
(MMA, SPNEA)

c. 1893–94
KNICKERBOCKER CLUB
Knickerbocker Club
cor. Fifth Avenue and 32nd Street
New York, New York
Interior decoration
(MMA, SPNEA)

1894
RIVES, Reginald
42 East 32nd Street
New York, New York
Interior decoration
(MMA, SPNEA)

1895–96
CUTTING, Bayard
24 East 72nd Street
New York, New York
Interior decoration
(AVERY, SPNEA)

after 1896
TAYLOR, Henry Augustus Coit
3 East 71st Street
New York, New York
Interior decoration
(BA, MMA, SPNEA); DE
Comments: Design by McKim,
   Mead & White, 1894–96

1897
BOWDOIN, George Sullivan
39 Park Avenue
New York, New York
Alterations and interior decoration
(BA, MMA, SPNEA); DE

1897
CUTTING, R. Fulton
(St. David's School)
Madison and 89th Street
New York, New York
Interior decoration
(AVERY, BA)

1897
FRELINGHUYSEN, Sarah B.
27 West 48th Street
New York, New York
Interior decoration
(AVERY)

1897
WILDERMING, Lucius K.
18 East 77th Street
New York, New York
Interior decoration
(SPNEA, MMA)

1897–1898
SORCHAN, Charlotte Hunnewell
   (Mrs. Victor)
267 Madison Avenue
New York, New York
Interior decoration
(AVERY, BA, MMA); DE

1899–1901
KING, Ethel Rhinelander (Mrs.
   LeRoy)
18 and 20 East 84th Street
New York, New York
Alterations and interior decoration
(AVERY, MMA)

1899–1901
KING, George Gordon
16 East 84th Street
New York, New York
Interior decoration
(MMA, SPNEA); E/A

1900–1
WINTHROP, Egerton
23 East 33rd Street
New York, New York
Interior decoration
(AVERY, BA, SPNEA)

1901
LAWRENCE, J. J.
Fifth Avenue at East 89th Street
New York, New York
(SPNEA); UN

1901
MARBURY, Elizabeth and
DE WOLFE, Elsie
122 East 17th Street
New York, New York
Interior decoration
(AVERY); EX

1903
CLARK, D. Crawford
(Irish American Historical Society)
991 Fifth Avenue
New York, New York
Interior decoration
(MMA); EX

c. 1903 – 10
CLEWS, Henry
630 Fifth Avenue
New York, New York
Interior decoration
(MMA, SPNEA); DE

c. 1903 – 10
HARRISON, Francis B.
876 Fifth Avenue
New York, New York
Interior decoration
(AVERY, MMA, SPNEA)

c. 1903 – 10
STURGIS, Frank K.
17 East 51st Street
New York, New York
Building design and interior
    decoration
(AVERY, BA, MMA, SPNEA); DE

c. 1904
WEBB, Leila Howard Griswold
    (Mrs. H. Walter)
15 East 51st Street
New York, New York
Building design and interior
    decoration
(AVERY, MMA, SPNEA); DE
Comments: Leila Webb married
    Codman in October of that year

1908
HAWKES, McDougall and Eva
    Van C. Morris
8 East 53rd Street
New York, New York
Interior decoration
(AVERY, MMA, SPNEA)

1908 – 10
BURDEN, Harriette H. Griswold
    (Mrs. Joseph Warren)
160 East 70th Street
New York, New York
(MMA)

1908 – 11
HAVEN, J. Woodward
(Acquavella Gallery)
18 East 79th Street
New York, New York
Building design and interior
    decoration
(AVERY, BA, MMA, SPNEA); EX

after 1908
MORSE, E. Rollins
(Venezuelan Consulate)
7 East 51st Street
New York, New York
Building design and interior
    decoration
(AVERY, BA, SPNEA); E/A
Comments: Sold to C. P. Kling,
    1910, Acct. book #1, MMA

1909
STEWART, John Aikman and
    Mary Capron
16 West 53rd Street
New York, New York
Interior decoration
(MMA, SPNEA)

1910
DE WOLFE, Elsie
131 East 71 Street
New York, New York
Alterations and interior decoration
(BA, MMA); E/A

1910
DE WOLFE, Elsie and
    MARBURY, Elizabeth
103 East 35th Street
New York, New York
(SPNEA); UN

1910
FARQUHAR, Percival
1080 Fifth Avenue
New York, New York
Alterations and interior decoration
(BA, MMA, SPNEA); DE

1910 – 11
BULL, Charles C.
30 West 52nd Street
New York, New York
Interior decoration
(MMA)

1910 – 11
DE WOLFE, Elsie and
    MARBURY, Elizabeth
123 East 55th Street
New York, New York
Alterations and interior decoration

c. 1910 – 17
KISSEL, Caroline Thorn (Mrs.
    Gustav)
12 East 55th Street
New York, New York
Alterations
(SPNEA)

c. 1910 – 17
WISSMAN, Francis de R. and
    Helen Jones
9 East 96th Street
New York, New York
Building design
(AVERY, SPNEA); NE

c. 1911 – 17
SPEYER, James
Fifth Avenue at 87th Street
New York, New York
Alterations
(AVERY)
Comments: Design by Horace
    Trumbauer

1912
BRICE, Helen Mill
Fifth Avenue
New York, New York
Building design
(AVERY, SPNEA)

1912
BRONSON, Sara Gracie King
    (Mrs. Frederic)
1142 Park Avenue
New York, New York
Alterations and interior decoration
(AVERY, BA, MMA, SPNEA)

1912
CODMAN, Ogden Jr.
(Manhattan Country Day School)

7 East 96th Street
New York, New York
Building design and interior
　decoration
(AVERY, MMA, SPNEA); EX

1912
EMERY, Leila Alexander (Mrs.
　John J.)
5 East 68th Street
New York, New York
Alterations and interior decoration
(AVERY, MMA, SPNEA)

1912
GERARD, James W.
1134 Fifth Avenue
New York, New York
Building design
(SPNEA)

1912
LANE, James Warren and Eva
　Metcalf Bliss
49 East 52nd Street
New York, New York
(MMA)

1912
METROPOLITAN CLUB
Metropolitan Club
(Canadian Club)
11 East 60th Street
New York, New York
Construction of east wing and
　interior decoration
(BA, MMA, SPNEA); EX

1912
SANDS, E. Louise and Anna
11 East 84th Street
New York, New York
Interior decoration
(BA, MMA, SPNEA); EX

1912–14
STRAUS, Herbert N.
1142–1144 Park Avenue
New York, New York
Interior decoration
(AVERY, MMA)

1913
GARDINER, David
3 East 82nd Street
New York, New York
Alterations and interior decoration
(MMA, SPNEA)

1913–15
HUNTINGTON, Archer M.
(National Academy of Design)
1083 Fifth Avenue and 3 East 89th
　Street
New York, New York
Building design and interior
　decoration
(AVERY, MMA, SPNEA); EX
Comments: Work at 3 E. 89th St.
　preceded that at 1083 5th Avenue

1915
DAHLGREN, Lucy Drexel (Mrs.
　Eric B.)
(Paul Springer Foundation)
15 East 96th Street
New York, New York
Building design and interior
　decoration
(MMA, SPNEA); E/A

after 1915
WAINWRIGHT, S.
123 East 55th Street
New York, New York
(AVERY)
Comments: Former residence of
　Elsie de Wolfe

1916
LIVINGSTON, Susan de Peyster
　(Mrs. Robert E.)
(Emerson School)
12 East 96th Street
New York, New York
Building design and interior
　decoration
(BA, SPNEA); E/A

c. 1916
TRIMBLE, Walter and
　SHEARSON, Edward
11 and 13 East 96th Street
New York, New York
Building design
(AVERY); NE

RHODE ISLAND

CODMAN, Ogden Jr.
Newport, Rhode Island
(AVERY); NE

CUTTING, Marion Ramsay (Mrs.
　F. Brockholst)

Newport, Rhode Island
Interior decoration
(AVERY, SPNEA); NE

1883
OGDEN, Margaret Van C. (Mrs.
　John Doughty)
Mapleshade
Newport, Rhode Island
Interior decoration
(BA, SPNEA)

1893
BROWN, Harold
Newport, Rhode Island
Interior decoration
(AVERY, BA, MMA, SPNEA); EX

1893
WHARTON, Edward R. and
　Edith
Land's End
Newport, Rhode Island
Alteration, interior decoration,
　landscape design
(AVERY, BERK, MMA, SPNEA); E/A
Comments: Landscape design by
　Beatrix Farrand

1894–95
VANDERBILT, Cornelius II
The Breakers
Newport, Rhode Island
Interior decoration
(AVERY, MMA, SPNEA); EX
Comments: Design by Richard
　Morris Hunt

1895–96
POMEROY, Edith Burnet (Mrs.
　Charles Coolidge)
Seabeach
Newport, Rhode Island
Building design and interior
　decoration
(BA, MMA, SPNEA); E/A

c. 1895–96
COATS, Alfred M.
Landfall
Newport, Rhode Island
Building design and interior
　decoration
(AVERY, BA, MMA,); E/A

c. 1896–97
THAYER, Nathaniel
Edgemere

Newport, Rhode Island
Interior decoration and addition
(BA, MMA); E/A

1896—98
VAN ALEN, J. J.
Wakehurst
Newport, Rhode Island
Landscape design
(AVERY, UNIVERSITY OF
CALIFORNIA/BERKELEY, MMA);
EX
Comments: Garden designed with
Beatrix Farrand

1900
MILLER, William Starr
High Tide
Newport, Rhode Island
Interior decoration
(SPNEA); EX
Comments: Design by Warren and
Wetmore

c. 1900
MORSE, E. Rollins
Villa Rosa
Newport, Rhode Island
Building design and interior
decoration
(AVERY, BA, MMA); DE

c. 1900
WINTHROP, Egerton
Quatrel
Newport, Rhode Island
Interior decoration
(BA, MMA, SPNEA); EX
Comments: Design by Thomas A.
Tefft, 1853—54

1902—3
SLATER, E. Hope Gammell
Hopedene
Newport, Rhode Island
Interior decoration
(BA, MMA, SPNEA); E/A
Comments: Design by Peabody and
Stearns

1902—3
STURGIS, Frank K.
Faxon Lodge
Newport, Rhode Island
Building design and interior
decoration
(BA, MMA, SPNEA); E/A

1903
WETMORE, George Peabody
Château-sur-Mer
(Property of the Preservation
Society of Newport County)
Newport, Rhode Island
Interior decoration ("Green Salon")
(AVERY, BA, MMA, SPNEA); EX

1910
CODMAN, Martha
Berkeley Villa
Bellevue Ave. at Berkeley Street
Newport, Rhode Island
Building design and interior
decoration
(AVERY, BA, MMA, SPNEA); EX

c. 1901
COATS, Alfred M.
(Property of Brown University)
13 Brown Street
Providence, Rhode Island
Building design and interior
decoration
(BA, MMA, SPNEA); E/A

c. 1903—10
ST. JOHN'S CHURCH
St. John's Church
44 Benefit Street
Providence, Rhode Island
Alterations and interior decoration
(SPNEA); NE

1917
UPDIKE, Daniel Berkeley
Magee Street at George Street
Providence, Rhode Island
Alteration and remodeling designs
(SPNEA); NE

INCOMPLETE ENTRIES

COCKRAN, W. Bourke
The Cedars
Port Washington, New York
(BA)

FOWLER, Arthur A.
Peapack, New Jersey
(AVERY)

GERARD, Jason
New York, New York
(AVERY)

HARRISON, Francis B.
576 Fifth Avenue
New York, New York
(AVERY)

HESSEL
(SPNEA)

ISELIN, Adrian
New Rochelle, New York
Landscape design
(AVERY)

KAHN, Otto
(AVERY)

KANE
Boston, Massachusetts
(SPNEA)

LONG VIEW REALTY
COMPANY
Long View, New Jersey
(AVERY)

METROPOLITAN OPERA
HOUSE
New York, New York
(AVERY)

MCLELLEN, George
Princeton, New Jersey
(AVERY)

RIDING CLUB
New York, New York
(AVERY)

ROCHE, Burke
Newport, Rhode Island
(AVERY)

ROGERS, Archibald
Hyde Park, New York
(AVERY)

SILSBEE, George S.
Boston, Massachusetts
Interior decoration
(BA, MMA)

SNELLING, Anna L. Rodman
(Mrs. Howard)
South Lincoln, Massachusetts
Interior decoration
(BA)

STEWART, J. A.
Morristown, New Jersey
(AVERY, MMA)

WARREN, Mrs. S. D.
Waltham, Massachusetts
(AVERY)

WASHINGTON CLUB
(AVERY)

WHITNEY, H. P.
Newport, Rhode Island
(AVERY)

WHITNEY, W. C.
Building design
(AVERY)

1891–92
CODMAN, Charles R.
Building design
(SPNEA)

c. 1903–10
BLAINE, J. G. III
Building design

c. 1903–10
STILLMAN, J. A.
Tarrytown, New York
Building design
(SPNEA)

1917
COOKE, H. W.
(SPNEA)

CONTRIBUTORS

PAULINE C. METCALF has written numerous articles on Ogden Codman for such publications as *Antiques Magazine* and *House and Garden*. In the field of architectural history, Ms. Metcalf has concentrated on nineteenth- and twentieth-century American architecture and decorative arts. She has combined this career with her work as an interior designer, specializing in historic houses.

NICHOLAS KING is Director of the New York Foreign Press (USIA) and a regular contributor to the *Baltimore Sun, The Wall Street Journal*, and *The National Review*.

CHRISTOPHER MONKHOUSE is Curator of Decorative Arts at the Museum of Art, Rhode Island School of Design. He is the coauthor of *Buildings on Paper: Rhode Island Architectural Drawings 1835–1945* and *American Furniture in Pendleton House* and has written extensively on American decorative arts and furniture.

HENRY HOPE REED is the President of Classical America and one of its founders. He is the author of many articles and books, including *The New York Public Library: Its Architecture and Decoration* and *The United States Capitol: Its Architecture and Decoration*.

RICHARD GUY WILSON is Professor of Architecture at the School of Architecture at the University of Virginia. He has written extensively on American architecture and furniture. Among his publications are *The American Renaissance, 1876–1917, Machine Age America, 1920–41, McKim, Mead & White—Architects*, and *The AIA Gold Medal*.

ILLUSTRATION CREDITS

58 The Metropolitan Museum of Art, Gift of the Estate of Ogden Codman, Jr., 1951 (51.644.112)

59 Society for the Preservation of New England Antiquities Archives, Ogden Codman Architectural Drawing Collection (12055-B)

60 top The Metropolitan Museum of Art

60 bottom Society for the Preservation of New England Antiquities Archives (1993-B)

61 top The Metropolitan Museum of Art, Gift of the Estate of Ogden Codman, Jr., 1951 (51.644.144/37)

61 bottom Society for the Preservation of New England Antiquities Archives, Haskell Architectural Photographer (4698-B)

62 Society for the Preservation of New England Antiquities Archives, Ogden Codman Architectural Drawing Collection (14505-B)

67 The Metropolitan Museum of Art, Gift of the Estate of Ogden Codman, Jr., 1951 (51.644.63/13, 51.644.63/17)

68 The Metropolitan Museum of Art, Gift of the Estate of Ogden Codman, Jr., 1951 (51.644.78/2)

69 top The Metropolitan Museum of Art, Gift of the Estate of Ogden Codman Jr., 1951 (51.644.78/8)

69 center Society for the Preservation of New England Antiquities Archives (11224-B)

69 bottom The Metropolitan Museum of Art, Gift of the Estate of Ogden Codman, Jr., 1951 (51.644.78/14–15)

70 The Metropolitan Museum of Art, Gift of the Estate of Ogden Codman, Jr., 1951 (51.644.78/13)

71 Courtesy of Edward Lee Cave

72 Courtesy of the owners, photograph by Jean-Jacques L'Heritier

73 Avery Architectural and Fine Arts Library, Columbia University, Ogden Codman Collection

76 The Metropolitan Museum of Art, Gift of the Estate of Ogden Codman, Jr., 1951 (51.644.82/12–13, 64.577.17)

77 . The Metropolitan Museum of Art, Gift of the Estate of Ogden Codman, Jr., 1951 (51.644.76/32, 51.644.76/36–30)

78 The Metropolitan Museum of Art, Gift of the Estate of Ogden Codman, Jr., 1951 (51.644.76/11)

79 Courtesy of Pauline C. Metcalf

80 The Metropolitan Museum of Art, Gift of the Estate of Ogden Codman, Jr., 1951 (51.644.77/44)

81 The Metropolitan Museum of Art, Gift of the Estate of Ogden Codman, Jr., 1951 (51.644.144/29)

82 top The Metropolitan Museum of Art, Gift of the Estate of Ogden Codman, Jr., 1951 (51.644.90)

82 bottom Reprinted from *American Homes and Gardens* 2 (February 1906)

83 top The Metropolitan Museum of Art, Gift of the Estate of Ogden Codman, Jr., 1951 (51.644.78/4)

83 bottom Reprinted from *American Architect and Building News* 7 (October 18, 1902)

84 Edith Wharton Restoration, Inc., The Mount, Lenox, Massachusetts, photograph by Warren Fowler

85 top Avery Architectural and Fine Arts Library, Columbia University, Ogden Codman Collection (1000.009.02186)

85 bottom The Metropolitan Museum of Art, Gift of the Estate of Ogden Codman, Jr., 1951 (51.644.145/18)

86 top left The Metropolitan Museum of Art, Gift of the Estate of Ogden Codman, Jr., 1951 (51.644.70/4)

86 top right The Society for the Preservation of New England Antiquities Archives, Codman Family Photograph Collection (14520-B)

86 bottom The Collection of American Literature, Beinecke Rare Book and Manuscript Library, Yale University

87 top The Metropolitan Museum of Art, Gift of the Estate of Ogden Codman, Jr., 1951 (51.644.145/39)

87 center Avery Architectural and Fine Arts Library, Columbia University, Ogden Codman Collection (1000.009.03395)

87 bottom Reprinted from Daniel Marot, *Das Ornamentwerk* (Berlin, 1892)

88 Society for the Preservation of New England Antiquities Archives, Codman Family Photograph Collection (11541-B)

89 top Courtesy of the owners, photograph by Jean-Jacques L'Heritier

89 bottom Collection of Nicholas King

90 The Metropolitan Museum of Art, Gift of the Estate of Ogden Codman, Jr., 1951 (51.644.78/7, 51.644.80/16)

91 top The Metropolitan Museum of Art, Gift of the Estate of Ogden Codman, Jr., 1951 (51.644.100)

91 bottom Nassau County Museum of Fine Art, Mattie Edwards Hewitt Collection

92 Society for the Preservation of New England Antiquities Archives, Codman Family Photograph Collection (14525-B)

93 right Society for the Preservation of New England Antiquities Archives, Ogden Codman Architectural Drawing Collection (9507-B)

93 left Society for the Preservation of New England Antiquities Archives, Ogden Codman Architectural Drawing Collection (9505-B)

94 top left Photograph by Richard Cheek, courtesy of The Magazine Antiques

94 top right Nassau County Museum of Fine Art, Mattie Edwards Hewitt Collection

94 bottom Reprinted from James Paine, *Plans, elevations and sections of noblemen's and gentlemen's houses* (England, 1767)

96 top Society for the Preservation of New England Antiquities Archives, Ogden Codman Architectural Drawing Collection (11553-B)

96 bottom Nassau County Museum of Fine Art, Mattie Edwards Hewitt Collection

97 Society for the Preservation of New England Antiquities Archives, Ogden Codman Architectural Drawing Collection (11552-B, 11551-B)

98 Courtesy of the owners

99 Reprinted from Ogden Codman, *La Leopolda: A Description* (Paris, 1939)

100–103 Society for the Preservation of New England Antiquities Archives, Codman Family Photograph Collection (14504-B, 14311-B, 14512-B, 14312-B)

104 Society for the Preservation of New England Antiquities Archives, Codman Family Photograph Collection (14514-B, 14517-B)

106 Society for the Preservation of New England Antiquities Archives, Codman Family Photograph Collection (14515-B)

107 The Metropolitan Museum of Art, Gift of the Estate of Ogden Codman, Jr., 1951 (51.644.80/8, 51.644.80/9)

108 The Metropolitan Museum of Art, Gift of the Estate of Ogden Codman, Jr., 1951 (51.644.80/12, 51.644.80/11)

112, 113 Avery Architectural and

INDEX

Italics indicates page number of an illustration; **bold face** indicates color plate